D1228796

The Oral Art and Literature of the Kazakhs of Russian Central Asia

THE ORAL ART AND LITERATURE OF THE KAZAKHS OF RUSSIAN CENTRAL ASIA

Thomas G. Winner

Durham, N. C.
DUKE UNIVERSITY PRESS
1958

CAMBRIDGE UNIVERSITY PRESS, LONDON, N.W.I, ENGLAND

LIBRARY OF CONGRESS CATALOGUE CARD NUMBER
58-7995

PRINTED IN THE UNITED STATES OF AMERICA
BY THE SEEMAN PRINTERY, INC., DURHAM, N. C.

FOREWORD

IT SHOULD BE NOTED that while Kazakh literary texts in Russian translation are freely available, texts in the original Kazakh are somewhat scarce in the Western World. All original sources which could be obtained were carefully examined, but at the time that this study was made it was not possible to carry on extensive research within the Soviet Union. For this reason I have not thought it appropriate to consider, in any final sense, the independent aesthetic qualities of the Kazakh literature and oral art. Rather, I have adopted a social approach, which I feel to be a fruitful one both because of the traditionally social nature of Kazakh folk literature and because of the youth of modern literature in the Western sense in Kazakhstan.

The present study was initiated in 1947-48 and made possible by two grants by the American Council of Learned Societies. Further research, both in the United States and in Europe, aided by a year's grant of the Ford Foundation in 1951-52, resulted in the present study. My sincere thanks are due to both the American Council of Learned Societies and to the Ford Foundation for their generous aid. My thanks are also due to the Duke University Research Council, which supported much of my research and made the publication of this study possible.

There are many individuals to whom I am indebted for criticism and suggestions. My primary debt of gratitude is to my former teacher, Professor Ernest J. Simmons of the Department of Slavic Languages and Literatures at Columbia University, who has offered me tireless help and criticism and who has encouraged my work from its inception. I am also indebted to Professor Karl Heinrich Menges, who introduced me into the mysteries of the Ural-Altaic languages. Special thanks are also due to Miss Violet Connolly of the Research Department of the British Foreign Office, who placed many materials at my disposal;

to Mr. J. C. W. Horne, Assistant Keeper of the British Museum who never lost patience in helping me find needed materials; to the Kazakh colony in Munich for receiving me so generously, and especially to Mr. Asan Kaigy for supplying me with valuable information about his native land; and to Professor N. Poppe of the University of Washington for valuable information about the bard Džambul. Professor Lawrence Krader kindly read the manuscript, and many thanks are due him for his helpful suggestions.

Durham, N. C. *T.G.W.*

TABLE OF CONTENTS

FOREWORD v

INTRODUCTION xi

The Historical Setting xi

The Russian Conquest xiii

I. THE KAZAKH CULTURE PATTERN 3

The Economic Organization of the Kazakhs 3

Socio-political Structure of the Kazakhs 5

Religious Beliefs of the Kazakhs 9

Role of Women 13

Education 15

The Kazakh Legal System 16

Effects of Russian Colonial Policy on the Culture of the Kazakhs 17

II. EARLY FOLKLORE 25

The Setting: Central Asiatic Oral Traditions 25

The Main Types of Kazakh Folklore 29

The Ajtys: *Songs at Celebrations* 29

Ritual Songs 34

Tales and Legends 45

III. FOLKLORE: THE HEROIC EPOS 54

Some Characteristics of the Epos of the Central Asiatic Nomads 54

Trends in the Development of the Kazakh Heroic Epos 60

Formal Characteristics of the Kazakh Epic 68

The Main Kazakh Epic Figures 71

IV. FOLKLORE IN THE NINETEENTH CENTURY: REFLECTIONS OF RUSSIAN RULE 86

Bukhar Džyrau (c. 1693-1787) 87

The Folklore of Revolt 89
Poetry of Resignation 95

V. The Growth of a Kazakh Intelligentsia and of a Written Literature 99
The Nineteenth Century 99
Čoqan Valikhanov (c. 1837-1865) 101
Ibraj Altynsaryn (1841-1899) 107
Abaj Qunanbayev (1845-1904) 110
The Early Twentieth Century 120
The Emergence of a Kazakh National Press 120
Growth of a National Intelligentsia 122
The Westerners 123
sultan mahmud toruajgyrov (1893-1920) 123
omar qarašev (1876-1921) 125
other "western" writers 126
The Nationalists: Bajtursonov 128
Concluding Remarks 131

VI. Cultural Developments of Soviet Kazakhstan 133
Historical Background 133
"Crimes Based on Customs" 137
Education and the New Alphabet 139
The Anti-illiteracy Program 142

VII. Kazakh Soviet Oral Art 146
Oral Art on the Eve of the Revolution 146
The Soviet Period 150
Attitudes towards the Oral Tradition 150
Modern Oral Creations 156
General Characteristics of the New Oral Art 159

VIII. Early Soviet Kazakh Literature 173
Kazakh Literature and Cultural Considerations 173
Growth of Kazakh Literature 175
Revolution and War Communism (1918-1922) 178
intellectual currents 178
literary trends during the period of revolution and war communism 180

The Reconstruction and the NEP Period (1923-1927) 186
Literary Trends during the Period of the First Five-Year Plan (1928-1932) 190
Concluding Remarks 192

IX. KAZAKH POETRY AFTER 1932 193

GENERAL TRENDS 193
POETRY 198
The Older Generation of Poets 201
SABIT MUQANOV 201
OTHER POETS OF THE OLDER GENERATION 207
The Younger Generation of Poets 209
ASQAR TOQMAGAMBETOV 209
TAHIR DŽARUQOV 215
ABDYLDA TADŽYBAJEV 224
Concluding Remarks 234

X. KAZAKH PROSE AFTER 1932 235

APPENDIX: KAZAKH THEATER AND DRAMA 255

INDEX 259

INTRODUCTION

The Historical Setting[1]

Geographically, economically, and culturally Central Asia can be divided into two main areas which have experienced widely divergent historical developments. The rich oasis regions of the south were conducive to a settled mode of life based on intensive agriculture in irrigated fields. The potential richness of this region, as well as its geographic position as the only known trade route to the Far East and to India, made the southern oasis regions a constant prey to incursions.

The north, on the other hand, with its vast arid steppes, remained for a long period the domain of nomadic tribes whose mobility helped to protect them from the incursions which constantly threatened their southern neighbors. The nomadic groups, who were in constant competition for the best grazing lands and who never hesitated to enrich themselves by plundering the rich areas to the south of them, developed a fierce and warlike culture.

[1] These few remarks are meant to characterize only briefly the historical setting of the Kazakhs. Since the subject of Kazakh history has been treated amply elsewhere, no details are attempted here. Those interested in studies of Kazakh history can be referred to such works as:

M. Abdykalykov and A. Pankratova, eds., *Istoriya Kazakhskoi SSR* (Alma-Ata, 1943); Akademiya Nauk SSR, Institut Istorii, *Materialy po istorii Kazakhskoi SSR* (Moscow, 1940); V. V. Barthold, *Die geographischen und historischen Erforschungen des Orients mit besonderer Berücksichtigung der russischen Arbeiten* (Leipzig, 1913); Barthold, *Turkestan down to the Mongol Invasion* (London, 1928); Barthold, *Zwölf Vorlesungen über die Türken Mittelasiens* (Berlin, 1935); René Grousset, *L'Empire des steppes. Attila, Gengiz-kan, Tamerlan* (Paris, 1939); Muhammed Haidar, *Tarīkh-i-Rašīdi*, N. Elias, ed. (London, 1898); A. I. Levshin, *Opisanie kirgiz-kazatskikh ord i stepei* (St. Petersburg, 1832) (translated into French as *Déscription des hordes et des steppes des Kirghiz-Kazakhs* [Paris, 1840]); R. Majerczak, "Renseignements historiques sur les Kazakhs ou Kirghizes-Kazaks depuis la fondation de la horde Kazake jusq'au XIXe siècle," *Revue du Monde Musulman*, XLIII (1921), 54-220; and many other studies.

There were other broad cultural differences between the northern and the southern peoples of Central Asia. The south remained Iranian linguistically for a long period of time and fell under the strong sway of Islam. The north, on the other hand, remained basically Turkic from the sixth century onward, when Turkic culture become dominant in the area, and was not touched by the Arabic conquests of the eighth century. Thus it was also that the northern nomads were not converted to the new religion of Islam, which the Arabs had introduced to the southern areas which they had conquered. The gradual acceptance of Mohammedanism by the nomadic Turks of the north began, it seems, only after the tenth century,[2] but Mohammedanism was never fully accepted by these peoples, who retained many of their early shamanistic rites and beliefs.

The most significant tribal group of northern Central Asia, the Kazakhs, today inhabit an area roughly corresponding in size to that of continental Europe without its Iberian and Scandinavian peninsular appendages, but they number only about six million people. Linguistically they are Turks, speaking one of the eastern Turkic languages. They were, until the Russian conquest, essentially horse-raising nomads, who also raised cattle, sheep, goats, and camels and who wandered, in planned migrations, in search of fodder.

Relatively little is known about the history of the Kazakhs before the Russian conquest. There are many and varied theories about their origin, but none are historically verifiable. One version identifies them as a tribal group which had split off from the Uzbek tribal confederacy during the fifteenth century, when the latter had begun to move into the fertile southern oasis lands in conquest of the Timuride empire. As Uzbek confederate unity began to crumble under the impact of the new settled economy, the Kazakhs maintained their nomadic way of life and became the most significant and powerful nomadic tribal federation of Central Asia. The Kazakh federation, however, which could maintain a certain unity only in the face of strong external threat of war, gradually broke into three distinct tribal groupings, the

[2] See Barthold, *Zwölf Vorlesungen . . .*, p. 59.

so-called "hordes" (in Kazakh *Žüs* [*džüs*])[3] which were formed at some time between the sixteenth and eighteenth centuries. These were the same groups which the Russians later met when they entered the territory of the Kazakhs: The Old Horde (*Ulu Žüs*), which controlled the grazing lands in Semirechye as well as the territory between the rivers Chu and Syr Darya; the Middle Horde (*Orta Žüs*), which in summer utilized pastures on the banks of the rivers Irtysh, Tobol, and Ishim and in winter migrated to the river Sary-su and the lowlands of the Syr Darya; the Young Horde (*Kišši Žüs*), which spent summers in what is now the district of Aq-tübe (the Russian Aktyubinsk) and wintered on the shores of the rivers Ural (*Džajyq*) and Ilek.[4]

The Russian Conquest

The first Russian penetration of Central Asia took place at the end of the sixteenth century with the conquest of some of the northern marginal regions. It was not until the eighteenth century, however, during the reigns of Peter the Great and Catherine II, that substantial inroads into Central Asia were made with the conquest of a considerable part of the Kazakh Steppe. However, a large-scale invasion of Central Asia did not occur until the nineteenth century. After completing their conquest of the Kazakh Steppe, the Russians absorbed the southern khanates; in 1864 they captured Tashkent and three years later the entire area was incorporated into the Russian empire as the Turkestan Government-General under a special governor-general. The khanate of Kokand was simply subjugated, while the khanates of Bukhara and Khiva became Russian vassals, independent in name only. By 1881, with the fall of the Turkmen fortress Gök-tepe, the Russians controlled all of Central Asia.

Russian policy to maintain control over the regions where they were in complete control called for the abolition of the conquered national cultures. Thus in Kazakhstan the traditional power of the khan and the tribal sultans was replaced by Russian

[3] From Kazakh züs (*džüs*)—"hundred."
[4] See Abdykalykov, Pankratova, *op. cit.*, pp. 109-110.

military and civilian administrators and the Kazakh traditional courts were replaced by Russian courts, the so-called border tribunals, which were subject to the governor-general in Orenburg. The political and national unity of the conquered peoples was disorientated by a new arrangement of the border lines and political zoning which cut through the old national lines. In general, the policy was one of Russification, which was carried out partly by the settling of Russian colonists interspersed with the local population, and partly by a concerted cultural policy, which will be discussed later.

The Oral Art and Literature of the Kazakhs of Russian Central Asia

Chapter I

THE KAZAKH CULTURE PATTERN

The Economic Organization of the Kazakhs

Kazakh economy before the Russian conquest, like that of the other Turkic steppe dwellers of Central Asia, was based on nomadism and cattle breeding. The Kazakh herds, which constituted the main wealth of the nomads, included sheep, goats, horses, camels, and cattle. The most important animals were the sheep, which also was the exchange medium of Kazakh society, and the horse, which was milked and, on special occasions, eaten and was the most admired and revered animal. The importance of the horse as a means of rapid mobility for the nomadic tribes of the vast steppe areas can hardly be exaggerated, and, quite naturally, the horse was a common subject in the folklore.

The problems which arose around the migrations of the various Kazakh tribes within the limited lands available were considerable. For a people who possessed as large herds as the Central Asiatic Turkic nomads, carefully planned migrations were important. Every cattle breeder had to look for a place most advantageous for his cattle. In winter the nomadic cattle herder had to find an area which would afford him maximum protection against the extreme cold and the wind, either a wooded pasture or a river valley, for at that time the most dreaded natural catastrophe, the *džut,* might occur, a condition caused by the freezing over of previously thawed snow. The resulting crust of ice made it impossible for the cattle to dig through the snow for fodder. The constant fear of the *džut* contributed to the insecurity of the tribes in winter, when a single catastrophe could wipe out an entire herd. Thus there is the Kazakh proverb "A hero perishes from one bullet, but a rich man can perish from one *džut*."[1] In summer it was important that the cattle have adequate grazing grounds and that sufficient water be available at lake shores or river banks. Thus the migration of the nomads followed a set pattern and revolved around two primary poles, the requirements of winter and those of summer. Since it was the winter camping area which had to meet the most rigorous conditions, it was this land which was valued most highly and which set the upper limit on population. Radloff wrote that "all battles . . . during the past centuries must always be regarded as a striving for the best winter places."[2] In general, the great dependence on the herds, the difficult environmental conditions, and the shortage of desirable land laid the basis for considerable economic insecurity and conflict.

After the sixteenth century certain changes took place in the Kazakh economy. Until that time wealth (in terms primarily of cattle and secondarily of grazing lands) was not concentrated to any great extent in the hands of any particular group. Though an aristocracy based on birth held political power, it does not seem probable that there was a great deal of economic stratification. Gradually, however, as the Kazakhs were able to increase their holdings as a result of their conquest of some of the richer southern areas, wealth began to be concentrated in the hands of a limited number of families. A further change in Kazakh economy was the introduction of a small amount of agriculture, mainly in the southern regions which the Kazakhs captured from the Uzbeks and from the Iranian Tadzhiks. Southern agriculture was intensive, utilizing the highly developed irrigation system which had been taken over from the Uzbeks and the Tadzhiks. Some agriculture had existed also in the northern steppe regions, but it seems to have been an extensive system of agriculture, not based on irrigation. Cultivation was unpopular among the nomads and was generally carried out only by the poorer groups, though after the southern conquests a limited section of the aristocracy became settled also. The poor

[1] Abdykalykov, Pankratova, *op. cit.*, p. 120.
[2] Radloff, *Aus Sibirien: lose Blätter aus meinem Tagebuch* (Leipzig, 1893), I, 415.

Kazakh who took up agriculture usually gave what cattle he possessed to his clan for pasturing and, in return, shared his crop with his fellow clansmen.

The conquest of the southern regions encouraged trade between the urban people of the south and the Kazakhs, who bartered their livestock products for bread and craft products.[3] Many Kazakh sultans and khans, as well as artisans and traders, were drawn to the cities. Another factor which further increased Kazakh trade was the beginning, in the sixteenth century, of commercial relations with the Russians.

In spite of the introduction of some agriculture and trade, Kazakh economy remained based primarily on herding and nomadism until the Russian conquest. Wealth became increasingly concentrated, but its nature did not change. The effect of this trend on Kazakh social organization was, however, most profound.

Socio-political Structure of the Kazakhs

Knowledge of the early social and political organization of the Kazakhs is limited both because of the scarcity of source materials and because the Kazakhs seemed to lack a strict terminology defining social units. Designations and exact functions of units, whether united by blood, social, or political ties, are unclear, and the result is a general confusion in the literature and an arbitrary use of terms which are not clearly defined nor well understood. It is possible that one explanation for the general confusion is the lack of cohesiveness of at least the larger social units, causing the border line between the various groups to be vague. The definitions offered here, after examination of the various sources, appear to the writer to be, at least provisionally, the most probable ones.

Early Kazakh society was based on the patriarchal family. Several related families were grouped into a permanent organiza-

[3] The existence of some degree of urban civilization in the eighteenth century among the nomadic Kazakhs is testified to by F. Skibin, the envoy of Peter the Great to the Kazakh khan Teüke, who counted twenty to thirty-two Kazakh towns. Quoted in Abdykalykov, Pankratova, *op. cit.*, pp. 124-25.

tion, the *aul*. In winter several auls combined to form the clan, which carried out co-operative labor and held herds and winter land. In the summer, clan members maintained close relations, although they were separated in different *auls*. The *aul* was, it appears, a part of the clan, but not identical with it. It should rather be considered a subclan. Such a subclan, also called *taipas*[4] in Kazakh (*qyrq*[5] in Kirghiz),[6] was usually administered by the *aqsaqal* (the "white beard"), generally the oldest member of the largest family. The clan (*urū or rū*)[7] was a fairly large and complex organization, since it comprised, according to Kazakh tradition, all individuals who could trace a relationship within a period of seven generations (*džeti ata*).[8]

As the interests of the individual *auls* comprising a clan clashed frequently, an authority was required to maintain equilibrium and carry out judgments in cases of conflicts. Radloff says that "this authority is concentrated in persons who are distinguished by riches, mental faculties, and a sense of justice."[9] Such arbiters (Kazakh *bi*) gradually rose to a position of political leadership over the clan.

Several clans formed a tribe and several tribes formed a tribal confederation (*äl*).[10] The tribes were ruled by sultans. It is not

[4] *taipas:* from Arabic *tā'ifa*—"tribe, clan."

[5] *qyrq*—"forty."

[6] See M. A. Czaplicka, *The Turks of Central Asia in History and at the Present Day* (Oxford, 1918), pp. 40-42.

[7] The designation of the term *urū* for clan is not quite clear. Vámbéry indicates that this is the clan and defines it as being "as well the household standing under one family father, as also the sum of the closer relatives" (A. Vámbéry, *Die primitive Kultur des Türko-Tatarischen Volkes* [Leipzig, 1879], p. 134). Hudson, on the other hand, basing himself primarily on Vladimirtsov's definition of the Mongol term *urux* or *uruġ* as meaning "descendant, offshoot of a given gens" (B. Ya. Vladimirtsov, *Obshchestvenny stroi Mongolov: Mongol'ski kochevoi feodalizm* [Leningrad, 1934], p. 59.), defines it as meaning just any related group and states that the Kazakhs have no exact distinction for their various tribal units. He claims that the application of conventional tribal nomenclature to Kazakh social structure would only be misleading. (See Alfred E. Hudson, *Kazak Social Structure* [New Haven, Yale University Press, 1938], pp. 17-24.) This statement is supported by Majerczak, who states that the Kazakh use this designation indiscriminately for the tribe, the clan, and the subclan. (See R. Majerczak, "Renseignements. . . ," pp. 62-63.)

[8] Cf. A. Vámbéry, *loc. cit.*

[9] Radloff, *Aus Sibirien,* I, 513.

[10] The term *äl* was already in use in the earliest Turkic monuments, the

clear just how an individual obtained the position of sultan though it is known that eligibility was limited to the aristocracy. The tribal confederations were led by khans. There is also little information about the origin of the position of the khan. Although the position was hereditary, there was no definite rule of succession and consequently much strife resulted.[11] Radloff thinks that the position of the khan was based primarily on usurpations,[12] and he is supported in this by Barthold, who writes:

> The khans, the representatives of state power, who under favorable conditions succeed in subjugating the people, appear only under extraordinary circumstances, and even in these cases the khans have usurped their power on their own initiative, without having been appointed or elected by anybody.[13]

There is very little information concerning the degree of social stratification among the early Kazakhs. It is known definitely only that in early times the whole of Kazakh society was divided into two groups: the ordinary people—*qara süjök* (the black bones), and the hereditary aristocracy—*aq süjök* (the white bones), who claimed descent from Dzhingiz-khan. The latter made up the dynasties of the khans and sultans while the former composed the clan population and clan leaders.

It would seem, however, that the important unit in early Kazakh society was the clan, around which centered most of the social, economic, and political life. Themes of family and clan loyalty run quite consistently through the folklore. Thus the following two proverbs clearly demonstrate the importance of the clan in early Kazakh history: "It is better to be a herder in one's own clan than to be a king in an alien clan,"[14] and "Those who do not know their seven ancestors are traitors" (*džeti atasyn bilmegen mürtöd*).[15] In times of peace the hereditary aristoc-

---

eighth-century memorial inscriptions which were found in the Orkhon region of northern Mongolia, and is translated by Radloff as: people, tribe, tribal community (*Volk, Volksstamm, Stammgemeinschaft*); see Radloff, *Alttürkische Inschriften der Mongolei* (St. Petersburg, 1895), p. 93 and *passim*.

[11] Barthold, *Turkestan* . . . , p. 60. [12] Radloff, *Aus Sibirien* . . . , I, 515.

[13] Barthold, *Zwölf Vorlesungen* . . . , p. 11.

[14] Waldemar Jochelson, *Peoples of Asiatic Russia* (New York: American Museum of Natural History, 1928), pp. 84-85.

[15] Ibrahim Altynsaryn, *Kirgizskaya Khrestomatiya* (Orenburg, 1906), p. 140.

racy was probably not a very important factor in the everyday life of the average person.

By the seventeenth century the increase in wealth as a result of the conquest of some of the rich southern agricultural areas and the limited introduction of agriculture had brought about a marked change in Kazakh social organization. Individual families were able to increase their cattle holdings to the point where clan winter lands could no longer support the cattle. Moreover, such families were forced to travel separately because of the inadequacy of water supplies for such large herds along the road. Finally, the increase in cattle caused more pressure on the limited grazing grounds resulting in sharpened intertribal wars and invasions, resettlement of the population, and disruption of the clan units. Thus, the clan often split and a new unit, the *ajmaq*,[16] composed of elements from the various clans, was formed. Nevertheless many clan traditions, such as mutual aid, marriage, and other kinship traditions,[17] survived. But the important clan function of the group management of herds and pastures ceased to exist.[18]

With the growth of large individual holdings of cattle and pasture a new aristocracy based on the new wealth emerged in addition to the traditional hereditary aristocracy of the *aq süjök*. At the same time many of the poorer Kazakhs were dispossessed of their herds and forced to become hired workers (*džalšy*).[19] Finally there was a small slave group (*qul*) composed of foreigners (probably war captives),[20] individuals who could be bought

[16] Abdykalykov, Pankratova, *op. cit.*, p. 125.

[17] Akademiya Nauk, Institut istorii, *Materialy . . .*, IV, 6.

[18] There is considerable disagreement in the sources as to the extent of any communal ownership of herds and pastures. There seems to be no doubt, however, that early holdings were relatively small and unstable and at least partially communal, and that concentration of wealth and the development of larger private holdings was an historically late development. Cf. V. Riazanovski, "Customary Laws of the Kirghiz," *Chinese Social & Political Science Review* (Peiping), XXI, 2 (1937-38), 202; Abdykalykov, Pankratova, *op. cit.*, pp. 125-27; Radloff, *Aus Sibirien . . .*, I, 127, 146, 417; Hudson, *op. cit.*, pp. 34-35; P. Pogorelski, "K voprosu o teorii i praktike osedaniya kochevnikov," *Revolyutsionny Vostok* (Moscow, 1934), No. 5, p. 182.

[19] Hudson, *op. cit.*, p. 27.

[20] The term *qul* in the sense of "slave" is already found in the Orkhon inscriptions. Also in the times of the Orkhon inscriptions, the group of the *qul* seems to have consisted primarily of war captives. E.g., in the Bilgä-

and sold but who had the right to acquire property.[21] There was in addition one group, the *tölöngüts,* who apparently formed the personal bodyguard of the sultans and the khans.[22]

Religious Beliefs of the Kazakhs

The world view of the early Kazakhs was, as was that of all nomadic Turks of Central Asia, based on shamanistic beliefs, although Mohammedanism was superficially accepted. The Orkhon memorial inscriptions contain some scanty information on the beliefs of the early Turks. With the information offered by these sources and with the help of analogies to the beliefs of the Turks of the Altai region, among whom shamanistic beliefs were retained more persistently than among other groups, Radloff[23] and Thomsen[24] have reconstructed the following picture of the shamanistic beliefs and mythology of the early Turks.

The world was believed to consist of a number of strata. Seventeen strata formed heaven, or the "realm of light," and seven or nine strata formed the underworld, or the "realm of darkness." The surface of the earth on which man lives was pictured as between heaven and the underworld.[25] The supreme ruler and

---

khan inscription it said of the sons of the leaders of the defeated people that they "became slaves" (*bäglik ury oghlyn qul boldy*) (Vilhelm Thomsen, *Inscriptions de l'Orkhon,* Mémoires de la Societé Finno-Ougrienne, V [Helsingfors, 1896], p. 106; Radloff, *Alttürkische . . . ,* p. 55).

[21] Abdykalykov, Pankratova, *op. cit.,* p. 130; Hudson, *op. cit.,* p. 59.

[22] *Ibid.,* pp. 59-60. It seems that this group originally consisted of herdsmen who placed themselves voluntarily under the protection of a khan or sultan and, in return for this service, received the use of cattle. Some of the *tölöngüts,* however, seem to have been liberated slaves. Cf. Radloff, *Aus Sibirien . . . ,* I, 526, G. Togzhanov, "O kazakhskom feodalizme," *Revolyutsionny Vostok* (Moscow, 1933), 6, pp. 126-27. While most authorities agree that the relationship of the *tölöngüt* to his master was essentially a voluntary one, it seems that after the Russian occupation this situation changed radically and the *tölöngüt,* just like the *qul,* was now bound to serve his master for life. See F. Zobin, *K voprosu o nevol'nikakh, rabakh i tyulengutakh v Kirgizskoi stepi,* Pamyatnaya kniga Semipalatinskoi oblasti na 1920 g., vyp. IV, p. 37, in Akademiya Nauk, *Materialy . . . ,* IV, 11-12.

[23] Radloff, *Aus Sibirien . . . ,* II, 1 ff.; *Alttürkische . . . , passim.*

[24] V. Thomsen, "Alttürkische Inschriften aus der Mongolei," *Zeitschrift der deutschen Morgenländischen Gesellschaft,* N.F., III (Leipzig, 1924); *Inscriptions . . . , passim.*

[25] Cf. in the Orkhon inscriptions: *Özä kök tängri asra jaghyz jär (jir) qylynduqda ikin ara kiši oghly qylynmyš* ("after the blue heaven above and the

creator of heaven and earth (*tängri*)[26] resided in the topmost stratum of heaven. The heavenly strata were also inhabited by a number of benign spirits or deities. Thus there was the goddess Umai,[27] who is mentioned in the Orkhon inscriptions and who was evidently considered as the protecting spirit of little children. The souls of the deceased were believed to reside in one of the higher strata, while the souls of evil persons were believed to people the underworld. Not only were heaven and the underworld inhabited by numerous spirits, but there also were a number of spirits—friendly to man—who were believed to inhabit the surface of the earth. These were called collectively *jär-sub*[28] (literally: earth-water), and were believed to be found at the tops of high mountains and at the sources of rivers. As man did not dare to communicate directly with the spirits of heaven, the souls of deceased ancestors served as intermediaries. It was difficult, however, to communicate with the ancestors, and thus it was preferable to employ a shaman for this purpose.

Further beliefs of the early Turks can be deduced from their burial customs. It seems to have been the custom to erect some form of monument (*balbal*)[29] over the grave of a hero on which enemies killed in battle were symbolically represented, probably in the belief that the spirits of these enemies would serve the deceased in the other world. Such monuments are found

dark earth below had been created, the sons of man were created in between the two"), Thomsen, *Inscriptions* . . . , p. 97; Radloff, *Alttürkische* . . . , p. 43.

[26] The word *tängri* occurs in the Orkhon inscriptions both in the meaning of "heaven" and in the meaning of "god of heaven." E.g., *öd tängri jašar:* "heaven [or rather, the god of heaven, TGW] lives eternally" (while man is mortal), Radloff, *Alttürkische* . . . , p. 28. Thomsen here reads *jasar* instead of *jašar* and translates: "heaven [the god of heaven, TGW] arranges the time" (when man must die), Thomsen, *Inscriptions* . . . , p. 113; Thomsen, "Alttürkische . . . ," p. 156. In the pure meaning of "heaven" or "sky" we find *tängri* in such expressions as *kök tängri,* "the blue heaven" (as opposed to *jaghyz jär,* "the dark earth," i.e., the underworld), Radloff, *Alttürkische* . . . , p. 43; Thomsen, *Inscriptions* . . . , p. 97. The Kazakh ethnographer Valikhanov speaks of *tängri* as meaning not a personified god, but rather "heaven" under whose influence man found himself. Čoqan Valikhanov, *Sochineniya,* Zapiski Imp. Russkogo Geogr. Obshchestva, XXIX, St. Petersburg (1904), p. 13.

[27] Radloff, *Alttürkische* . . . ," pp. 18-19; Thomsen *Inscriptions* . . . , pp. 108-154.

[28] Radloff, *Alttürkische* . . . , p. 9; Thomsen, *Inscriptions* . . . , p. 100.

[29] Radloff, *Alttürkische* . . . , pp. 247, 277; Thomsen, *Inscriptions* . . . , p. 132.

throughout the regions inhabited by Turkic people and range as far west and north as the southern Russian steppes where they are called, according to Russian folkways, *kamennye baby* (literally: stone women). Barthold also reports a belief of the early Turks in reincarnation. The soul was believed to enter the body of a bird or an insect and thus the Turks spoke of the deceased as *üčdü* (he has flown away).[30] In the west, long after their Islamization, the Turks said of the deceased: *Šunqar bołdy* (he became a falcon).[31]

There seem to have existed strong elements of fire worship among the Kazakhs, probably originating in influence from the Persian Mazdaists. Fire was considered holy. There was a taboo against spitting into it and it was frequently referred to not by its common Kazakh name (*aulie*), but, as among the Mongols, as "mother."[32]

From modern ethnology we have further evidence of shamanism recently practiced. It was found in the late nineteenth century that the shaman (Kazakh: *baqsa*) still performed the old arts of healing, invoked the aid of the spirits, and induced a semihysterical or hysterical state. Radloff describes the healing activities of the Kazakh shaman in the following way:

> When the shaman arrives at the house of the diseased, he brings with him his instrument, the *qobyz* which has attached to its top bells, or metal rings . . . . He accompanies his song with this instrument. During his singing, he often attains such a state of trance [*Verzückung*] that he has to be held down by several people. Great *baqsas* in this state are completely without sensation; they touch red-hot iron, insert several inches of a needle into their skin, lick red-hot iron, step on red hot iron, so that the soles of their feet sizzle.[33]

There were two types of disease recognized among the Kazakhs, with different shamanistic therapies indicated for each. Light diseases (*učuq*), accompanied by fever and nausea, had

[30] Barthold, *Zwölf Vorlesungen* . . . , p. 20.
[31] *Ibid.*, p. 21.
[32] Valikhanov, *op. cit.*, p. 15.
[33] Radloff, *Proben der Volksliteratur der türkischen Stämme Süd-Sibiriens* (St. Petersburg, 1870), III, 60 n.

their origin, according to popular beliefs, in food which had been spoiled by spirits. Such illnesses were cured by a shamanistic ceremony consisting of thrice sprinkling the patient with hot and cold water. Serious disease, *qaghyndy,* was also believed to be caused by evil spirits, which the shaman attempted to dispel by beating the patient with animal lungs.[34]

The penetration of Mohammedanism among the Kazakhs was a slow process. The Arab invasion of southern Central Asia, which brought about the conversion of the sedentary Turks and Iranians, had no influence on the religious life of the northern Turks. As late as the tenth century, Arab geographers still describe the northern Turks as being totally indifferent to Mohammedanism, although, according to Barthold[35] the situation was at that time already beginning to change. By the eleventh century there were somewhat more successful attempts at proselytism by the Mohammedan Karakhanides who carried on a relentless struggle against the "infidel" Turkic tribes in the near north of the oasis regions. But the vast majority of nomadic Turks further north in the steppe regions remained virtually immune to this new monotheistic religion. Systematic attempts at conversion were made by missionaries belonging to the sect of the Ṣūfī, but even their influence seems to have remained limited to the Turks living near the oasis regions. The first large-scale conversions of the Kazakhs to Mohammedanism began in the seventeenth century[36] under the influence of contact with the Mohammedan sedentary Uzbeks.

One obstacle to quick and complete acceptance of Islam by the nomads was the unsuitability of many Mohammedan tenets and rites, such as the strict dietary and sanitary laws, to a nomadic way of life. Valikhanov tells us that before the Russian conquest of the Kazakh steppe, Mohammedan religious consciousness was so shallow that "not a single steppe fighter (*batyr*) knew who Mohammed was."[37] A Western observer, Schuyler, confirms Valikhanov's observations, saying that:

[34] Valikhanov, *op. cit.,* p. 19. [35] Barthold, *Zwölf Vorlesungen* . . . , p. 59

[36] H. Vámbéry, *Das Türkenvolk in seinen ethnologischen und ethnographischen Beziehungen* (Leipzig, 1885), p. 299.

[37] Valikhanov, *op. cit.,* p. 191.

> It is only externally that they are Moslems. On being asked what religion they have . . . they will say they do not know, but at the same time they would repel with vigor any insinuations that they were not good Moslems.[38]

Unlike conditions among the sedentary Islamized Turks, the language of the Islamized nomads has not shown much Arabic or Persian influence. Moreover, these nomads had little regard for the Mohammedan dietary laws except in regard to the abstention from pork; they did not adhere strictly to the Mohammedan prayers and fasts; they did not always carry out the Mohammedan circumcision rites; and they neither veiled nor secluded their women, since this would have interfered with the heavy burden of women's work in nomadic society. Although Mohammedanism was never completely accepted by the nomads, it influenced the traditional shamanistic rites and customs which survived and many elements of the Islamic ritual were incorporated into the shamanistic rites. Thus the shaman used the Moslem insignia of the *aṣā,* the Moslem ornamented staff, and in prayers he used the name of Mohammed.[39] But at the same time he enacted the entire ceremonial of trancelike frenzy described earlier. When healing the sick he chanted magical lines which showed the influence of Mohammedan prayers as well as shamanistic formulae.[40]

Role of Women

The role of women in Kazakh society created a considerable social problem which was reflected most eloquently in the folklore and literature. The woman was considered an economic asset in terms of the work she could accomplish. The rich nomad was able to buy several wives (the wife was purchased for a bride price—*qalym*) and polygamy was a sign of male status. Women were allowed to live in, and run, their own households and sometimes could even own property. (The husband tradi-

[38] Eugene Schuyler, *Turkistan, Notes of a Journey in Russian Turkistan, Khokand, Bukhara and Kuldja* (New York, 1876), I, 37-38.
[39] Radloff, *Proben* . . . , III, 60, 61.
[40] Vámbéry, *Das Türkenvolk* . . . , pp. 301-2; Radloff, *loc. cit.*

tionally lived in the large *yurt* [*džurt*][41] surrounded by the smaller structures of his wives.) Nevertheless, the attitudes toward women and the arduous work required of them, which included tending and watching the cattle, cleaning the *yurt*, cooking, milking the animals, making felt rugs, and in general carrying out the most menial tasks, in addition to the duties of rearing children,[42] made their position difficult. A woman in this culture was always subject to the will of a superior. As a young girl she was expected to carry out the menial chores in the household of her parents, where she was ruled by her father, opposition to whose will was considered, after the adoption of Islam, as a violation of Mohammedan customary law (*'adāt*). It was, however, after marriage that her greatest trials began. As marriage was considered an economic arrangement between the future husband and his parents-in-law, the bride herself could take no part in the plans or negotiations. After the marriage ceremony the young wife moved to the husband's compound, where she became subject to the will of her husband and his older wives. (The first wife [Kazakh: *baj-biše*] occupied a favored position and thus enjoyed a more agreeable married life than the younger wives.) Men were allowed complete authority over their wives, even to the extent of killing them, for which the customary punishment was none or quite negligible, while the punishment for any offense on the part of the wife was extremely severe. The customary punishment for adultery on the part of the woman was to hurl the offender down a deep precipice. The husband could divorce his wife on a considerable number of grounds, thus forcing her to return to her family, where she usually was not welcomed because of the duty thus imposed to return the *qalym*.[43]

The nomadic Turks accepted only those aspects of Mohammedan attitudes toward women which were suited to their society. Thus the *'adāt* (Mohammedan customary law) was useful in enforcing the idea of the superior status of the male members of

[41] The *yurt* (*džurt*) is the tent-like conical felt structure in which the nomadic Turks of Central Asia live.

[42] See George P. Murdock, *Our Primitive Contemporaries* (New York, 1934), p. 158.

[43] Hudson, *op. cit.*, p. 51.

society, and there was no conflict between the traditional nomadic polygamous household, in which the woman did the menial and heavy work, and Mohammedan family organization. On the other hand, those aspects of Mohammedan customs concerning women which could not be easily integrated into nomadic life, such as the seclusion and veiling of women, were not adopted, and nomadic women retained the right to run their own households and to own a limited amount of property.

Education

Before the steppe Turks were converted to Mohammedanism education was of a primitive order and probably was limited to the learning of tribal economic pursuits, crafts, and lore. It was only after the introduction of Islam that the Kazakhs began to have a very limited number of organized schools and teachers. The schools were, however, primarily religious and were designed solely for the education of the clergy. The substance of the requirements were memorization of the religious tenets of Islam and of the most important sections of the Koran. There were two types of schools, the *mekteb,* the lower religious school, and the *medrese,* the higher theological school. All teachers were Mohammedan priests of various ranks. Methods of instruction in the religious institutions reflected the narrow character of Mohammedan education. The stress placed on attainment of factual knowledge caused the student to spend a great deal of time learning texts by heart while the implications of the materials were often lost to him. Moreover, most of the memorizing, at least in the *medrese,* was in the Arabic language, of which the Turkic children knew little.

An incidental but important by-product of this education, however, was the study of some Oriental poetry, particularly Arab and Persian religious poetry, in the original language. The price of education was prohibitive to any but the rich as the parents were obliged to pay the teacher for every assignment which the student mastered. The result was a small educated class, most of whom were members of the Mohammedan clergy.

The Kazakh Legal System

It is fortunate for the student of Central Asiatic cultures that the laws of the Kazakhs were codified in the seventeenth century under Khan Teüke,[44] and while the orginal documents have not been preserved, we have at least a partial record of them from the records of the Russian colonial administration and as a result of ethnographic researches by Russian scholars in the nineteenth century. The period of the reign of Khan Teüke over the Kazakhs was one of rapid change and increasing social stratification; and, as might be expected, the codified law of which we have knowledge is primarily concerned with property rights and with the political and social hierarchy of the Kazakh tribes and confederation. Particularly revealing for this study is the criminal code because of its close bearing on the Kazakh social and economic structure.

In addition to the early concept of Kazakh justice based on the traditional law of blood revenge (in which the relatives of a victim took upon themselves the obligation of punishing the criminal) there was a second method of administration of justice in which society played a role. Either by agreement or by a sentence imposed by the judge (*bi*) (a traditional Kazakh official who held this position by virtue of his knowledge of tribal law)[45] punishment of the offender might be limited to the payment of a *qūn.*[46] The *qūn,* like the Anglo-Saxon *wergild,* implied a fixed scale of payment for each offense, e.g., one thousand sheep for the murder of a man or five hundred sheep for the murder of a woman.[47] The *qūn* scale also provided for fixed payments for mutilation of part of the body. Thus, for example, injury to one finger called for the payment of one hundred

[44] S. V. Yushkov, ed., *Materialy po kazakhskomu obychnomu pravu,* Akademiya Nauk Kazakhskoi SSR (Alma-Ata, 1948), p. 3.

[45] Valikhanov, *op. cit.,* p. 161.

[46] From Persian *xūn:* "blood."

[47] Radloff, *Aus Sibirien . . . ,* I, 523-24.

sheep.[48] Social stratification among the Kazakhs is well expressed by the *qūn* scale. While the *qūn* for murder of a commoner called for payment of one thousand sheep, the *qūn* for murder of a sultan was equal to that for seven commoners.[49] An insult to a member of the aristocracy had to be atoned with nine head of cattle.[50] The *qūn* laws also provide an interesting picture of the patriarchal, autocratic family relations among the nomadic Kazakhs. Thus parents were not punished for killing their children, and a man who had killed his wife had to pay only a relatively small *qūn,* but a woman who had killed her husband was immediately executed unless she was pregnant.[51]

Effect of Russian Colonial Policy on the Culture of the Kazakhs

The effects of the Russian occupation and the ensuing colonial policy on the culture of the Turkic nomads were far reaching and brought about the disintegration of much of the traditional nomadic culture. As a result of the Russian attempt to reorganize and change the basic structure of Kazakh society and also as an almost inevitable consequence of contact with the more complex Russian economy, drastic changes took place in all aspects of Kazakh culture, and in particular in Kazakh economy. Kazakhstan became an important route for Russian trade with the Orient, particularly with Persia and India but also with the southern Uzbek khanates. The large-scale influx of Russian manufactured goods sharply diminished the traditional home production of clothes and tools. The Russians established fairs in the larger towns of the Kazakh territory where the cattle breeder sold his cattle for cash and was thus able to buy the products of Russian industry. This development caused a great change in the nature of nomadic cattle breeding, which had been primarily for use of the tribe and the clan, but which now developed into breeding for the market. Moreover, the already sharpened social differentiation among the Kazakhs was increased

[48] Yushkov, ed., *op. cit.,* p. 78.
[49] *Ibid.,* p. 282.
[50] *Ibid.,* pp. 35-43.
[51] A. I. Levshin, *op. cit.,* III, 170-74; Abdykalykov, Pankratova, *op. cit.,* p. 116.

as the cattle-poor herder had few things to sell and thus could not buy the Russian products which formerly had been made in home industry, while many large cattle breeders became merchants or cattle traders, and even began to settle in the towns.

The Russian land policy in particular brought about great changes in the Kazakh nomadic economy and eventually made it necessary for many to undertake agricultural pursuits. Under the Temporary Statute of 1869 all Kazakh land became Russian crown property, and the Kazakh cattle breeder was allowed to use the land only by paying a heavy tax to the Russians.[52] Each Kazakh was obliged to carry a passport and traveling from one district or subdistrict to another was sharply curtailed. This restriction had a disastrous effect on the nomadic economy, based as it was on free migration from winter to summer areas, for it frequently occurred that the winter and summer grazing grounds were located in different Russian administrative zones.

A large-scale program of colonization of the Kazakh steppes by Russian and Ukrainian peasants caused a further disruption of the original distribution of land. In 1861 the Russian government issued the "Temporary Rule for the Colonization of the Kirghiz[53] Steppes by the Rural Population" (*Vremennye pravila po pereseleniyu v kirgizkiye stepi sel'skikh obyvatelei*), according to which each peasant-colonizer received forty-five *desyatinas*[54] per head. In the 1880's the Russians settled a large number of T'ungans and Uighurs in Semirechye.[55] By 1895 this Russian

[52] *Aziatskaya Rossiya,* izd. Pereselencheskogo Upravleniya (St. Petersburg, 1914), I, 159.

[53] Kirghiz was the term erroneously applied to the Kazakhs by the Russians. This term was generally used even after the establishment of Soviet power in the area. It was only in April, 1925, that the name was officially changed to Kazakh.

[54] One *desyatina* equals 2.7 acres.

[55] The T'ungans are Chinese Moslems, located primarily in Kansu Province, the Ili Valley, and the cities on the northern edge of the Tien-Shan mountains, who had risen unsuccessfully against the Manchu dynasty, and whose rebellion had been bloodily suppressed by Chinese troops. The Uighurs are a Turkic, sedentary people, the bulk of whom inhabit the oasis regions of Chinese Turkestan (Sinkiang). They represent the dominant Turkic group of this westernmost Chinese province. In 1863 the Uighurs rose in revolt against the Chinese authorities and under the leadership of the famous Ya'qūb Beg set up an independent Turkic state with the capital at Kashgar, but by 1877 the Manchu general Tso Tsung-t'ang had succeeded in destroying Ya'qūb

colonization policy had taken on such proportions that, according to the statistics of the Russian Colonization Authority, in the Ural and Turgai districts the Kazakhs were deprived of twenty million *desyatinas* of land.[56] Frequently the best grazing lands were given to the Russian colonizers. In addition, the Russians constructed military Cossack fortifications in the steppes (the so-called *stanitsy*).[57] Around these stations there stretched a belt of several miles which was forbidden territory to the local population.

As a result of the land policy and of the colonization program, by 1895, according to the data of the Russian Colonization Authority, only 37.7 percent of the households in the district of Semipalatinsk were still nomadic,[58] and by 1908 it is reported that in the Chimkent district only 16.6 percent of the population maintained a purely nomadic way of life.[59] (This figure is somewhat misleading, however, since agriculture continued to be very much looked down upon and in many cases agricultural pursuits were taken up only as a necessary evil, to be abandoned in favor of nomadism as soon as the individual had again amassed enough cattle to sustain himself.)[60] It was primarily the poorer Kazakhs who were forced to settle because they were unable to support themselves on the very long migrations, while the large cattle breeders took over most of the remaining land for grazing purposes.

The Russians, following a conscious policy of Russification, undertook a number of reforms seriously detrimental to the

---

Beg's realm and in re-establishing, at the cost of much bloodshed, Chinese authority over the rebellious Mohammedans. Large numbers of both groups fled across the Russian border and sought protection under the tsar. The tsarist government was only too glad to utilize the two groups in its aim of establishing non-Kazakh settlements in the Kazakh territory. See Owen Lattimore, *Pivot of Asia* (Boston, 1950).

[56] Abdykalykov and Pankratova, *op. cit.*, pp. 287-92.

[57] It was in one of these Cossack stations that the major part of Pushkin's tale *The Captain's Daughter* takes place.

[58] Abdykalykov and Pankratova, *op. cit.*, pp. 304-9.

[59] T. Ryskulov, "Sovremenny Kazakhstan," *Novy Vostok* (Moscow), No. 12 (Dec., 1926), p. 107.

[60] S. I. Rudenko, "Ocherk byta Kazakov basseina rek Uila i Sagyza," S. F. Baronov, A. N. Bukeikhan, S. I. Rudenko, *Kazaki, antropologicheskiye ocherki* (Leningrad, 1927), p. 8.

Kazakh socio-political structure, rooted as it was in a tribal, patriarchal way of life. Through a series of administrative decrees the traditional tribal hierarchy of the khans and the sultans was replaced by a new Russian-imposed administration. The institution of new administrative regions and boundaries cut through the traditional tribal boundary lines, and, as a result, the Kazakhs were deprived of all local autonomy and tribal and national unity.

The first steps in the accomplishment of this policy were the Igelstroem Reforms of 1786.[61] In these reforms the Russians sharply limited the political jurisdiction of the khan by making him directly responsible to the Russian administration and by making his election by the tribal aristocracy subject to the approval of the Russian colonial administration. The khan, who had hitherto been the supreme ruler of the tribal confederation of the Kazakhs,[62] was reduced to the role of an obedient servant of the Russian administration.[63] Simultaneously the Russians brought about the breakdown of the traditional Kazakh legal structure and the court system by limiting the jurisdiction of the tribal judges (*bi*) to purely local affairs. Most of the functions of the *bi* were taken over by newly organized Russian courts, the border and district tribunals (*pogranichnye sudy*), which were composed primarily of Russian officials with a few members of the upper Kazakh aristocracy, and were subject to the governor-general in Orenburg. Subservient to the border tribunals and responsible for the justice in the various territorial subdivisions were the district tribunals, which were administered by Kazakh officials appointed by the Russians.[64]

In 1824 the Russians abolished the institution of the khan completely and transferred his power to a group of sultans, each of whom ruled over a different district of the Kazakh steppes. That these sultans no longer ruled as national Kazakh adminis-

[61] Abdykalykov and Pankratova, *op. cit.,* pp. 180-81.
[62] Although his power was frequently sharply limited and restricted, there had never been an authority higher than the khan.
[63] Majerczak, "Renseignements . . . ," pp. 130-31; Abdykalykov and Pankratova, *op. cit.,* p. 180.
[64] Majerczak, "Renseignements . . . ," p. 128.

trators, but purely as executors of Russian colonial policy, is evidenced by the fact that each of them received a guard of two hundred Russian Cossack soldiers.[65]

After occupying the entire region inhabited by the Kazakhs, the Russians, in 1868, finally abolished the position of the sultan. They then divided the Kazakh steppes into four Russian provinces (*oblast'*) (*Turgai, Akmolinsk, Semipalatinsk, Semirechiye*) without regard for previous tribal lines and placed at the head of the administration of each of these districts a Russian military governor. Each province was subdivided, according to the Russian administrative system, into districts and the districts again into subdistricts (Russian: *volost'*; Kazakh: *bolus*). Local rule of a kind extended up to, and through, the district administration, but the election of officials had to be confirmed by the Russian Government. Above the district level the administration was taken over completely by the Russians.[66]

It was the promulgation of the "Temporary Statute," one year later in 1869, which completed the destruction of all tribal organization. As a result of this statute the Kazakh administrative districts were further revised so as to destroy the last vestiges of territorial unity of the tribes and clans.[67] Russian administrators replaced Kazakh officials even at the level of the *volost'*, which, under the new statute, was to be ruled by a Russian governor appointed by the tsar. The "Temporary Statute" further provided that all Kazakh elections, local or regional, were to be confirmed by the Russian Government, which also obtained power to recall all dignitaries on a moment's notice. Under the new statute the traditional legal system was almost completely supplanted by the Russian police and court system and only less important local cases continued to be judged by the *bi*.[68]

These far-reaching economic, political, and social changes in Kazakh society created many new social problems and greatly

[65] Majerczak, "La justice chez les Kirgiz-Kazaks," *Revue du Monde Musulman*, XXXV (1917-18), 254; Majerczak, "Renseignements . . . ," p. 160.
[66] Majerczak, "La justice . . . ," pp. 256-57.
[67] Schuyler, *op. cit.*, I, 33.
[68] Abdykalykov and Pankratova, *op. cit.*, pp. 268-70.

intensified internal conflicts. A part of the Kazakh aristocracy took on jobs as administrators, thus obtaining favored positions and the best grazing lands. At the same time ever larger groups of the smaller herd owners were dispossessed of cattle and grazing lands and were forced to undertake agriculture, a transition which was not easy for them. Further, the Kazakhs, who had formerly been able to unite in the face of an enemy, were now split internally on attitudes toward the Russians.

In addition to upsetting the social and political structure of society and destroying the Kazakh national and tribal unity by gerrymandering of boundaries, the Russians also pursued a policy of Russification of Kazakh culture, a policy which was applied to all the national cultures. The means used to accomplish this was primarily that of education. One method which the Russians might have been expected to pursue, that of religious proselytism, was not followed to any significant extent. Actually religion was one of the few aspects of Kazakh culture which was allowed to remain relatively unchanged. Although there were some sporadic efforts to send Christian missionaries into the steppes,[69] the Russians seem to have avoided any concerted efforts to combat Islam. On the contrary, all available evidence indicates that the Russians actually fostered Mohammedanism by constructing mosques and importing Kazan-Tatar *mullās* for the carrying out of Moslem proselytizing activities.[70] As a result, Russian occupation fostered a considerable growth in Islamic conversions among the Kazakh groups which were in prolonged and intimate contact with the Russians.[71]

In their educational policy, however, the Russians made a

[69] In paragraphs 244-49 of the "Act on the Sibirian Kirghiz" (1822) reference is made to the desirability of Christian missionary work in the steppes. Cf. Levshin, *op. cit.*, III, 286-87.

[70] Valikhanov, *op. cit.*, p. 63.

[71] V. Grigorev writes the following: "An incontrovertible proof that the Mussulman propaganda in one or another form went into the Kirghiz steppes from the side of Russia is the circumstance that especially those Kirghiz who live along our lines have become Mussulman, while the old genuine Shamanism is kept up, even at the present time, among those Kirghiz particularly who wander in the neighborhood of Khiva, Bukhara, and what was formerly Khokand, that is, in really Mussulman countries . . ." ("The Russian Policy Regarding Central Asia. An Historical Sketch," in Schuyler, *op. cit.*, II, 405).

concerted effort to infuse their culture into every possible aspect of Kazakh cultural life and attempted to supplant the Kazakh language by Russian at least as the official state language of the area. The Russians further inaugurated an educational program in order to train native Kazakhs for work in the Russian administration. For this purpose a new school system was instituted which was to be one of the most important means for carrying out the Russification policy. In the territory of the Kazakhs the first Russian school was opened in Omsk in 1789 under the name of "Asiatic School" (*Aziatskaya Shkola*). Similar schools under the name of "Russo-native" or "Russo-Kirghiz" schools (*Russko-Tuzemnye* or *Russko-Kirgizskie Shkoly*) were opened in other towns of the Kazakh region, such as Uralsk (1841), Turgai (1869), Chimkent (1887), Türkistan (1888), Kazalinsk (1894), and Perovsk (1901). Later, during the early twentieth century, such schools were opened in the Kazakh towns of Aulie-Ata, Verny (Alma-Ata), Semipalatinsk, Petropavlovsk, Akmolinsk, and Kustanai.[72]

In addition to the Russian-administered schools, a small Kazakh educational movement developed which was responsible for the creation of a new type of secular school, the "new method" schools. These new schools denied the old religious, dogmatic educational methods and stressed in their stead an education based on the tenets of a broader, more Europeanized culture.[73] Instruction was in Kazakh in a cyrillic script.[74]

The new Russian and Kazakh schools did not, however, bring about any great change in the character of the educated class, which, though broader than that of pre-Russian days, was still limited to those who could meet qualifications of wealth, sex, and birth. Thus the students chosen were usually the children of the highest Kazakh dignitaries or of the richest members of society. The literate population was composed primarily of the clergy and the officials of the Russian administration, a minute fraction of the total population. In general the Russians at-

[72] Abdykalykov and Pankratova, *op. cit.*, pp. 298-99.
[73] *Ibid.*, p. 360.
[74] S. D. Asfendiarov, *Istoriya Kazakstana* (Alma-Ata, Moscow, 1935), I, 202.

tempted to limit the curriculum to the training necessary for administrative work.

The educational program of the Russians did succeed in providing trained native officials and did bring about, to some extent, the Russification of Kazakh culture. But a far more profound effect of the new education was the encouragement of the development of Kazakh nationalism. The Russian educator was presented with the age-old problem of colonial administrators. A consequence of educating colonial peoples, in this case of training interpreters and scribes in the Russian language, was to open to them channels to the study of Western thought which might eventually be used against the ruling power. Thus the newly trained Kazakh officialdom soon became acquainted with Russian philosophy and literature and eventually with the liberal, democratic, and nationalist thought of the period. A new intelligentsia emerged, and it was from this group that the leaders of the Kazakh independence movement were drawn.

In the light of an historical perspective one can only conclude that while the Russians were able to effect vast changes in Kazakh culture and to destroy some aspects of it, the Russification policy itself failed; and this conclusion can be applied as well to the rest of the Central Asiatic nomadic peoples. Although the Russians were successful at first in breaking down national and tribal unity, eventually their policies acted to solidify the national feelings of the Kazakhs. The new nationalist movement led by the growing intelligentsia was to take on proportions unlike any of the earlier atempts at unity, in spite of all the efforts of the Russians to combat such a development. The new Kazakh spirit was reflected most eloquently and passionately in the folklore and literature of the nomads.

Chapter II

EARLY FOLKLORE

The Setting: Central Asiatic Oral Traditions

The early history of Central Asia was replete with migrations and intermixtures of the many nomadic groups inhabiting that area, and the earliest folklore traditions of these peoples were carried from one group to another until it has become difficult to determine to which group particular traits originally belonged. In considering the oral art of the Turkic peoples of Central Asia it is necessary to make a clear distinction between the creations of the nomadic Turks, such as the Kazakhs, Kirghiz, and Turkmen, and those of the Turks who—like the Uzbeks—eventually adopted a sedentary agricultural mode of life. Not only did the artistic products of the two groups diverge in subject matter, but they developed many different genres and types. Until the nineteenth century, nomadic art was composed almost entirely of oral productions, distinguished by a well-developed epic tradition. Among the sedentary Turks, however, epic folk traditions gradually lost much of their vitality, but these peoples developed a considerable treasure of written literary works at a far earlier period than did the nomads.

The Turks who conquered the southern oasis regions found themselves in the midst of a civilization which placed great emphasis on the arts, particularly on architecture and literature. These Turkic groups rapidly adopted the Irano-Arabic tradition of the arts. It was not until the nineteenth century, however, that their northern neighbors began to develop a comparable literary tradition as a result partly of the influence of the Turko-Irano-Arabic literatures of the south, but mainly as a result of the Russian conquest with the consequent influence of Russian literature and Western literary currents.

Nomadic Central Asia has presented the world with an almost inexhaustible reservoir of folklore productions representing a wide variety of genres from the simple song to ceremonial songs, tales, legends, fantastic stories, and finally the heroic epos. This folklore heritage of the nomadic peoples is clearly a product of their whole way of life and culture. The ceremonial songs reflect the existence of definite, prescribed tribal and clan rites. The tales and legends suggest a strong tradition of tribal lore and mythology. The heroic epos, which was most highly developed by the nomads, indicates a tradition of struggle and warfare for conquest or for defense against transgressors which was carried out by groups large enough to have created a national spirit and a sense of tribal history. The economy of the nomads was geared to warfare over grazing lands with neighboring tribal federations and excursionary wars against the settled populations of the south. Such a life provided fertile ground for development of a widespread and tenacious epic tradition, which, similar to epic traditions the world over, has immortalized warlike heroes who, by their great bravery and strength or by their supernatural powers, have led their people to victory or safety. These traditions of the nomads have remained a vital force and a living part of their society even to this day.

The original composers of the folk creations remained to a large extent unknown. Songs, legends, tales, or epics commemorating particular events were composed by bards[1] (in a few cases their identities have been preserved) or originated in improvisation by groups at gatherings or at communal work. They were then handed down from generation to generation by oral transmission. The most widespread method of distribution was that of the wandering bard, who traveled from tribal *aul* to *aul* and either simply recited tales in prose or verse or sang his songs or epics, frequently to the accompaniment of primitive string instruments. These productions underwent, in the course of time, considerable alteration. The bards, relying entirely on

[1] The most common Kazakh term for the bard is *aqyn*. If the bard specializes in the performance of epic songs, he is called *džyršy*. A bard who also carries out shamanistic functions is called *baqsy* or *bajan*.

memory, frequently introduced variations in the texts or their own individual interpretation of the subject matter. Similarly, the tunes to which the bards sang the songs were frequently the result of improvisation.[2]

Systematic efforts at scientific recordings of Central Asiatic oral art were not made until the nineteenth and particularly the twentieth century when Russian ethnographic and linguistic expeditions equipped with modern recording devices went to Central Asia in search of these texts. The recordings of Central Asiatic folklore made in the nineteenth century or earlier, however, are also of great significance. Three works of outstanding importance have survived. The first of these, which provides information about the very early nomadic folk-art, is Mahmūd al-Kāshgarī's *Dīwān lughāt at-Turk,* a dictionary of a Central Asiatic Turkic language closely related to ancient Uighur, compiled in Baghdad in c. 1077 in Arabic by an emigré Turk from Central Asia. This work contains, in the manner of lexical explanations, a great wealth of Central Asiatic folklore, particularly poetry and proverbs. The *Dīwān* is of particular importance because it gives us not only an insight into the earliest folklore heritage of the Central Asiatic Turks and of their shamanistic customs and rites, but also because it is the first work to give us information about the vernacular of the early Turkic tribes.[3] The second work is the recordings of folklore of the Turkic tribes and the translations of their texts into Russian and German by the Russian linguist and ethnographer Vasili Vasilevich (Wilhelm) Radloff.[4] The third important collection of texts,

[2] The tradition of the wandering bardsman, which has been carried on to the present day, has its counterparts in varied cultures, such as the Osman Turkish, Azerbaidzhan, and Armenian *ašyq,* the Russian *skazitel'nitsy,* the Serbo-Croat *guslari or pjevači,* and the medieval troubadours. In few cultures, however, does this tradition seem to have developed to such an intricate art as in that of the nomadic peoples of Central Asia.

[3] For a discussion of the significance of this work and for folklore excerpts from it, see C. Brockelmann, "Altturkestanische Volkspoesie," *Asia Major* (introductory volume), (London, 1922), pp. 1-22 (part one) and in *Asia Major,* II (1922), 110-24 (part two). Also: C. Brockelmann, "Altturkestanische Volksweisheit," *Ostasiatische Zeitschrift* (Berlin), VIII (1920), Heft 1-4, 49-73.

[4] Radloff, *Proben . . .* (translations) ; *Obraztsy narodnoi literatury tyurk-*

though a much more limited one than Radloff's, is that of the nineteenth-century Kazakh ethnographer Čoqan Valikhanov, who described a number of epics for the Imperial Geographic Society in St. Petersburg.[5]

These source materials reveal, in addition to the developing national character of the various folklore traditions, the frequently supranational character of many of the elements of form and of content in Central Asiatic folklore. G. N. Potanin, in his well-known work,[6] has traced a great number of Oriental, Central Asiatic, and Mongol elements in the European epic of the Middle Ages, and traces of such similarities, or borrowings of subject-matter, have been noted and indexed in particular by members of the Finnish School of folklorists. The outstanding example of a folklore complex which has spread throughout Central Asia is that of the heroic epic, which seems to have been handed from people to people across national boundaries. Thus not only are there many specific epics shared by several nationalities, but there are also common epic characters which appear in the epics of many of the nations of Central Asia. A common and dynamic epic tradition with specific characteristics and traits seems to have pervaded all the Central Asiatic nomadic Turkic cultures.

The Kazakh folklore tradition grew out of the vast and rich folklore heritage of Central Asia. Much of Kazakh folklore can actually be traced to the very early period considerably before the formation of the Kazakh federation as there are frequent references in the texts to events which occurred among the individual, and still independent, tribes. As the Kazakh nation grew, there developed a most expressive and often powerful oral art which played an important part in all Kazakh cultural activity and which lays before us much of the story of the Kazakh way of life.

---

skikh plemyon zhivushchikh v yuzhnoi Sibiri i Dzungarskoi stepi (St. Petersburg, 1866-1907) (original texts in cyrillic transcription).

[5] Valikhanov, *op. cit.*, pp. 201-8, 223-64, and *passim*.

[6] G. N. Potanin, *Vostochnyie motivy v srednevekom yevropeiskom epose* (Moscow, 1899), izdaniye Imperatorskogo Obshchestva Lyubitelei Yestestvoznaniya, Antropologii i Etnografii.

The Main Types of Kazakh Folklore

The Kazakhs have been traditionally an enormously musical people. Songs of all kinds and epics which were improvised and sung by wandering bards (*aqyn, džyršy*) to the accompainment of various primitive stringed instruments, such as the *dombra, qobyz,* or the *čybyzga,*[7] make up their remarkable folklore heritage.[8] All phases of Kazakh life—birth, marriage, battle, mourning, and death—were recorded in song. The wandering bards (*aqyn*) or epic singers (*džyršy*) not only composed their own songs, but also collected them from various tribes and clans, or from other *aqyns* and spread them by recitation from memory, thus causing the songs and epics to receive extremely wide circulation.

The Ajtys: *Songs at Celebrations*

An integral part of every large Kazakh celebration, side by side with such attractions as wrestling matches, horse races, and games, was the *ajtys.*[9] The *ajtys* was, in the truest sense, a sing-

[7] The *dombra* is a "plucking" stringed instrument, somewhat similar to the Russian *balalaika.* The *qobyz* is a two-stringed instrument with an alto pitch. It has a round body, open at the top, and a fingerboard which curves upward, so that the strings cannot be depressed to touch it. (See Valikhanov, *op. cit.,* p. 227.) According to Radloff, it is the instrument most frequently used by the shaman; and when used to accompany shamanistic rites, it is often adorned with bells and pieces of metal (Radloff, *Proben . . .* , III, 60 n.). The *čybyzga* is a primitive woodwind instrument, made of wood or—more commonly—of leather. For a description of the last two mentioned instruments, see A. I. Levshin, *op. cit.,* III, 140-41. Of these three main Kazakh instruments, it is the *dombra* which seems to have been—and still remains—the one most commonly and widely used.

[8] In addition to oral art, the Kazakhs also produced a considerable body of "booksongs," songs of predominantly religious character written by the clergy for the propagation of Islam. These works were of somewhat later origin, as the Kazakhs were converted to Mohammedanism relatively late in their history. They betray clearly the fact that they were written under the influence of the Arabic and Persian cultures dominant in the Islamic world. The "booksongs" and works of similar character composed the entire written literature of the Kazakhs. The development of a Kazakh tradition of written literature of any proportions did not occur until the latter part of the nineteenth century. As knowledge of the "booksongs" was limited to a small group and as these works did not leave a significant imprint on the culture, they are only mentioned by way of a footnote in this study. For reference, see Radloff, *Proben . . .* , III, xix, 408-856.

[9] *ajtys:* the literal meaning of this word is "dialogue, conversation, speech," from the stem *aj-t-,* "to cause to say."

ing competition between two individuals,[10] professional bards or amateurs, or two groups. In such duels the words were generally improvised and the most successful improviser was declared the winner. The content of the songs was usually drawn from everyday life. Each party might recite as many simple tales as could be recalled or the competition might be carried on in the form of a witty debate, or a mock love duel in words and song. Sometimes the competing parties vied with each in singing the praise of a distinguished guest or tribal potentate.[11] The following song is a selection from one of the competition songs recorded by Radloff and illustrates the relatively sophisticated character of these songs. Radloff tells us that the *ajtys* at which this song was sung took place at a feast, and that the participants were a young man who had recently been captured as a horse thief and a young girl from the tribe that captured him. The horse thief was brought to the feast in chains:

Qyz: Qarqaramnyn üšü ajdas ajda,
qolan qara šašymnyn tübül sajda
tep tek džatqan elimdi tez büldürgön,
ajtysamyn aghalar džajau kajda.

Džigit: Qarqarannyn ol üšü šajda bolar
izdägängä asylyq pajda bolar.
Sonša derdan men keldim džajau izdäp
ajtysamyn, qyz Opan qajda bolar.

Q.: Džermän kökkö tensälip dželsön džigit,
džermän kökkö tensälip džürsön džigit,
eginšinin atyndaj kišänin bar
rūndu sonda surajmyn n'elsin džigit?

Dž: Rūmmdu surasan Baghanaly,
bajlyqminän džylqymyz kök alaly
. . . .
at kötünö salmajmymba sen balany

[10] An informant (Mr. Asan Kaigy, a contemporary Kazakh writer, now living in Munich) told the author that in the very frequent song duels between a man and a woman, the prize for the man was a night with his opponent. There are, according to this informant, no set rules about what constitutes winning, but he asserts that the loser knows when he is beaten and generally gives up voluntarily.

[11] See Levshin, *op. cit.*, III, 139.

Q.: Barmaq qajda? Bazargha kelmäk qajda
ötö šaup elimdi almaq qajda?
Bizdin eldä džalan but džajau džürüp
at kötünö Opandy salmaq qajda?

Dž: Ölündü ajtyp, Opanym džön ölörsün,
bujuruq kelsä aldadan send' ölörsün,
Aman Džoldun Naur Qul džip kelsäm.
Alaqandaj sen Najman džergä enärsin.

Q.: Džön söilös käribim džöndügündü
negä ajtasyn au sorlu beldigindi,
bizdin eldä džalan but džalau džürüp,
negä au sorlu ajtasyn beldigindi?

Dž: Ölön bilsäm tamaghym kenäj ajtamyn
söz mänisin bilmäsäm, negä ajtamyn?
Bajbišänin balasy basyn östüm,
beldik ajtpaj e balam neni ajtamyn,

. . . .

Dž: Qatty džutup saumal qanghym keldi,
taghy birgä Opanmän jürgüm keldi,
eldägi esär qylyq eskä tüsüp
Opanyn aq tösünö mingim keldi.

Q.: Bir qamšym bar qolumda segiz örmö,
al közünö tīmäsin mennän körmö!
ekki ajaqty kisigä minämin dep.[12]

Translation[13]

Girl: The tip of my hat-feather weaves back and fro,
The roots of my black hair are soft.
He who has suddenly disturbed my peaceful people,
He who has come on foot—who is he? Brothers, I shall sing [of this].

Man: The tip of your hat-feather weaves back and fro,
He who searches shall have excellent profit.
From far away I came walking and searching:
Who is the girl, Opan?[14] [Of this] I shall sing.

[12] Radloff, *Obraztsy* . . . , III, pp. 38-40.
[13] All translations into English, unless otherwise identified, are by the author of this study.
[14] The name of the girl, his opponent.

Girl: Even if you, oh youth, have ridden, weaving, through heaven and earth,
Even if you are riding, weaving, through heaven and earth,
Still now your feet are bound by fetters, like those of the horse of the peasant laborer.
I ask your name. What is your tribe, oh youth?

Man: My tribe, since you ask, is the Baganaly tribe,
Rich are we in gray and many colored herds of horses
. . . .
Shall I not take you, my child, and place you behind me on the horse?

Girl: How will you take me, riding through [the land of] my people?
Since in our land you must now go barefoot and on foot,
How will you manage to place Opan behind you on a horse?

Man: When you sing, Opan, you arrange [your words],
When God so orders, you will die.
When I order the Naur men of Aman Džol to assemble[15]
You, Najman,[16] will sink into the earth [small] as a hand.

Girl: Oh, speak as it behooves you, poor man,
Oh, unfortunate one, why are you praising your excellence.
Since you find yourself now amongst us, with naked feet and horseless,
Oh, unfortunate man, why are you praising your perfection?

Man: If I know a song, I sing—clearing my throat,
If I did not know the meaning of speech—then, what should I say,
As the oldest wife's son I have grown up better.
[Why then] should I not praise my good points, what [else] should I say
. . . .

[15] He apparently alludes to the heroes of his tribe.
[16] Najman: a Kazakh tribe of the Middle Horde, apparently the tribe of Opan.

Man: Now that I have drunk sufficiently of *qumys,*[17] my thirst is quenched.
But now I should like to stay with Opan,
Now I remember the silly customs of my people
And I would like to mount Opan's white breasts.

Girl: In my hand I hold a whip, an eight-thonged whip.
May it not hit your eyes, and do not complain about me [then]
If you want to mount a two-legged human being,
May you never [again] behold hairy-tailed cattle.[18]

. . . .

Although this "duet" contains characteristic folklore epithets and turns of speech such as the repetitions of key phrases, such devices usually served only as a skeleton around which the song was improvised. It should be noted, however, that while the words in these singing competitions were frequently improvised, the tunes to which the songs were sung were generally limited to one of a number of stock melodies to which the words were adapted.[19]

There were occasions when the *ajtys* was apparently not based on free improvisation but was carried out in the framework of a strictly prescribed ritual. Some reports even claim that all *ajtys* were based on such strictly prescribed form. The modern Kazakh writer Mukhtar Auezov, who contends that the form of the *ajtys* was strictly prescribed, declares that the following rules were invariably followed: the winner was required to sing twenty-four couplets of four lines each;[20] the first six couplets must contain praise of the "king" and "queen" "elected" by the participants of the festival at which the *ajtys* was performed; the next three couplets must include a compliment to the neighbors of the singer; in the following six couplets it was required that consideration be given to the cattle and possessions of the singer or the host; next there were prescribed three purely fantastical or nonsense couplets followed by five couplets about the

[17] *qumys* (kumiss) : a slightly intoxicating drink, made of fermented mare's milk. A favorite drink among the Central Asiatic nomads.
[18] Radloff, *Proben . . . ,* III, 48-52.
[19] See Levshin, *op. cit.,* III, 140.
[20] This was found to be true of the *ajtys* studied by this author.

love of the singer; finally, there was a concluding couplet the subject of which could be chosen by the singer, but the last couplet was to be so constructed that the lines could be read backwards and the sense still maintained.[21] In none of the texts studied were all these rules followed, although in most of the texts some of the rules were followed but in a most flexible manner. It seems clear that the rules remained primarily formal, while the content in general was more often left to the imagination of the performer. While complete adherence to these rules was undoubtedly rare, it is evident that the *ajtys* was a very complicated form of singing. Its widespread distribution testifies to the musical and poetic ability of the Kazakh people. The *ajtys* was of particular importance because it was in such competitions that the career of almost all the professional *aqyns* began. Only after conquering his opponents in several *ajtys* and holding his ground in singing competitions with older and recognized *aqyns,* could the young singer claim to be a professional bard.[22]

Ritual Songs

Kazakh ritual songs are of great interest not only because of their aesthetic value, but also because of the insight they provide into culturally prescribed attitudes of the people toward outstanding events in their lives. Many of the ritual songs, in contrast to other song forms of the Kazakhs, were not improvised but were performed according to fixed texts and music. The most widespread ritual songs were those which accompanied shamanistic rites, wedding songs corresponding to the various stages of the wedding ceremony, farewell songs (*qostasū*), songs relating sad news (*estirtū*), sympathy or condolence songs (*könülajtū*), and mourning songs (*džoqtau*). In addition to these there was also a wide range of less important ritual songs, such as songs sung at the occasion of childbirth, cursing songs, and religious ritual songs of various kinds.

[21] Mukhtar Auezov, "Kazakhshki epos i dorevolyutsionny folklor," Leonid Sobolev, ed., *Pesni stepei, antologiya kazakhskoi literatury* (Moscow, 1940), pp. 15-16.

[22] *Ibid.*, p. 16.

An important part in the lives of the early Kazakhs was played by shamanistic rites, many of which continued to be performed after the conversion to Mohammedanism. Shamanistic rites were frequently accompanied by ritual dances and songs.[23] The dual religious influences in Kazakh life were revealed in the songs in which it was not uncommon to find Mohammedan and shamanistic elements intermingled, as is illustrated in the following selection:

> Oh help me first, oh God!
> We are here, if you will help,
> Fulfil the supplication
> Oh give to the woman [who has not yet borne] children.
> Good God, merciful God!
> God, the prince, God the Master!
> My God first created Heaven,
> Then he created the earth;
> I pray first to God,
> Then I pray to Muhammed.
> To the first we are slaves,
> Of the second we are followers;
> The third is [God] the heaven [*sic*].[24]
>
> The fourth are the four Califs,
> The eighty-eight noble ones
> . . . .
> The saints at Mecca,
> The saints at Medina.[25]

In the next few lines of this invocation of saints the *baqsy* suddenly deviates from the traditional Mohammedan hagiolatry and calls on the pagan spirits:

> Dzhingiz-Khan, the saint,
> The girl-saint
> On top of the red mountain,
> The cattle-saint,

[23] The Kazakh term for shamanistic songs is *baqsy džyry,* from *baqsy:* shaman, and *džyr:* song (from *džyrlamaq*—to declaim).

[24] Cf. *tängri* of the shamanistic beliefs. Occurs as early as the Orkhon inscriptions. See *supra,* chap. i.

[25] Radloff, *Proben . . . ,* III, 60-61. For different versions, see J. Castagné, "Magie et exorcisme chez les Kazak—Kirghizes et autres peuples turks orientaux," *Revue des Études Islamiques* (Paris), IV (1930), 77-79; Sobolev, *Pesni . . . ,* pp. 138-40.

On the ram-mountain,
The bald saint,
The elk on the mountain,
The dragon which comes forth from the mountain. . . .[26]

In another shamanistic invocation the *baqsy* calls not on the shamanistic spirits, but on the Mohammedan devil, *šajtān* ("Hey, devil, what do you need, why do you not go away from me . . . ?" [*Ej, šajtan, senin nin bar aulaq žürmöj* . . . ?]), but then continues by addressing the devil in traditional shamanistic formulae, sacrificing to him and threatening him:

If you will not listen to me,
If you will not go home soon,
Then let the dead sacred ancestors
Persecute you.
. . . .
Are these sheep lungs not enough for you?
Are they not to be considered lungs?[27]

If you will not take the lungs and go home,
. . . .
I will throw myself on you and
In this way cut your head off.[28]

There were three main types of ritual songs for the occasion of marriage which were prescribed for each successive stage of the wedding ceremony. The *džar-džar*[29] was sung immediately preceding or following the ceremony; the *synsū* ("the weeping of the bride") or *qyz tanysū* ("the girl's farewell") was sung at the moment the bride left the parental home; and finally the *bet ašar* ("the uncovering of the face") was sung at the occasion of the arrival of the bride at the home of the groom. Most wedding songs were dramatic in character, composed of a dialogue-like singing of a group of young men and a group of young women. Wedding songs reveal to us quite clearly early bridal customs such

[26] Radloff, *Proben* . . . , III, 61-62.
[27] Animal lungs are sacrificed to the evil spirits by the healing shaman.
[28] M. Miropiyev, ed. and transl., *Demonologicheskiye razskazy Kirgizov*, Zapiski Imperatorskogo Russkogo Geograficheskogo Obshchestva po otdeleniyu etnografii, tom X, vypusk 3, 50.
[29] *džar-džar:* lit. "friend-friend."

as bride purchase, the levirate, and polygamy, as well as the typical attitude towards woman in Kazakh society.

The first of the group of wedding songs, the *džar-džar,* is sung in the form of a dialogue between a group of young men and a group of young women. The new life facing the young bride is described in turn from the point of view of the man and from that of the woman. In the gay song of the young men (*džigittär*) the woman is told that she must abandon her family *džurt* and her friends, that she must now dedicate her entire life to her new, and frequently unknown, husband and to his family. The bride is persuaded not to postpone the farewell to her mother, for her mother will be replaced by her mother-in-law, her father will be replaced by her father-in-law, and her former home will be replaced by her own *džurt* in the *aul* of her husband. In a jesting manner the girl is asked to be reasonable in adapting herself to this change in her life. Each light-hearted stanza of the young men is answered by a doleful, mournful stanza sung by a chorus of the young girls (*qyzlar*), who bemoan the bride's future, the loss of freedom entailed in marriage, the passing of youth, and the sad parting from home and the loved ones. The following is an excerpt from a common *džar-džar:*

Girls: A pattern, just like a verse, is placed on the felt, *džar-džar,*
The barren mares are being slaughtered for the feast, *dž. dž.*
But I shall implore my mother to beg my father, *dž.-dž.*
To let me stay at home with my own people, *dž.-dž.*

Young men: Beautiful is youth with its young fire, *džar-džar,*
Like a lovely bird, to strangers you will go, *dž.-dž.*
Now in your father you must place no more hope, *dž.-dž.*
You will be carried off by him who paid the *qalym,*[30] *dž.-dž.*[31]

Some of the *džar-džar* songs are more complex, as the following one which was recorded by Radloff:

[30] The bride-price.
[31] Abdykalykov and Pankratova, *op. cit.,* pp. 136-37.

Džigittär: Bir tolarsaq, bir tobuq sanda bolar, džar! džar!
qyrq kisinin aqyldy qanda bolar, dž. dž.
ākämai dep džylama baghus qyzdar, dž. dž.
ākan üšün qain atan onda bolar, dž. dž.

Qyzlar: Džazghy turghu aqša qar džaumaq qaida? dž! dž!
qulun taidai aiqasqan on džaq qaida, dž! dž!
azar džaqsy bolsada qain atamyz, dž! dž!
ainalain ākamdāi bolmaq qaida? dž! dž!

Džigittär: Bir tolarsaq, bir tobuq sanda bolar, džar! džar!
qyrq kisinin aqyldy qanda bolar, dž. dž.
Šešemäi dep džylama bajghus qyzdar, dž. dž.
Šešen üšün qain enän onda bolar, dž. dž.

Qyzlar: Džazghy turghu aqša qar džaumaq qaida? dž! dž!
qulun taidai aiqasqan on džaq qaida, dž! dž!
azar džaqsy bolsada qain enämiz, dž. dž.
ainalain šešämdäi bolmaq qaida, dž. dž.[32]
Etc.

Translation

Young men: The leg has a bone and a kneecap, *dž. dž.*
The khan has the intelligence of forty people, *dž. dž.*
Do not cry for your father, poor girl, *dž. dž.*
Your father's place will be taken by your father-in-law, *dž. dž.*

Girls: Oh, where is the falling of white snow in spring, *dž. dž.*
Where is the right side, where we used to play like fillies, *dž. dž.*
However good my father-in-law may be, *dž. dž.*
I want to go back, because like a father he cannot be. *Dž. dž.*

Men: The leg has a bone and a knee-cap, *dž. dž.*
The sultan has the intelligence of forty people, *dž. dž.*
Do not cry for your mother, poor girl, *dž. dž.*
Your mother's place will be taken by your mother-in-law. *Dž. dž.*

Girls: Oh, where is the falling of white snow in spring, *dž. dž.*
Where is the right side, where we used to play like fillies, *dž. dž.?*
However good my mother-in-law may be, *dž. dž.*
Etc.

[32] Radloff, *Obraztsy . . .*, III, 7.

The repetition of the stanzas is varied only by the insertion of the various members of the family and of the bride's friendship circle.[33]

The *synsū*[34] ("the weeping of the bride") or *qyz tanysū* ("the girl's farewell"), the traditional song of farewell sung at the time of departure of the bride for her husband's *aul,* generally followed the *džar džar*. As Kazakh rules of exogamy provided that marriage could take place only between partners who were unrelated by blood for at least seven generations, few young girls married into nearby *auls*. Instead, marriages were preferably concluded between people of far distant groups. Thus the departure of the bride meant for her a departure into a strange land in order to submit to a marriage which was frequently not of her choosing or was even against her will. In the *synsū* not only the personal grief of the bride, but also the plight of womanhood in general, was lamented.

According to tradition during the performance of the *synsū* the bride, with her friends, visited all the *džurts* of her relatives and friends in her own and in nearby *auls*. This frequently turned into a mournful procession of all the women of the neighboring *auls* at which occasion the bride poured forth all her misery and voiced her protest, frequently with bitter irony, at having to part from family and friends and from the freedom of youth.

A goose swims with the stream in a little brook,
A young woman must now forsake her native home.
If you drip blood into water, the water will carry it away speedily
And if you are married, a stranger will carry you far away.

. . . .

It is as if you shot me straight in the breast, oh dear father.
You sold me for a herd of horses, dear father.
You have more room now in the *džurt,* dear father,
And in it, there is no room for me any more, dear father.[35]

When the bride finally arrived at the *aul* of the bridegroom,

[33] For a complete German translation, see Radloff, *Proben . . . ,* III, 8-10.
[34] From *synsy*—to complain, whine.
[35] Sobolev, ed., *Pesni . . . ,* p. 131. For another version see Radloff, *Proben . . . ,* III, 15.

she was met by her new family and by the dignitaries of the husband's *aul* with the song *bet ašar* ("uncovering the face"), which accompanied the first ceremonial unveiling of the bride before the groom's family. This song portrays the unwritten law of the Kazakh patriarchal family. It outlines, in detail, the duties of the young wife towards her husband and his family and, in general, circumscribes the bride's position in the household. The bride herself did not participate in the singing of this song. She was expected to listen in silence and to remember the admonitions contained in it.

Tān ertän turup, kelinšäk,
Qaqandama, kelinšäk!
Üj artynda mal kelzä
Baqandama kelinšäk!

. . . .

Auzun murnun süröndöp
Ösök ajtpö, kelinšäk!
Qain aghanyn aldynan
Kezip ötpö, kelinšäk![36]

Translation

Rising in the early morning, little bride,
Never walk upright,[37] little bride.

When cattle comes near the *džurt,*
Never hit at it with the *džurt* stakes.

. . . .

Never speak lies, little bride,
Grimacing with mouth and nose.
Never pass your husband's elder brother,[38] little bride.[39]

In the following section the young bride is warned against neglect of performance of her wifely duties in a manner which

[36] Radloff, *Obraztsy . . .*, III, 10-11.

[37] Young wives were required to walk with bowed head. See Radloff, *Proben . . .*, III, 13.

[38] The wife was forbidden by custom to pass older members of the family, who always preceded her. (See Radloff, *loc. cit.*) In the case of the husband's elder brother this rule may have been enforced in a particularly rigid fashion as, according to the custom of the levirate, the older brother might become the husband of the woman in the event of her first husband's death.

[39] Radloff, *Proben . . .*, III, 13.

leaves little doubt as to the hostility with which the newcomer was met:

Džaman qatynyn belgisi
är nedän džoq ülgüsü,
sasyq bolady isi
iš kelmädi kelisi.
Talqan tüjüp kep berär,
qaryny tojsun dep berär.
. . . .
Ajaq bolar qumghana,
qolun malyp džughany,
üstü basy boq bolup
qas qudaidyn urghany.
Šylanšu džürör džalbangdap,
balaghy džürör salbangdap
mandai šašy burqurap
eki emšägi salaktap.[40]

Translation

The sign of an evil wife is
That she knows not the customs,
That she is of evil smell,
And not good for anything.
She gives you burned grain,
Saying: "May you fill your stomach on this."
. . . .
She uses the eating dish for a washing utensil
And dips her hands in it while washing.
Her external appearance, her head are dirty.
[Such a wife] is a punishment of God.
Her headkerchief hangs fluttering in the wind.
Her pants hang disorderly over her boots,
Her hair sticks out of her head covering,
And her breasts sag down.[41]

The farewell songs (*qostasū*)[42] include a great variety of songs which were frequently improvised and performed at the most diverse occasions of separations and departures. The Kazakh heroic epos is filled with examples of such songs. A

[40] Radloff, *Obraztsy* . . . , III, 10-11.
[41] Radloff, *Proben* . . . , III, 13.
[42] From *qostas*—to bid farewell.

qostasū might be sung as a farewell to one's native land, to a friend or lover, or even to a favorite horse. Finally, such a song might be sung as a farewell to life. In the latter case an individual might compose "a last testament" in which he related his last wishes, sang of the sadness of death, and recounted his unfulfilled dreams. In the periods of forced migrations caused by outside aggression (e.g., the Oirats, the Russians, etc.) the *qostasū,* particularly in the form of a farewell to family and native land, was most widespread. There is preserved a *qostasū* composed by the eighteenth-century *aqyn,* Bukhar Džyrau, during the forced migration of a group of Kazakhs from their traditional grazing grounds as a result of pressure from the Dzungars:

> A caravan is marching from the heights of the Q̰ara
> Tau.
> . . . .
> How hard it is to bid farewell to our native land.
> Tears stream from dark eyes. . . .
>
> What times we must live in! Oh, times of misery!
> The tears from my eyes form seas and lakes.
> Oh what times of hardship!
> Happiness and riches have forsaken us.
> Dust rises from the wandering caravan,
> Worse than the icy storms of December.[43]

The *estirtū,* the song of sad news, was the traditional means of bringing word to an individual of the death of a friend or relative. This song form is also amply represented in the heroic epos. The singer cautiously approaches the subject by drawing a number of analogies from nature, from animal life, and from history which symbolize the temporary nature of life on earth. Only at the very end of the song is there any mention of the actual death which the song reports. The *estirtū* is generally followed by the *könül*[44] *ajtu* ("the speaking of the heart"), the song of consolation.

There exists the following legend concerning the *estirtū:* The son of a powerful khan, Džošy-Khan,[45] had been killed

[43] Abdykalykov, Pankratova, *op. cit.,* pp. 170-71.
[44] *könül*—"heart, soul."
[45] Džuči-Khan, Dzhingis-Khan's son.

by a horse. His entourage was afraid to inform the khan of the death of his son. However, the khan himself, having already guessed the reason for the failure of his son to return as scheduled, demanded of his son's friends: "Tell me what happened to my son. But know that I shall kill the person who informs me of his death, by pouring hot lead into his mouth." The son's friends held council and finally solved their dilemma by transmitting the sad news to the khan not by words, but by the mournful sounds of the *qobyz.* The khan understood the message of the music and in order to fulfil his threat he ordered the *qobyz* punished. A hole was drilled in the instrument through which hot lead was poured. Since that time, the legend goes, the *qobyz* has a hole on top.[46] Later the *aqyns* invented the following words for this wordless *estirtū:*

The *qobyz* sings. Oh listen Džošy-Khan,
What it speaks of, enchained by sadness.

From distant dusty steppes,
A wild horse, lame, but sly, had run away.
Over the hills, trampling dry bushy weeds,
He ran into the limitless steppe;
The hunter boy had frightened him,
The hunter boy whom you know well, oh Džošy-Khan.
And bolting after the lame horse, without separating,
Was a whole tribe of wild horses,
A tribe which hitherto had always
Pastured in the foggy vale.
And then a two-year-old *tulpar,*[47] in passioned heat

Into the herd of wild horses carried the boy.
What can one do? In life it's Allāh only who is free,
And death, as always, stands behind us, at our shoulder. . . .
The slyest of the wild horse herd
Was the lame one. And when the playful *tulpar* [of your son]
Was chasing after him, the evil wild horse
Bit to death your son.
And trampling on the dead boy (since they have no pity)

[46] Cf. the Kazakh folktale "Ker-bugha Quiši" in A. Melkov, *Materialy po kirgizskoi etnografii,* Trudy Obshchestva Izucheniya Kirgizskogo Kraya (Orenburg), III (1922), 169-70.

[47] *Tulpar,* the legendary horse of the epic heroes, hence, a good horse in general. Here the horse on which Džošy-Khan's son was riding is meant.

The wild horse herd galloped on.
The people could not speak of this,
And but in tunes of songs expressed their sorrow.
Oh, ruler, the *qobyz* sings to you,
Believe the tune of sorrow, Džošy-Khan.[48]

The following is a typical *könül ajtū:*

There is no horse in the whole world with whole hoofs,
There is no tree which, preserving all its leaves,
Would rustle under the sun. There is no falcon with
whole wings.
There are no people in the world whose whole kin are still alive.
If there were no battles, there would be no blood.
From pine tree seeds no red sprout would arise.
Ask those who have whitened in years, the wisest elders:
Is it possible that man should not die?
Is there a man anywhere who would not curse his fate,
Without sadness in his heart and without a wrinkle on his face?
Inescapable death, such is the fate of all men:
Just like your son, so also they
Will find peace in the grave.[49]

The song of mourning, or weeping song (*džoqtau* or *džoqtaghan džyr*), has a great number of variations. According to tradition the closest female relative of the deceased observed mourning ceremonies for one year; and the wives, daughters, sisters or the mother of the deceased were obliged to perform a *džoqtau* at every sunrise and sunset.[50] Men performed mourning rites only on extraordinary occasions such as the commemoration of an important tribal dignitary at special mourning feasts.[51] The *džoqtau,* which was frequently improvised,[52] consisted of two basic parts: the enumeration of the good qualities and the riches of the deceased and the expression of grief over his death. The latter part was frequently highly symbolic in content and hyperbolic in form:

al dadan kaitty nazarym,
betimnän ketti ažarym
qan iänmiz ketkändä

[48] Sobolev, ed., *Pesni . . .*, pp. 135-36.
[49] *Ibid.*, p. 137.
[50] Abdykalykov, Pankratova, *op. cit.*, p. 139.
[51] Radloff, *Proben . . .*, III, 22 n.
[52] *Ibid.*

bir kündö ketti bazarym.
Džazda künü bolghanda
Künün közü bailanghan
aq sunqar üšüp ainalghan.[53]

Translation

My gaze turned away from God,
All color disappeared from my face,
When my prince and master went away.
When spring came, also my *bāzār*[54] went away.
The sun's rays were darkened,
My white falcon flew away[55] and turned
around [i.e., died].[56]

Tales and Legends

Tales and legends of the most varied kinds are abundant in Kazakh folklore. The most widespread genres are the following: legends and historical tales, many of which are almost epic in character and deal with the aspirations of the people for better grazing land or with the struggle against intruding neighbors, comical tales, traditional love tales, fairy tales, animal stories, children's stories, and demonological tales. In addition, there is a large group of tales which reflects the influence of story cycles and literary works of other cultures. Thus there are Kazakh tales based on the *Arabian Nights,* the Indian "parrot tale" cycle (the *Śukasaptati*), the eleventh-century epos *Šāhnāme* by the Persian poet Firdūsī, the Türkmen heroic epos *Köroghly,* and the romances of the Čagatai poet 'Alī-Šīr Nawā'ī.

Kazakh tales and legends were spread, as were the songs and

[53] Radloff, *Obraztsy* . . . , III, 21.

[54] "*Bāzār* originally means a market place. The term is also used in many Turkic languages to designate the day corresponding to our Sunday. Here it refers to the crowds of guests who, like the crowds in the *bāzār,* used to fill the *džurt* of the deceased. A previous passage makes clear the use of night" (Radloff, *Proben* . . . , III, 24).

[55] The use of the falcon symbol here corroborates Barthold's thesis of a belief in reincarnation among the early Central Asian Turks. The soul was believed to enter the body of a bird or insect, and thus the Turks spoke of the deceased as üčdü (he has flown away). Long after their Islamization the Turks said of their deceased: *šunqar boldy* (he became a falcon). Cf. Barthold, *Zwölf Vorlesungen* . . . , pp. 20-21.

[56] For German translation see Radloff, *Proben* . . . , III, 25.

epics, by wandering storytellers. A good storyteller, Levshin tells us, was able to enliven his stories by a large number of dramatic elements. He could imitate sounds of nature and sounds of animals, add to the description by gestures and movements of his body and identify himself completely with the hero. Levshin writes that "In all the tales of these people there is evidenced a flaming imagination and a tendency to poetic enthusiasm."[57] Generally legends and tales were recited and were accompanied by the music of the *dombra* or the *qobyz;* and both instruments were frequently used to reproduce the sounds of nature and cries of animals as they occurred in the tale. Before a performance the storyteller usually gave a short synopsis of the legend which ended with the traditional phrase—"And now listen how the *dombra* tells about it."[58]

Kazakh legends and historical tales are typically preoccupied with the ever-present problems of the struggle for existence in nomadic society. Common themes were the threats of storms and drought and the never-ending search for better pasture lands and for a better future in general. A typical tale is that of Asan Qajghy,[59] a legendary figure who was said to have lived in the sixteenth century, during the reign of Kazakh khan Žanybek. Asan, saddened by the fate of his people who could not solve the problems of poor grazing land, decided to look for the promised land where "the days would be sorrowless and the land rich, where there would be no hatred and where the skylarks would peacefully build their nests on the backs of the sheep."[60] He traveled on a swift camel all over the steppes, but was unable to find the promised land. He then promised his people to lead them into unknown lands where he hoped to find better conditions. But he died and so could not fulfil his promise. The motif of this tale, the age-long yearning of the people for better living conditions and their fear that their dreams were hopless and could not be fulfilled, is repeated in many other tales. Not in all Kazakh tales is the search for the promised land unsuccess-

[57] Levshin, *op. cit.,* III, 140.
[58] Abdykalykov, Pankratova, *op cit.,* p. 145.
[59] *Ibid.,* pp. 141-42.
[60] *Ibid.,* p. 142.

ful. In the tale *Župar-qoryghy* the heroine succeeds in leading her children to a new land, a rich valley whither her whole tribe eventually follows.[61]

The Kazakh tale about Qorqyt, "the legendary father of Kazakh music," expresses the respect of the Kazakhs for their musical heritage. Qorqyt, unable to accept the idea of death, flees from people to eternal nature. But nature in the shape of trees, mountains, steppes, and forests tells him that even she does not have the power of immortality. Qorqyt then fashions from the wood of the tree *Šyrghaj* the first *qobyz* and plays on it the first Kazakh song—thus at last finding immortality in art.[62]

A large part of the repertoire of Kazakh tales might be termed comical stories. They can be found in great variety, but most frequently they celebrate the famous Central Asiatic rogue and mocker Aldar Qos, who is probably an adaptation of the Osman Turkish Hodža Nasr-ed-Dīn. This gay character, who reminds us of Till Eulenspiegel of Western literature and folklore, occurs in various guises in the folklore of most of the Central Asiatic Turkic tribes.[63] Through his sly wit Aldar Qos is able to outsmart everyone including devils who come to take possession of him and the greedy miser who refuses to extend the traditional Kazakh hospitality to travelers but who ends by giving Aldar almost all his possessions, even a beautiful daughter.[64] The sharp ridicule of avarice, superstition, and stupidity in the comical stories exemplifies Kazakh humor at its best.

The most popular tales are probably traditional love tales with their ever-present theme of the obstacles the lovers must overcome in order to become united. While some of these tales are purely lyrical romances, others—similar to the Aldar Qos cycle—are highly didactic in their elevation of the qualities of wit and intellect. An example of the latter type is the legend

[61] *Ibid.*, pp. 140-41.

[62] Auezov, "Kazakhski epos . . . ," p. 15; Castagné, "Magie . . . ," pp. 61-63.

[63] In Türkmen tales Aldar Qos occurs frequently, both under the name of Aldar Qos and under such variations as Äpendi, Džapbaqlar, Äsen Polat, etc. See G. Veselkov, *Ocherki Turkmenskoi literatury* (Turkmengiz, Ashkhabad, 1945), p. 24.

[64] For examples of these tales, see Sobolev, ed., *Pesni . . .* , pp. 166-73.

cycle about the imaginary hero, Žirenše-šešän,[65] a man of extraordinary intelligence and wit,[66] and his beautiful and equally witty wife, Qarašaš.[67]

A typical recorded version of this cycle[68] begins with the standard phrase: "There lived a wise man named Žirenše-šešän," and continues by enumerating his excellent qualities: "The mind of this man was deep and without limits, just like the sea, and the speech that flowed from his mouth was like the song of the lark." But he was extremely poor. Once while on a trip with some friends, they were stopped by a swollen river. At the river bank they met a group of women and inquired of them where they could find the nearest ford. A young girl, whom her friends called "beautiful Qarašaš," stepped forward. "She was dressed in old and ragged clothes, but she shone with unheard of beauty. Her eyes were like stars, her mouth like the moon, and her figure was lithe as a rod." Žirenše and Qarašaš both spoke in riddles, in language which only the wise could understand.

"There are two fords," Qarašaš told the travelers. One is "near but yet far and the other one, to the right, is far and yet near." Only Žirenše understood and took the farther but shallow ford, while his companions almost drowned in the near but deep ford.

Žirenše married Qarašaš, who was a poor as he. The khan, however, having heard of the great intelligence of Qarašaš, attempted to obtain her from Žirenše. He gave Žirenše a series of dangerous and difficult tasks, threatening him with death if he failed to carry them out. Thus Žirenše was ordered under penalty of death to appear before the khan at a time which was neither day nor night, to come neither on foot nor on horseback, and neither to remain in the street nor to enter the courtyard of the palace. With the help of his clever wife, Žirenše found

[65] The epithet *sešän* might suggest Mongol origin of this legendary figure, since it is derived from Mongol *sečän:* "clever, wise."

[66] Hence the epithet *sešän.*

[67] Qarašaš: "Blackhair."

[68] "Mudry Zhirenshe i krasavitsa Karashash," Sobolev, ed., *Pesni* . . . , pp. 152-57.

a way out. He appeared at the khan's palace at dusk riding a billy-goat and stopped under the very cross-beam of the entrance gate. Because of their superior wits, Žirenše and Qarašaš were finally able to outsmart the khan, who gave up his pursuit of Qarašaš.

Qarašaš died while Žirenše was hunting. His friends rode to meet him to inform him of his loss, but unable to tell him the news straight away, they approached the subject in a roundabout fashion:[69]

"You have always been famous for your wisdom, Žirenše," they told him. "Tell us! What does a man lose when his father dies?"

"When the father dies," Žirenše answered, "it is as if the walls of the fortress, which had protected the man from misfortune, had collapsed."

"And what," his friends continued, "does man lose when his mother dies?"

"When a mother dies the spring of love, which has nourished man, has dried out."

"And with what do you compare the death of a brother?"

"When a brother dies," Žirenše answered, "it is as if the right wing were broken."

"Tell us now, finally, oh wise Žirenše, with what would you compare the death of a beloved wife?"

Žirenše answered, "When a beloved wife dies, it is as if the handle of the whip were broken."

Then the friends cautioned him: "Look well, Žirenše, whether the handle of your whip is whole." And Žirenše, guessing the sad news, fell dead over his whip, which broke under him.

This tale illustrates two well-known folklore themes: the struggle of two lovers against difficult odds, and the successful hero whose superior intelligence helps him overcome all obstacles. The picture of an individual whose wits are so sharp that he can outtalk all adversaries is most common in Kazakh folklore,[70] and the name Žirenše has become a common Kazakh

[69] Cf. *supra,* the discussion of the "song of sad news." (*estirtū*).
[70] Cf. also the figure of Aldar Qos, *supra.*

epithet applied to people with a gift of oratory.[71] Many of the other leading *dramatis personae* of Kazakh legends have also become appellatives by which the Kazakhs characterize people, such as the wit Aldar Qos, the legendary miser Qarynbaj who took away the cattle from the people, and the visionary Asan Qajghy[72] who attempted to lead his people to a better land.[73]

Fairy tales also compose an important part of the Kazakh folklore heritage. These tales also exhibit many traits present in mythology and folklore the world over. There is the ever-recurring theme of magical healing qualities of certain objects of nature and of the bodies of certain animals. Thus in Kazakh tales the powdered bones of a black dog are attributed the power to resurrect the dead;[74] and special trees, if touched, can restore sight and limbs.[75] We also meet such legendary figures as the hero who can hear over great distances or who can even hear the thoughts of other people,[76] the hero who understands the language of animals,[77] the talking animals,[78] and the magic horse which can not only talk but can fly and traverse "a month's distance in six paces."[79] And finally there are the magic implements like the comb which can be transformed into a forest to trap pursuing enemies, the mirror which can be transformed into a lake to drown the enemy,[80] the magic wand with which one can bewitch human beings,[81] and the magical objects which have the power to bring riches to their owners.[82] (Cf. the Russian *skatert'-samobranka* and the German *Tischlein-deck-dich.*)

[71] Abdykalykov, Pankratova, *op. cit.*, p. 142; Auezov, "Kazakhski epos . . . ," p. 15.
[72] See *supra*.
[73] Auezov, "Kazakhski epos . . . ," p. 15.
[74] "Wie der Gute und Böse Gefährten waren," Radloff, *Proben* . . . , III, 345.
[75] *Ibid.*, p. 344.
[76] "Ešigäldi," *ibid.*, pp. 332-343; "Der angelnde Jüngling," *ibid.*, pp. 395-402; "Qara Kös Sulū," *ibid.*, pp. 402-407.
[77] "Des Kan's Tochter," *ibid.*, pp. 347-55.
[78] "Dudar Qyz," *ibid.*, pp. 373-87; "Der angelnde Jüngling," *ibid.*, pp. 395-402.
[79] "Dudar Qyz," *ibid.*, p. 381.
[80] *Ibid.*
[81] "Bogaty i bedny," Sobolev, ed., *Pesni* . . . , pp. 158-65.
[82] *Ibid.*

Of particular importance in Kazakh culture are animal stories, including stories about the domesticated animals which form the basis of the livelihood of the Kazakhs (sheep, goats, camels, cows, horses),[83] and tales about wild animals, particularly the bear, wolf, and fox, the beasts of prey which are the greatest enemies of the cattlebreeders.[84] Domesticated animals are frequently ascribed human attributes and are typically represented as man's helpmates and friends. They are sometimes depicted as more intelligent and witty than both man and beast of prey.[85] The wolf and the fox are important figures in Kazakh folklore, as they are in the folklore of the Occident. As in Western tales, the fox is traditionally depicted as the epitome of slyness and craftiness, though he is not always crafty enough to avoid being outsmarted by his intended victims, while the wolf is usually depicted as the most despicable of beasts of prey, as the destroyer of herds, the gravedigger, the carrion eater, in short, as the greatest enemy of herd and man. Frequently, in the shape of the werewolf, the wolf is pictured as a symbol of everything evil: he kills newborn babies, eats man's remains, and ravishes his wives and daughters.[86] Another figure which is also found in Western tales is the many-headed dragon (*džalmaus*) whom the hero kills in battle.[87]

Of particular interest because of their didactic tendencies are children's tales. Most tales for children are fantasies. The heroes are usually small animals (birds, insects, etc.) which, despite their relative weakness, become victors over both human

[83] Domesticated animals frequently play important roles in genres other than animal tales. Cattle are important in the description of the riches of the hero as well as in the depiction of the bride price (*qalym*) in the heroic epos and the legend. The horse, as man's most trusted friend, is depicted in almost all epic songs.

[84] See "Die List des Fuchses," Radloff, *Proben* . . . , III, 369-72; "Lisa, verblyud, volk, lev i perepyolka," Sobolev, Auezov, *op. cit.*, pp. 204-7; "Lisa, medved i pastukh," *ibid.*, pp. 208-10; "Dikar," *Trudy Obshchestva Izucheniya Kirgizskogo Kraya* (Orenburg), III (1922), 144-49.

[85] See "Khrabry osel," Sobolev, ed., *Pesni* . . . , pp. 211-13.

[86] See "Dudar Qyz," also Abdykalykov, Pankratova, *op. cit.*, p. 140.

[87] See "Der angelnde Jüngling," "Bogaty i bedny," "Dudar Qyz." Also "Žalmaus-Kempir," in Miropiyev, *op. cit.*, pp. 32-38. The *džalmaus* frequently takes on human form, most frequently that of an old woman. Because of the magical qualities of this animal, it might better be treated as a demonological character than as belonging in the category of animal stories.

beings and beasts of prey. The aim of these tales is evidently to evoke the child's confidence in his own strength. A typical children's tale tells of Quwyršyq, a small creature smilar to Däumling in the Grimms' collection, who was adopted by a childless old man and who, in turn, became the benefactor of the family. One day when he was sitting down in the shade of a leaf to rest from work, the leaf under which he was sitting was swallowed by a camel and Quwyršyq was accidentally swallowed with it. The camel, after eating the leaf and Quwyršyq, was in turn eaten by a wolf. Quwyršyq now found himself in the wolf's stomach, but instead of giving up he made the wolf's life miserable by warning the shepherds by his shouts of the approach of the wolf. After many adventures Quwyršyq was freed from the wolf's stomach and returned home with great riches.[88]

Tales about demons and spirits reveal the shamanistic as well as Mohammedan influence in Kazakh beliefs. Thus spirits, which have their origin in the early shamanistic beliefs of the nomads, frequently react not only to shamanistic incantations, but also to Mohammedan prayer formulae. The spirits in Kazakh folk tales are generally hostile to man and most demonological tales are concerned with man's struggle against them. All spirits appear to man in disguise, as animals or people, and often in the shape of young, beautiful girls who lure men to their doom.

Some spirits are relatively harmless, such as the little devils (*šajtān*) who frequently appear in the shape of young women who torture their male victims, but are no direct danger to human lives. They are frequently vulnerable to Mohammedan prayers.[89] More dangerous spirits, however, attack people and sometimes kill them, an act which is frequently symbolized by the stealing of lungs. It appears that lungs, animal or human, are an important life symbol in Kazakh tradition. Spirits may appear in the shape of lungs. Death can be cheated by recovering the lungs from the spirit. In shamanistic healing rites, the *baqsa* may sacrifice animal lungs to the disease-causing spirits. Such a lung-robber is the *albasty,* who appears in animal shape

[88] Abdykalykov, Pankratova, *op. cit.,* p. 141.
[89] See Miropiyev, *op. cit.*, p. 9.

(usually as a fox or a male goat[90]) and kills women in childbirth by stealing their lungs. The *džalmaus-kempir,* who eats human flesh, also sometimes appears in the shape of lungs before revealing herself.[91]

The *žez-tyrnaq* (lit. "copper claws") is another spirit who threatens human life. This spirit, which frequently appears in the guise of a young girl, kills by means of her long metal claws. The *žez-tyrnaq,* however, can be cheated by covering a wood stump or stone with human clothes. When the spirit has dug her claws deep into this trap she cannot withdraw them and can easily be killed.[92] The *küldirgiš,* another spirit which appears as a young woman, is probably the most libidinally symbolic of the spirits, for she kills young men by tickling them to death.[93] Some evil spirits, while not appearing in female disguise, tempt the hero by offering him beautiful women. If he cannot withstand the temptation, he is blinded.[94] A particularly dangerous spirit is the *ubbe,* a water demon who lives at the bottoms of lakes and rivers, in a large sub-marine city. When people hear their names called from the water, they know that they must not go swimming, for the *ubbe* will pull them down and make them his slaves.[95]

[90] Note that the male goat is a common satanic symbol in Western folklore as well.

[91] See Miropiyev, *op. cit.,* p. 32: "Once a rich man went to the lake to let his horses drink. While he was watering the horses, a lung appeared in the water and approached the shore. The rich man pushed it away, but it remained in its previous place. The rich man began to push it anew, but it did not move, but grew larger and larger. . . . The rich man pushed it again. Suddenly the lungs became transformed into a *džalmaus-kempir,* which arose, caught the rich man by the beard and did not let go. . . ."

[92] See *ibid.,* pp. 15-23.

[93] See *ibid.,* pp. 39-40.

[94] See *ibid.,* p. 43.

[95] See *ibid.,* p. 31.

CHAPTER III

FOLKLORE
THE HEROIC EPOS[1]

Some Characteristics of the Epos of the Central Asiatic Nomads

The most important folklore complex, not only among the Kazakhs, but among all the Central Asiatic nomads, is that of the heroic epos. The Central Asiatic epos seems to epitomize the very spirit of the culture of the Turkic nomads. The hero of the epos usually symbolizes the cultural conception of the ideal personality; and the epos itself seems to mirror the cultural ideals of the nomads, their conception of honor and prestige, of chivalry, love, and war.

The intensive development of the epos in the nomadic culture, as well as the content of the epics themselves, suggests a considerable antiquity for the whole epic complex. Certain early documents also provide convincing evidence of the early appearance of this most important folklore form. The Orkhon inscriptions, the earliest known written documents of the Central Asiatic Turks, contain strong elements of the epic tradition. These inscriptions are concerned with the history of the Turkic Qaghanate, a powerful federation of nomadic tribes in northern Mongolia which existed from the sixth to the eighth centuries.[2]

[1] The best collections of the Kazakh epos which are available to the Western student are contained in the original in Radloff's *Obraztsy* . . . and in translation in Radloff's *Proben* . . . and Sobolev's *Pesni.* . . .The most complete modern collections of these epics in the original Kazakh published in Soviet Kazakhstan (Qalynžan, Bekkhožin, *Ädebijettik oqū qytaby* ["Literary Reader"] [Alma-Ata, 1939]; *Batyrlar džyry* [Alma-Ata], Kaz. Academy of Sciences [1939-]) are not available outside the Soviet Union.

[2] Written evidence of these tribes has been recovered not only from their own grave inscriptions, but also from the chronicles of the Chinese with whom these Turks were in constant warfare, in the records of the T'ang dynasty (A.D. 618-905), the T'ang-šu. See Edouard Chavannes, "Documents sur les T'oukiue (Turcs) occidentaux," *Sbornik trudov Orkhonskoi ekspeditsii,*

Most of the Orkhon inscriptions were dedicated to the ruler of the Turks, Bilgä-Qaghan, and to his younger brother and military leader, Kül-Tegin. The whole story of the Turkic Qaghanate is related beginning with the rule of the first *qaghan* Bumyn (Tumen of the Chinese chronicles). The struggles to attain independence from the Chinese and the constant raids and attacks of the Orkhon Turks against neighboring and related tribes, such as the Oghuz, Qyrqyz, and Türgeš, are all described.

Certain passages of the Orkhon inscriptions contain rhythmic patterns and rhyme schemes which foreshadow the style and structure of the later heroic epic:

Tabghač budunqa bäglik ury oghlin qul bolty
Silik qyz oghlin kün bolty.
Türk bäglär Türk atin ytty
Tabghačghy bäglär Tabghač atin tutupan
Tabghač qaghanqa körmüš
Älig jyl äšig küčüg bärmiš.
Ilgärü kün toghsuq-da
Bökli qaghan-qa tägi süläjü bärmiš.[3]

Your manly sons became slaves of the Chinese people,
Your pure maidens became slaves (of the Chinese people),
The Turkic *begs* abandoned their Turkic titles,
And after receiving Chinese titles, like Chinese *begs*
They looked into the eye of the Chinese *qaghan* [obeyed the Chinese *qaghan*]
For fifty years they gave their work and strength,
Forward towards sunrise[4] they went to Bökli-qaghan.

Not only are the rhythmic structure and rhyme scheme of these verses of interest, but also notable are the parallelism and repetition, so typical of the epic (cf. lines 1-2: ". . . ury oghlin qul [a male slave] bolty . . . silik qyz oghlin kün [female slave] bolty," and lines 3-4: "Türk bäglär Türk atyn . . . Tabghačghy bäglär Tabghač[5] atin . . ."). Radloff, who has observed this

Vol. VI, St. Peterburg, 1903. There Turks called themselves *kök Türk* (i.e., green or blue Turks) or simply Türk (see Radloff, *Alttürkische . . . , passim*), which became in Chinese t'u-kiüe.

[3] Radloff, *Alttürkische Inschriften der Mongolei, Neue Fole* (Sankt Peterburg, 1897,) p. 132.

[4] "Towards sunrise": i.e., towards the east.

[5] Tabghač—"Chinese."

form of narrative in his studies of the Kirghiz epos, asserts that it is typical of the Turkic epic in general.[6]

The epic character of these inscriptions emerges most clearly in the choice and treatment of subject matter. This is most dramatically illustrated in descriptions of the hero and in depictions of battle scenes. In typical epic fashion Bilgä-qaghan fights forty-seven campaigns and engages in twenty battles.[7] He is quoted in the inscription as saying:

With my younger brother Kül-tegin we . . . had come to the conclusion that the name and fame of the people which our forefathers had conquered, should not perish [and as a result] I have not slept nights on account of the Turkic people and have sat [still] in daytime. With my younger brother Kül-Tegin . . . we have conquered as much as was in our power [until we were dead tired]. . . .[8]

The following battle description also shows striking similarity to the later epics both in content and form which embodies such typical characteristics of epic style as slow, measured narrative, parallelism, and repetition.

In his [Kül-Tegin's] thirty-first year, we fought against the Čača-sünki. First he mounted the gray horse Tadyq-Sačuran, [this horse] fell; as his second horse he mounted the gray horse Yšbara-Jamtar and attacked, this horse fell there [*ol at anda ölti*]. For the third horse he mounted the brown saddled horse of Jäginsil-beg and attacked; this horse also fell there.[9]

Kül-Tegin mounted the white stallion of Bajyrqun and galloped toward the enemy. Grabbing a man, he threw him; he pierced him with his lance. . . . During this attack he spurred the white stallion of Bajyrqun so hard that his thighs broke the horse's ribs.[10]

The most convincing evidence of the antiquity of the epic in Turkic culture appears in a somewhat later document, Maḥmūd al-Kāšgarī's *Dīwān lughāt at-Turk* (*Dictionary of the Turkic Language,* c. 1077), mentioned earlier. In this work there are preserved a great number of fragments taken from early Turkic folklore, including a number of verses of such definite epic

[6] Radloff, *Proben* . . . , V, Introduction.
[7] Radloff, *Alttürkische* . . . , N. F., p. 134.
[8] *Ibid.,* p. 137.
[9] *Ibid.,* p. 139.
[10] *Ibid.,* pp. 140-41.

character that there remains little doubt that these were taken from epic poetry extant in Mahmūd's time. The largest of these epic fragments, from which the following lines are quoted, refers to the struggle of the Turks against the Tangut, with whom the Orkhon Turks were in a constant state of war:

> My noble horse was strong; to be strong it now saw its opportunity;
> The cloud rose and the sky was covered; fog came and hail.
> I followed [the wolf][11] and hurried. By traveling with speed
> I weakened my power. I pursued him with my steed;
> When he saw me he trembled.
> The heroes called to each other, eyed each other, fought with all weapons.
> The sword [covered with blood] would hardly fit into the sheath. . . .
> I called down, collected the tribe. Against the enemy I drew the bow.
> In battle I fought. When the enemy saw the men he hid his head.[12]

Another of these fragments describes the struggle of one of the Mohammedan Turkic tribes with the Buddhist Uighurs in the region of the river Ili. This fragment may refer to the period following the destruction by the Kirghiz of the nomadic Uighur empire on the Orkhon River in 840, for it was only after this event that the mass migration of Uighurs south towards the Ili region and East Türkistan took place.

> Like a wild mountain stream we ran down, against the cities we moved, we destroyed the idolatrous temples and laid our excrements on their idols.
> At night we attacked them, on all sides we lay in ambush, their locks we cut off. . . .
> We laid our insignia on the horses . . . against the miserable dogs we flew like birds.
> The red flag rose, the black dust rose. . . .[13]

Maḥmūd's work also contains two heroic weeping songs, a genre closely related to the heroic epic. Both of these fragments

[11] Probably the enemy (TGW).
[12] Brockelmann, "Altturkestanische Volkspoesie," I, 6-8.
[13] *Ibid.*, pp. 10-11.

also exhibit a great number of elements characteristic of the later epos.

The men howl together like wolves; while howling they tear their collars; their voices whistle like those of a singer; they
cry until their eyes become reddened.[14]

The fragments preserved by Maḥmūd al-Kāšgarī are permeated with the crude and rough heroic spirit and are characterized by liberal use of the clichés so widely employed in the heroic epos. Manliness is celebrated; bravery and the battle prowess of the heroes are hyperbolically described. When the heroes throw themselves on the enemy they "roar like lions,"[15] they "spread like a wild stream,"[16] they are so strong and brave that none can escape from them.[17]

The form and metric structure of these fragments anticipate—even more clearly than the Orkhon inscriptions—the later epic. The lines consist of seven to eight feet, just as in many Kazakh epics, and the rhyme scheme is very similar to that of the later Central Asiatic epos. The stanza consists of four lines, the first three of which usually rhyme, while the last line contains the rhyme which is constant throughout the whole poem. Thus we have: *a a a b, c c c b, d d d b,* etc. (e.g., oghradym, kökrädim, toghradym, tutar; alyqty, turuqty, taghyqty, jatar; artura, artura, oltura, butar, etc.).[18]

Other factors suggestive of the antiquity of the Central Asian epos are the many evidences of wide diffusion of epic traits and the occurrence of some epics which appear to be shared in almost identical forms in various national groups. There are indications that a number of such epics may have originated before the period of national separation of certain tribal groupings. Frequently it is difficult to determine with accuracy the exact national origin of a particular epic which may have traveled back and forth from one Turkic culture to another before it was first noted by the folklore scholar. Thus, most of the epics now considered Kazakh were actually products of the period before the formation of the Kazakh tribal federation. Even the contents of the

[14] *Ibid.*, p. 4. [15] *Ibid.*, p. 14. [16] *Ibid.*, p. 10.
[17] *Ibid.*, p. 15. [18] *Ibid.*, p. 15.

epics often fail to give us exact information about their national origin, for a great number of Central Asiatic epics pertain not to just one nationality, but to many of the Turkic and Mongol tribes, and are concerned not only with the problems of a particular nation, but with broad problems which affect the history of many or all of the Turkic nomads. Thus, some Kazakh epics are concerned with the common problems faced by the Turks as a result of Mongol domination of Central Asia. A number of Central Asiatic epics actually appear to be the composite product of a number of nations. Thus Orlov has stated that the Central Asiatic epos cannot be regarded as a purely national one.[19] Whether this supranational character of many of the epics in Central Asia is a result of diffusion or of a common historical past of many of these tribes under the Golden Horde and the Crimean and Kazan Khanates is sometimes difficult to determine and would depend partly on the age of the prototype. The fact remains that there is considerable identity of subject matter among the epics of the most variegated tribes, and some epics seem to be known in their entirety by many of the Central Asiatic Turkic tribes. Orlov reckons five epics known to the Kazakhs as belonging to this "international" group of epics: *Edige-batyr,*[20] which is told not only among the Kazakhs, but also among the Kirghiz, the Baraba, Taranči, and Crimean Tatars; *Qoblandy-batyr,*[21] which is known not only among the Kazakhs, but also a-

[19] A. S. Orlov, *Kazakhski geroicheski epos* (Moscow, 1945), p. 5.

[20] This epic is not included in Radloff's collection, but is available in Russian translation in fragments in Orlov, *op. cit.,* pp. 133-47. Orlov's text and synopsis are based on the MS literal translation of Sh. M. Bekmukhamedov in the Institut Yazyka, Literatury i Istorii of the Kazakh branch of the Soviet Academy of Sciences, *ibid.,* p. 6 n. The earliest recording is doubtless that of the Kazakh ethnographer, Valikhanov; see *Sochineniya,* pp. 223-64.

The epithet *batyr* after the name of the hero means simply "hero." Cf. the Mongol *baghatur,* a title given to heroes for their services. Cf. also later Mongol *bātor,* Hungarian *bátor,* and Russian *bogatyr.* According to Radloff the term *batyr* is used in modern Kazakh, Kirghiz, Türkmen, Kazan, and Crimean Tatar, and *batur* can be traced to the language of the Orkhon inscriptions (Radloff, *Opyt slovarya tyurskikh narechii* [Sankt Peterburg, 1911], IV, 1511-15).

[21] For a Russian translation of this epos, see Mark Tarlovski, transl., *Koblandy-batyr* (Alma-Ata, 1937), also Sobolev, ed., *Pesni . . . ,* pp. 17-29 (fragment). Some fragments are also contained in Orlov, *op. cit.,* pp. 34-49.

mong the Karakalpaks and the various Tatar groups; *Alpamyš-batyr,*[22] which is known among the Kazakhs as well as among the Karakalpaks and the Uzbeks;[23] *Šora-batyr*[24] (with variations of Šura-batyr and Čura-batyr), which can also be found among the Kirghiz and the various Tatar groups; and finally the Kazakh lyrical epos *Qozy Körpöš and Bayan Sulū,*[25] which is based on the Romeo and Juliet theme and is also known among the Oirat and as far East as the Uighurs in Chinese Turkestan.[26]

Not only are similar, or almost identical, epics found among various national groups in Central Asia, but also many epics found throughout Central Asia share common *dramatis personae* and thus seem to belong to common epic cycles.

Although it is clear that the epic traditions of the peoples of Central Asia were closely interwoven and drew much of their material from a common source, the various traditions also developed their own national character. Epics, whether adopted from other nations or shared in similar form by various nations, were integrated into the traditions of the nations of which they were a part, and thus they provide not only extensive information about the whole way of life of nomadic Central Asia, but compose individual expressions of the tribal groups of which they are a product.

Trends in the Development of the Kazakh Heroic Epos

The typical Kazakh epic was centered on the life and adventures of a national hero, his struggles and triumphs against his

[22] Orlov, *op. cit.,* pp. 10-33. His texts are based on the translation of Sh. M. Bekmukhamedov; cf *supra.*

[23] See C. M. Zhirmunski, Kh. T. Zarifov, *Uzbekski narodny geroicheski epos* (Moscow, 1947), pp. 60-110.

[24] Prose translation by A. Divayev, "Etnograficheskiye materialy," *Sbornik materialov dlya statistiki Syr-Darinskoi oblasti,* Vol. IV, also Orlov, *op. cit.,* pp. 87-114 (fragments).

[25] Radloff, *Proben . . . ,* III, 261-97; Sobolev, ed., *Pesni . . . ,* pp. 74-91 (fragments of M. Tarlovski's poetic translation). This was the poem which interested Pushkin so greatly when he visited the approaches to the Kazakh steppes in search of materials for his *History of Pugachev.* The first Russian partial abstract of this lyrical epos was made for Puskhin and copies of this translation have recently been found among his papers (*Vremennik Pushkinskoi komisii,* Vol. III, 1937, quoted in Orlov, *op. cit.,* p. 5 n.).

[26] Radloff, *Proben . . . ,* VI, 236-47.

or his nation's enemies. The basis for the story was very often an actual historical event, but, as Orlov states, such events represented merely the "historical substratum"[27] of the epic while much of the subject matter went far beyond the framework of the early period.

The basic repertory of the Kazakh heroic epos includes the following main epic productions: *Edige-batyr, Alpamyš-batyr,* and *Er-Kokča,*[28] concerned with the period of the "Golden Horde"; *Šora-batyr,* in which the destruction of the Kazan khanate is depicted; *Qoblandy-batyr, Qambara-batyr,*[29] *Er-Targhyn,*[30] and *Er-Sajn*[31] which tell of the struggle against the Kalmyks; and finally two epics of considerably later origin, *Ajman-Šolpan*[32] and *Uraq-batyr,*[33] set in the period of Russian conquest. The hero, in the early group of epics, is motivated by a strong social and national spirit. His strength and prowess, which he reveals in battles against tribal enemies, symbolize the wished-for strength of the group in the face of the enemy. The later epics are not as concerned with national symbolism. Personal motivation, love of family and wife, is given more importance, as the hero begins to fight not only for the interests of the tribal group but also for those of his immediate family or his beloved. The descriptive passages become more lyrical and frequently more emotional. Nevertheless, the *batyr* is still relatively stereotyped and highly idealized. He is characterized by the same general traits of superhuman strength, bravery, and incorruptible honor as is the *batyr* of the earlier group. In addition to these epics which are strictly heroic in character, mention should also be made of a group of lyrical epics, or love epics, the most commonly known of which are *Qozy Körpöš and Bayan Sulū* and *Qyz Džibek.*

[27] Orlov, *op. cit.,* p. 7 n.

[28] See Valikhanov, *op. cit.,* p. 225. The epithet *er* preceding the hero's name signifies "manly" or "brave."

[29] Sobolev, ed., *Pesni . . . ,* pp. 60-67 (fragment).

[30] Radloff, *Proben . . . ,* III, 153-205; Sobolev, ed., *Pesni . . . ,* pp. 47-59.

[31] Radloff, *Proben . . . ,* III, 205-261; Sobolev, ed., *Pesni . . . ,* pp. 30-46; Orlov, *op. cit.,* pp. 50-71 (fragments).

[32] Sobolev, ed., *Pesni . . . ,* pp. 108-126.

[33] Valikhanov, *op. cit.,* pp. 225-26 (résumé).

One of the most popular of the early epics is *Er-Targhyn,* which is available to the Western student in two translations, that of L. Penkovski[34] and that of Radloff.[35] This epos tells the story of the internal strife within the Crimean khanate. It takes place in the region of Western Kazakhstan between the rivers Volga (*Edil*) and Ural (*Džajyq*). The following is a short synopsis of the main events of the epos *Er-Targhyn.*

The hero Targhyn flees from his own tribe to the Crimea, after killing a high noble of his people. At this time in the Crimea there are forty khans, the most powerful of which is Aqša-khan. Targhyn lives with Aqša-khan's people incognito for many months. "No one knew that he was a hero."[36] Aqša-khan is engaged in constant warfare with two neighboring tribes whose fortress he besieges but is unable to take until Targhyn jumps into the breach and takes it singlehanded in the name of the true faith:

He who resembled a thousand heroes, Targhyn,
Knew that the people wanted to return home;
From God he asked orders,
Shortened the horses tail-leather,
Pulled up both belly-straps,
Mounted his horse,
"My death is good, too, oh my God," he said.
The nine hordes of the Torgaut,
The ten hordes of the Oimaut,
Beat their drums, beat their cymbals,
Made their warriors march before him.
"This is a difficult matter," he said.
In the name of God, the hero stormed towards them,
"Only God alone can help," he said.
Moving like a light-yellow camel
The hero galloped, spurring his horse
Sucking like the *džalmaus.*[37]
This hero paid no heed to the armies which were outside,
Stormed into the inside of the fortress.[38]

[34] Sobolev, ed., *Pesni . . .* , pp. 47-59 (fragments).
[35] Radloff, *Proben . . .* , III, 153-205.
[36] *Ibid.*, p. 153.
[37] The *džalmaus,* a vampire, occurs frequently in Kazakh legends and tales. Cf. *supra.*
[38] *Ibid.*, p. 154.

Thereafter Er-Targhyn is much honored by Aqša-khan and made the leader of his armies. The khan has a daughter of exquisite beauty.

She combed her hair with a comb,
Like the rich man's mare
She was slender in body;
When one looked at her face
It was like the rays of spring,
When one looked at her face,
It was white like wheat flour,
Freed from its shell;
Her eyebrows curved, like yellow bows,
Her eyelids were like piercing arrows,
Her waist was pliable;
Whoever looked at her, was unable to turn away his eyes.
She had hair like the *qulan*,[39] eyes like the sheep,
Her speech was superior to that of others,
Aq-Žunus was the name of this maiden.[40]

Hearing of the heroic exploits of Targhyn, Aq-Žunus bribes a servant to admit Targhyn to her quarters. She takes him into her tent and "they spent six to seven hours together, playing and joking."[41] Aq-Žunus falls in love with the hero, but another khan asks for her hand. She tells Targhyn that she will marry no one but him and asks him to prove his heroism by eloping with her. Targhyn mounts Aq-Žunus on a black horse of the khan and flees with her, and the angered Aqša-khan immediately calls his people and promises his daughter's hand to the man who returns Aq-Žunus and Targhyn to him. No one, however, can match the speed of the fleeing couple. Only one, the old and experienced *batyr* Qart-Qožaq, on his famed horse Qasqa-Azban finally overtakes them. Targhyn's horse snorts in warning and Targhyn, encouraged by Aq-Žunus, turns to meet the enemy. Seeing that Qart-Qožaq is an old man, Targhyn, true to the Kazakh tradition of veneration of old age, greets him politely. The unwritten code guides their words in the typical verbal exchange between the two heroes before battle which in-

[39] *qulan*—a wild horse.
[40] *Ibid.*, p. 155.
[41] *Ibid.*, p. 156.

cludes greetings and praise of the opponent, questions about names and intentions, and also boastings and threats. Qart-Qožaq, the older, begins by boasts. Targhyn learns that his opponent is a famous *batyr* from the Crimean khanate, descended from a long line of famous *batyrs*. Qart Qožaq had already made much booty:

> Wherever there was battle, I took my road,
> The prepared enemy I attacked,
> Straight through them I took my road.

But Qart Qožaq also extends the customary praises and greetings to his opponent:

> You yourself are a great wise man,
> You burn like lighted dry grass,
> Your manly bravery is without blemish.[42]

Qart Qožaq does not fail, however, to warn his opponent:

> If fate reaches me, I shall die,
> If fate does not catch up with me,
> I shall take from you
> The maid Aq-Žunus, who is at your side.

When the duel begins, Qožaq, being old and experienced, pities the young Targhyn and purposely shoots his arrow astray. He then persuades Targhyn that any further struggle against him is useless and Targhyn departs, leaving Aq-Žunus to the old Qožaq. Weeping, Aq-Žunus covers herself with a rug but Qožaq orders her to show him her entire body, adding that if he likes her body, he will take her, but "if only one little place does not please me, I will not take you."[43] Aq-Žunus refuses and sings with much feeling a song in which she depicts her own beauty and Qožaq's age. Qožaq relents and releases her to Targhyn.

Targhyn and Aq-Žunus continue their journey and soon come to the land of the Nogai, where they are received with much honor by the Nogai khan, Khanzada, who asks Targhyn's aid in the struggle against the Kalmyks. Targhyn agrees and with three Nogai *batyrs* he approaches the Kalmyks, who flee, afraid to join battle with the famed Targhyn. Targhyn then mounts a tree to

[42] *Ibid.*, p. 162.

[43] *Ibid.*, p. 165.

reconnoiter, but a branch breaks and he falls to the ground, dislocating his spine, making it impossible for him to move. Despite the great care of Khanzada, he does not recover; and when Khanzada has to move to his summer pastures, he leaves Targhyn and Aq-Žunus behind with food supplies for one week, planning to fetch them after completing his migration. After one week nobody returns to fetch them and they begin to starve. Feeling death approaching, Targhyn sings a deeply emotional song to his wife and his horse Tarlan, while Aq-Žunus sings a similar song to Targhyn. Both curse the faithless Nogai people. Furious at the thought that people would say that he did not die in battle, but only from a fall from a tree, Targhyn grabs his back, presses it hard and miraculously his joint jumps back into place and he recovers. He rejoins Khanzada, who begs his forgiveness for abandoning him, which Targhyn readily gives after learning that Khanzada had been encircled by Kalmyks and had thus been unable to rescue him. Khanzada again asks Targhyn's assistance against the Kalmyks. Targhyn defeats the Kalmyk *batyr* Dombaul in a duel and then single-handedly defeats the entire army of seven thousand Kalmyks. For twelve days and nights he fights. On the twelfth day not a single Kalmyk remains alive on the battlefield. Targhyn and his proud horse Tarlan have lost none of their courage, but physically, they present a sad picture.

> When he looked at his grey-white horse,
> From the hoofs, large as a fire site,
> Only something of the size of a thimble remained,
> Of the lips, large as two coat tails,
> Only the width of two fingers remained,
> Of the ears, which looked like cut reeds,
> Only a hand's width remained,
> Of the flowing mane
> Only a yard's width remained,
> Of the tail, which you could hardly embrace with both arms,
> Only a handful remained.
> When he looked at his own body,
> He was wounded in seventeen places.[44]

[44] *Ibid.*, pp. 199-200.

Khanzada had promised his daughter to Targhyn as a second wife, as payment for defeating the Kalmyks. But he betrays Targhyn and refuses to release his daughter. Targhyn departs in fury with Aq-Žunus, planning to make his peace with Aq-Žunus' father Aqša-khan, collect an army and with it revenge himself on Khanzada. Frightened, Khanzada sends messengers after Targhyn with rich gifts, and, thus mollified, Targhyn returns, is given large herds and land by Khanzada, and finally becomes himself a khan.

Thus living, Targhyn became old, and when death took him, he left this world. From Aq-Žunus he had a son Arda-Bī, who was also a great hero and a noble ruler. Arda-Bī had two sons; the oldest was Asy Keräj Myrza. Asy Keräi died in his twentieth year. There remained the younger son, the seven-year-old Aj-Qoša. This Aj-Qoša ruled over five *auls,* thus he was the ruler of the people—a prince; he mounted the throne, and, ruling over these five *auls,* he died.[45]

The central theme of the lyrical epics is often the struggle of two young people for happiness and love. The oldest and most popular of these lyrical epics is that of *Qozy Körpöš and Bayan Sulū,*[46] which is related to the motif of *Romeo and Juliet.* The story tells of the love of two young people, Qozy and Bayan, who have been promised to each other by their respective fathers before their birth.[47] Shortly after the birth of the two children, however, Qozy's father dies and Bayan's father, not wishing to marry his daughter to an orphan, promises her hand to Qodar,

[45] *Ibid.*, p. 205.

[46] The epithet *sulū* means "beauty." Bayan Sulū therefore simply means "Bayan the beautiful." Different versions of this love epic are recorded in Radloff (*Proben . . .*, III, 261-97) and Sobolev (*Pesni . . .*, pp. 74-91). The subject matter of this romance is widely distributed in Central Asia. It is found among the Uzbeks in the lyrical epos *Tahir and Zukhra* (see "Takhir i Zukhra, Uzbekskaya skazka," *Literatura i iskusstvo Uzbekistana* [Tashkent, 1940], I, 70-78), among the Turkmens (see Molla Nepes, *Zohre i Tahir* [Ashkhabad, 1943]), among the Turks of Siberia (see Radloff, *Proben . . .*, IV) and among the present-day Uighurs of Sinkiang (see Radloff, *Proben . . .*, VI, 236-46; G. Raquette, *Täji bilä Zohra eine osttürkische Variante der Sage von Tahir und Zohra* [Lund-Leipzig, 1930]; Gunnar Jarring, *Materials to the Knowledge of Eastern Turki* [Lund, 1946], pp. 3-34).

[47] In the epics of many cultures we find reflected the custom of uniting two families through agreements for marriage of the children. Such agreements sometimes took place even before the birth of the children.

another *batyr* of his tribe. The poem tells of the search of Qozy for Bayan and of Bayan for Qozy. When the two lovers finally find each other, Bayan's father and Qodar kill Qozy. Grief-stricken, Bayan kills herself over her lover's grave. But even death does not release the two lovers from persecution. Qodar, whom Bayan had slain before she killed herself, is laid in the grave between the two lovers, and between the beautiful flowers emerging from Bayan's and Qozy's grave, there grows the wild rose of Qodar's grave.[48]

The following scene should serve as an example of the quite different style of this type of epic and of its more emotional and lyrical quality as compared to the traditional heroic epics.

Bayan finds a body which she presumes to be that of Qozy, slain by Qodar, but then learns that Qozy is alive:

> My only one, do you lie here by [the action of] an arrow?
> The sun shines through your back, since your soul has fled.
>
> . . . .
>
> My only one, are you lying here blinking?
> When I see you, my soul burns like fire.
> For the sake of revenge I have brought Qodar here;
> Arise now Qozy, sing like a bird.
> My only one, are you stretched out on the earth?
> Smitten by the raven-feathered arrow,
> If you still possess the soul of the fly, arise;
> Bayan is coming to you, singing like a bird,
> My light, my guiding star, companion of my soul.
> Bayan has come to you, your dear friend.

Then she finds Qozy alive:

> Qozy stood, his arms spread wide apart.
> Oh you my light, my guiding star, my beloved!
> You truly noble one, my linen, my wide trouser leg!
> When you were invisible to my eyes, oh how did I feel then?
> You, united with me in the mother's womb, you my white throat!
> You my light, my brightness, my guiding star,
> You brightly burning candle!
> When you were invisible to my eyes, what was I then?
> Oh, you my candle, united to me in the mother's womb!
> My dearest beloved, my light!

[48] For Western folk themes which parallel this concluding episode, compare *Tristan and Isolde* and the English ballad "Barbara Allen."

Did my voice penetrate to your ears?
When you were not visible to my eyes, what was I then?
. . . .
Alas, were you not my waking hours and my dreams?
Were you not all my life, all my care?
Submerging me in heavy sorrow, where had you gone?[49]

Another Kazakh love epic is *Qyz-Džibek,*[50] which tells of the love between the young *džigit* Tölegen and the beautiful girl Qyz-Džibek[51] and of Qyz-Džibek's act of devotion and deference to the memory of her lover and husband when, after he is slain by another suitor, she submits to the custom of the levirate and marries Tölegen's brother. The poem has more lyrical elements than *Qozy* and in its formal aspects is frequently regarded as unexcelled in the Kazakh epic.

Formal Characteristics of the Kazakh Epic

The Kazakhs have no particular name for their heroic epics but call them simply *džyr* (song) or *qysa,* an Arabic loanword.[52] The authors of the epics are in most cases unknown. As the epic was not written down and as each performer (either the *aqyn* or the more specialized singer of epical songs, the *džyršy*) frequently changed the song to suit his own taste or to adjust it to a particular occasion, there developed a great number of variants of the main prototypes. The performance of the epic, like that of other folklore types, was characterized by a large degree of syncretism: gestures, exclamations, music, and songs were all elements of the epic performance.

The most common Kazakh epic style includes both prose and verse. Generally, the basic plot of the *džyr* was told in prose, while verse was employed to cite speeches of the hero or other main characters.[53] The versified parts were sung to the accompaniment of the *dombra* or the *qobyz* while the prose sections were usually declaimed in *recitativo,* also to the accompaniment of

[49] Radloff, *Proben* . . . , III, 294-96.
[50] Sobolev, ed., *Pesni* . . . , pp. 92-107 (fragments).
[51] *Džibek*—silk, thus Qyz-Džibek means "girl-silk."
[52] From Arabic *qyṣṣa,* "story," "tale."
[53] See Valikhanov, *op. cit.,* p. 225.

the musical instrument. There were some epics, however, which were composed entirely of poetic verse, while others were related entirely in prose. The poetic verse was usually syllabic, with no consistent rhyme scheme. Rhyme was not absent, however, and was frequently based, as it was in the other Turkic languages,[54] on the repetition of identical agglutinative elements of the word, such as the plural suffix-*lar,* or the verbal personal suffixes. Thus we find rhymes such as *atlar—Qazaqlar* and *alarmen—qalarmen.* In addition the musicality of the verse was commonly underlined by alliteration, tonal repetition, and assonance.

Characteristic of the Kazakh epic, as well as of the epics of most of the Central Asiatic nomads, is the abundant use of stereotyped clichés, composed of a few expressive words or sometimes several descriptive passages. Among the most typical of such clichés are those used to describe the hero in battle, such as:

> We shall fight like stallions!
> We shall dip the string of the yellow bow
> Into the red blood,
> And we shall draw it until it tears![55]

The militant appearance of the hero might be described in this typical fashion: when the hero is angry, "snow falls from his brows," "ice hangs from his eyelids,"[56] he "looks dark as a storm-cloud,"[57] "his eyebrows contract like stones."[58]

The use of clichés is generally common in the longer, more elaborate descriptive sections of the epic, as the descriptions of the saddling of the horse, the lamentations, the descriptions of horse races (*bajga*) among the heroes, bragging before battle or duel, and the dialogue of two heroes meeting on the road. The following depiction of the running of the horse shows similarities to the Western heroic epos:

[54] Zhirmunski, Zarifov, *op. cit.,* p. 438.
[55] Radloff, *Proben . . . ,* III, 235-36.
[56] *Tvorchestvo narodov SSSR* (*Almanakh*) (Moscow, 1937), I, 336 (*Qoblandy-batyr*); Radloff, *Proben . . . ,* III, 188 (*Er-Targhyn*).
[57] *Tvorchestvo narodov . . . ,* I, 366.
[58] Radloff, *Proben . . . ,* III, 195 (*Er-Targhyn*).

The hero rides, he rides,
Chases into the enemy's camp.
His horse whirls along,
Eagerly chewing the bit,
Beating with his hoofs along the road,
Competing with the quick-flighted bird,
Stretching his tender neck,
Pulling, pulling on the reins,
[So that] the youth's hands begin to numb.
The muscles are playing
On Bajšubar the *tulpar*.

The sparks, flying from under his four feet,
Are alight, like a fire of flint.
If you listen to the noise he makes,
He roars like a mountain waterfall.
. . . .
When you say "forward," the furry horse
Bypasses the quickflighted bird,
Whirls like the wind,
Flies like an arrow,
. . . .
He jumps over crevices, and
That which we see far ahead,
After a moment
Is left far behind.[59]

In the epos *Qoblandy-batyr* the hero fights two duels, one against the Kalmyk khan Qazan and one against the Kalmyk khan Alčagir, the descriptions of which form one of the best examples of the repetitive character of such passages. Although the two pasages occur quite far apart in the epic, they are completely identical, except for the names of the opponents.

Duel with Qazan

Quicker than lightning in the roaring storm
The lances began to dance;
Both, boiling with anger,
Gripped the cherry-wood handles;
The steel of the swords
Became bent like pretzels,
The earth was filled with horses foam,
And in a bloody stream snivel

[59] Orlov, *op. cit.*, p. 17.

Ran down the Kalmyk's face.
He stretched like a hungry polecat,
But the enemy's lance caught him,
So that never again would he ride on horseback.
Qoblan raised his lance,
Qazan died on the ground.[60]

Duel with Alčagir

Quicker than lightning in the roaring storm,
Rapidly the lances flashed;
Both, boiling with anger,
Gripped the cherry-wood handles;
The steel of the swords
Became bent like pretzels,
The earth was filled with horses foam,
And in a bloody stream snivel
Ran down the Kalmyk's face.
He stretched like a hungry polecat,
But the enemy's lance caught him,
So that never again would he ride on horseback.
Qoblan raised his lance,
Alčagir died on the ground.[61]

Radloff has observed that the use of clichés was not actually limited to any particular parts of the epic, and the epic singer had at his disposal, in addition to the standard clichés about hero, horse, and battle, stereotypes to describe the most diverse subjects as the birth and childhood of the hero, the price of weapons and brides, etc.[62]

The Main Kazakh Epic Figures

The Kazakh epic traditionally centers around a core of relatively constant *dramatis personae* who are characterized in a manner consistent enough to justify a number of generalizations about their treatment and role in the epic.

The central figure in the Kazakh epic is the warrior hero (*batyr*), who generally symbolizes the society's idealized virtues of bravery, military prowess, beauty, and physical strength. Above

[60] *Tvorchestvo narodov* . . . , I, 384.
[61] Sobolev, ed., *Pesni* . . . , p. 29.
[62] Radloff, *Proben* . . . , V, xvi.

all, the *batyr* possesses unshakable ideas of military honor. Thus Qoblandy-batyr, when escaping from captivity among the Kalmyks, refuses to accept aid from the Kalmyk girl whom he loves because he considers such a way to freedom degrading for a hero of his stature. In most cases the hero's unusual physical and intellectual strength become apparent in his earliest youth. Thus, the hero Alpamyš is able as a child to shoot from a big bow, and in his duel with the Kalmyk hero Qoqaldaš, he is strong enough to throw his adversary high into the air. As a child Alpamyš is so strong that if he accidentally strikes one of his playmates, his friend falls dead. Er-Sajn is so extraordinary that as an infant he refuses his mother's breast and finishes the marrow and fat of one fat mare every three days.

> When he was two years old,
> He was equal to the whole nation in strength.
> When he was three years old,
> From the horse which he mounted in the morning,
> He would not dismount till evening.
> When he was four years old,
> He already swung the lance of fir-wood. . . .[63]

Šora-batyr is also a most unusual infant.

> Šora developed unusually rapidly. When he was only forty days old he already smiled and was able to distinguish his parents from strangers. At one year of age he amazed everyone by his handsomeness, at two years he had grown so that he could not be recognized, at three he was lively as a bird, at four he entered school, at five he reached higher education, at ten he showed pride and bravery, at eleven he became a really handsome man with supple body and high stature and, finally at twelve years of age he became a fabulous hero, with athletic chest, shoulders, and muscles.[64]

Also Edige[65] distinguishes himself in childhood by superior intelligence and strength; he easily solves the difficult legal problems posed him by khan Tokhtamyš.[66]

According to folk tradition the epic heroes were not only

[63] "Sain Batyr," Radloff, *Proben* . . . , III, 217.
[64] Orlov, *op. cit.*, p. 89 n.
[65] Valikhanov, *op. cit.*, p. 233.
[66] Cf. Siegfried, who kills a dragon in his youth, and young Roland in the *Chanson de Roland,* who saves Charlemagne's armies.

endowed with superhuman strength, but were also often invulnerable.[67] Thus when Alpamyš is to be put to death by the Kalmyks, they learn that he cannot be burned, he cannot be drowned, a sword cannot cut him, a bullet cannot harm him, and he cannot die by hanging.[68] Not all Kazakh heroes, however, are invulnerable. Many of them are saved only by luck or by the aid of a friend, a woman, or a horse. Qoblandy-batyr, who is neither invulnerable nor invincible, is often saved only by the aid of the daughter of the Kalmyk khan.

In popular fantasy, even the birth of the *batyr* is frequently ascribed to miraculous or unusual circumstances, as is so common in folklore the world over in the depiction of an ideal leader or hero. The usual formula is that of the childless parents to whom a son is given either in answer to a call to a saint for help (*Alpamyš*) or in response to a dream in which a saint promises that a son will be born to them (*Er-Sajn, Šora-batyr*).[69] The explanation of the birth of Edige[70] does not follow the typical pattern. The hero is described as the son of the saint Baba-Toqty-Čačty-Azis and a water nymph.[71]

The epic rarely provides detailed preliminary descriptions of the hero's external characteristics. A picture of the hero emerges only during the course of the action, during the description of battles or tournaments and in the speeches of the heroes.

[67] Cf. Achilles and Siegfried. In contrast to the Western heroes, however, the invulnerable Turkic heroes rarely have a vulnerable spot.

[68] Orlov, *op. cit.*, p. 12.

[69] Zhirmunski and Zarifov have suggested the possible influence of the Biblical legend of the childless Abraham and Sarah on epics found in Mohammedan cultures. (See Zhirmunski, Zarifov, *op. cit.*, p. 79.)

[70] The epos about Edige shows certain marked differences from most other epics. It is more accurate historically; Edige is clearly identified as one of the chief sultans of Tokhtamyš-khan, one of the khans of the Golden Horde. The central theme of the *džyr* is not, as is usual, the heroic adventures of the *batyr,* but the mutual relations of the *batyr* and the Tokhtamyš. (Cf. Valikhanov, *op. cit.*, pp. 223-64.)

[71] Potanin has noted some parallels between this epos and the Biblical tale of David and Saul. Both Edige and David are shepherds before they are called for service to the court, both are suspected by their royal masters of coveting the throne, and this suspicion on the part of Saul as well as of Tokhtamyš is confirmed by a fortune teller; both royal masters attempt unsuccessfully to murder their councillors in order to rid themselves of the imagined threat to their position. (Cf. I Samuel, 18:8, 19:11-12 and Potanin, *op. cit.*, pp. 233-34.)

As the most important virtues of the *batyr* are military ones, his characteristics are most eloquently described in his struggle with the enemy. A detailed but symbolic description of the hero usually emerges in the traditional "praise of the hero" which is pronounced by his closest friend, his beloved, or by any accidental person the hero meets on his road. The description of the hero is characterized by typical epithets. He is compared most frequently to a horse but also to a wild and brave animal (a lion[72] or a wolf).[73] When referred to by his mother he is often compared to a filly,[74] a lamb,[75] or a young camel.[76]

The hero meets the enemy either alone or with a large army. In order to dramatize the *batyr's* superior battle strength, his enemy commonly appears to be invincible, or at least marked with apparent physical superiority. The *batyr* is frequently the first ever to defeat the opponent. The following passage describes Targhyn's battle against the Kalmyks:

> From his brows fell snow,
> On his eyelids ice began to form,
> His shoulder blades were broad, his neck long,
> For shooting his hand was long.
> . . . .
> When he let his horse go, in the morning, he caught up with it
> quickly.
> If he let it go now, he would catch up by noon,
> (With the horse) that had whinnied,
> Whose head one could not hold,
> Which, when its straps were foamy,
> Could traverse a month's road in six steps.
> . . . .
> When he saw Dumbaul, he galloped toward him,
> When he galloped, they shot at him,
> The arrow fell to the ground.

[72] See in the epos *Er-Targhyn:* "the noble-born lion," Radloff, *Proben . . .*, III, 180.

[73] *Ibid.*, p. 195. The wolf is a totemic animal in Kazakh culture.

[74] "He kicked like a young filly . . . ," "Sain Batyr" (*Er-Sajn*), *ibid.*, p. 249.

[75] Alpamyš' mother says about her son: "When my lamb will return tomorrow . . . ," Orlov, *op. cit.*, p. 27.

[76] ". . . like a light yellow camel the hero galloped . . . ," "Er Targhyn," Radloff, *Proben . . .* , III, 154. The camel is a common symbol of strength in Kazakh tradition.

From the tramping of his feet
Cracks, big as kettles, arose in the rock. . . .[77]

Or:

He played alone with the enemy,
Never ceased battle,
The raised lance
As long as it was whole, could not get its fill of blood.
After some time
He pulled from his belt the dagger,
Rode toward the enemy.
Many of the Kalmyk begged [for mercy],
Those who begged, he did not smite down.
By the neck he grabbed them,
And cut their throats.
When he looked,
He was no hero which man could bear.
He made snow fall from the trees.[78]

The heroine of the *džyr,* the hero's wife or beloved, is usually endowed with qualities similar to, or complementary to, those of the *batyr,* though they are not often developed as fully as those of the hero. It is interesting to note that in the epics not only of the Kazakhs, but of all the Turkic peoples of Central Asia, the heroine is depicted as equal in moral worth and intelligence to her husband or lover and that she is always highly idealized. It seems reasonable to assume that this attitude towards the woman in the folk fantasy of the Turkic peoples goes back to the period before Mohammedan influence. There are, however, some traces in the early epic of the later attitude toward woman in Kazakh society as inferior and subject to the will of the man. Thus in the epos *Qoblandy-batyr* the hero becomes angry at his faithful and wise wife Qurtqa because she has advised him to forego a planned campaign against the Kalmyks. His manly dignity is insulted and he is embarrassed before his fighting friends. Accordingly, he gallops home, intending to kill her, having been incited by his friend Qaraman.

[77] "Er-Targhyn," Radloff, *Proben* . . . , III, 188-189.
[78] *Ibid.,* pp. 196-97.

Woe to us,
If with a woman you have tied yourself.
I had dreamt of being drunk with slaughter,
And my dreams have died away.
With the khan I cannot measure my strength now,
And his *džurts* I cannot plunder.
We are not Qypčaqs,
We are not fighters,
We are no kind of horde,
If our heroic deeds are drowned in marriage bonds,
If anybody can spit at us,
If it's the womenfolk who are masters here. . . .[79]

But in this epos woman's wisdom wins out in the end and the hero recognizes that his wife is right and wiser than he. He apologizes rather sheepishly:

I am a gander, he said, a crooked-footed one,
I am the puddle in which the ganders sleep,
I am a cornflower after bloom
Which the donkeys chew in April
. . . .
You almost fell from my own hand,
It would be better if you would knock off my own head.
Is it so easy then to find a spouse
Who is equal to us [men]?[80]

Such episodes as Qoblandy's intended murder of his wife for what was considered an insult to his manly dignity are rather rare. In most cases the woman is almost as brave as her husband, or she surpasses him in intelligence and thus complements his manly bravery with her wits. So Qoblandy's wife Qurtqa is, as Mark Tarlovski puts it, "the bearer of reason; while he (Qoblandy) is the bearer of arms."[81] In *Er-Targhyn* the heroine Aq-Žunus is able, by her wit and womanly intuition, to extricate herself and Targhyn from a difficult situation. When Er-Targhyn's rival, the old and experienced fighter Qart Qožaq, threatens to take Aq-Žunus away after Er-Targhyn had conceded defeat in the duel, Aq-Žunus beguiles Qart Qožaq with a song

[79] "Qoblandy-Batyr," transl. Mark Tarlovski, *Tvorchestvo narodov*, p. 366.
[80] *Ibid.*, p. 367.
[81] *Ibid.*, p. 358.

in which she sings of her beauty, flatters Qart Qožaq by praising his past heroic exploits, but gives him to understand that she is not for him:

Your beard and moustache have become grey,
The veins in your body
Have all filled with water.
How can you think of pursuing a girl?
. . . .
Even if you kill me, I will not take you,
Think it a crime, if you like, I do not love you.
Even though formerly you were a hero,
Now your head is only
Like the grey dung which lies on the ground.

Qožaq, impressed by the fact that the girl has told him his entire life "as if she had lived by my side," feels that if she was right about his youth, she must also be right about his old age, and that it must be as she says, that she is not for him. He returns her to Targhyn and lets both of them go.[82]

In *Er-Sajn,* the Kalmyks capture the hero's wife and mother and attempt to use the two women to entrap the hero. Both women implore the hero not to attempt to liberate them, as he would be in danger of being captured himself in the process. "For you," his mother says, "my light, I will gladly sacrifice myself." And his wife Aju-Bikeš advises him,

Do not excite yourself, oh hero Sajn,
That your wife is with the enemy!
Say that they (wife and mother) went away when we quarreled.[83]

It is the characterization of the woman which serves as the main center of lyrical digression, of colorful and emotional expression. Her beauty is described in hyperbolic terms, with wide use of metaphorical devices. Aq-Žunus in the epos *Er-Targhyn* is compared to a "young mare," her eyelashes are like "arrows placed in a row," her "hair is fragrant," and her "eyes are like those of a sheep."[84] And Aju-Bikeš, in the epos *Er-*

[82] Radloff, Proben . . . , III, 168.
[83] *Ibid.,* pp. 254-55.
[84] Orlov, *op. cit.,* p. 80.

Sajn, is described as "slim as a switch," her face "pink as an apple."[85] When Sajn is looking for a wife the people tell him about Aju-Bikeš:

> She has black hair like a *qulan,*
> She stretches like a pheasant,
> Through her throat one can see the food she ate,
> When she looks toward the sun,
> Sunshine is mirrored in her face.[86]

The love between the hero and his wife or beloved is frequently expressed in highly emotional passages. Thus when the wounded Targhyn and his beloved believe death to await them, they each sing a lyrical song in which Targhyn takes leave of the woman he loves and of his faithful horse, and Aq-Žunus sings farewell to Targhyn:

> When my lion was alive
> I wore stockings with gold,
> . . . .
> Oh God, why did you treat so badly
> The noble-born lion.
> You have forgotten his noble soul.
> . . . .
> If you go away, my beloved,
> What shall I do, if I have to remain behind?
> Tell me truthfully,
> Are you going?
> What will I do without you?[87]

In general, it may be said that in the earlier epics the element of romantic love, though it plays an important role, is commonly subordinated to the more important theme for which it serves as the background, the prowess of the hero.[88]

[85] Radloff, *Proben* . . . , III, 255.
[86] *Ibid.,* p. 226.
[87] *Ibid.,* p. 181.
[88] In sharp contrast is the epos of the southern Turks, particularly of the Uzbeks, in which, presumably under the more intensive influence of Iranian culture, romantic love is given a far more important position. Love scenes are described in the most elevated and frequently sensual tones, and detailed self-analyses of the emotions of the hero and heroine are typical. Traces of this treatment of love can be found also in the epos of the Kazakhs, but they only faintly reflect the metaphorical, colorful passages in the southern cycles. These trends in the southern epic must be looked upon in the context of the

An important figure in the Kazakh epos is the friend who is united to the hero through the ties of a "friendship-in-arms." In some of the Turkic epics the actual ritual of fraternization by exchanging or drinking each other's blood or sucking at the same breast is described.[89] But more generally the ritual is not described and we may assume that such rituals were probably not of great importance among the Turkic peoples. In the Kazakh epics we find typically a description of two inseparable heroes who were not necessarily united by a ritual tie. The friend is often drawn in such a way as to bring into relief the excellent qualities of the hero. Like Qaraman in *Qoblandy-batyr,* he may be greedy, haughty, and even a little treacherous. Or he may play the role of a comical character, in which case he may even be depicted as somewhat of a fool.

Apart from this group of *dramatis personae,* there are usually two groups in the Kazakh epos who are treated in a more formal fashion: the enemies of the hero, usually depicted without much differentiation in the darkest possible colors, and the immediate family of the *batyr.* The enemies, depicted with great hatred, consistently use unfair tricks to subdue the hero. The one tactic permissible in regard to them is to put them to the sword. In many epics the enemies are depicted as infidels and the struggle against them as a struggle for Islam.

In the following selection the enemy is addressed by Qoblandy as he is about to fight a duel with the Kalmyk khan Qazan:

Why should you know,
You abortion,
You who are shallow of brain and whose mug is ugly,
In whose beard, there are few hairs
Why should you know, who I am and who were my forebears. . . ?[90]

And Qoblandy describes the wounded enemy:

general decline of the epic tradition among the settled people under Iranian and Arab influence, and the gradual transition to lyric poetry and more sophisticated forms of art.

[89] E.g., the Kirghiz epic cycle *Manas,* in which the hero, Manas, and his Chinese friend, Alambet, become "milk brothers" after they have drunk from the breast of Manas' mother.

[90] *Tvorchestvo narodov . . . ,* I, 383.

And in a bloody stream
Snivel flowed all over the Kalmyk's face.[91]

The *batyr's* family, as relatively passive epic figures, have only a limited role in the action of the epic. They are utilized for the insertion of long, lyrical monologues usually in the form of epic laments which frequently compose the most beautiful parts of the epic. The laments are usually highly emotional and rhetorical in character and further aid in embellishing the character of the hero. In *Qoblandy-batyr,* the hero's mother, Analyq, after she has accompanied him part of the way toward his campaign against the Kalmyks, returns singing the following song, which is similar to the farewell song (*qostasū*):

I am the unhappy Analyq,
The most miserable poor wretch. . .
How can we return without Qoblandy?
How can we catch up with the dear son?
My tears flow down like large *aryqs*[92]
Flowing down the silent flats of the steppe,
Oh, Allah, mover of planets,
Incomparable one, oh life giver.
Oh, his prophet, Mohammed,
Whose protection is sweeter than anything else in the world.
After all, it is only thirty years
Since my Qoblandy saw the light of day,
And already he is a real *batyr*.

Then follows an enumeration of the heroic qualities of Qoblandy, after which the mother again turns to Mohammed:

I will give you a sacrifice for my son—
Oh, be merciful to us, Mohammed.
My only son, so much desired,
Was given me by Allah to care for.
Gathering with supernatural strength
The fruits of the merciful seed,
You have weighted me for nine moons,
You have thrust asunder in pain my belly.
True to yourself, oh my offshoot,
You saw snow, when you were born.

[91] *Ibid.*, p. 384.
[92] *aryq*—an irrigation canal.

You saw a mournful day, when first you were born.
Among silken covers
With lullabies you lay
In the beautiful cradle.
You grew so fast, so stormily,
Oh my rosy baby.

. . . .

Oh most merciful Ḥaẓret,[93]
Object of my thought,
None is left for us,
Save him, oh Prophet Mohammed,
For the years of our old age.[94]

Bitter resentment is revealed in the song sung by Alpamyš' father, Baj-Börü[95] (*Alpamyš-batyr*), who in Alpamyš' absence has been subjugated by his adopted son and forced to be a camel herder. While driving the unwilling camels the father sings about his longing for his son and laments his fate, peppering his lamentation with angry shouts to his animals:

I am weeping, I am turning to God
With the salt of the tears of my eyes,
Fulfil my prayer,
Oh creator, my God.
(*Araj,*[96] beasts, *araj.*)
Oh creator,
Will my Alpamyš return?
Did he see the tears in my eyes?
Will God, the creator,
Return to me him who has been absent so long?
(*Araj,* beasts, *araj.*)
On the heights of Qara Tau, a juniper tree is growing.
My son's wife now goes without silks.
(I am chasing you, but you keep straying away,
Little camel, given to my care by the hated one;
Araj, beasts, *araj.*)

A white tree grows on the mountain,
The maidens hang around their necks
Carnations and beads, one next to the other—

[93] Ḥaẓret—a high ecclesiastic title ("Excellency,") here used for Mohammed.
[94] *Tvorchestvo narodov* . . . , I, 375-77.
[95] *Baj-Börü:* "rich wolf."
[96] *Araj*—a call used to spur on the beasts.

(Here I am driving you, but you don't go where you are
supposed to,
May you die, having been left without a master.
Araj, beasts, *araj.*
May not one of you remain in health.
Here I drive you, but you go without reason,
May you be without master and die.
Araj, beasts, *araj.*)
. . . .
With these words I am pouring out the sadness of my soul.
In my old age I must suffer misery
From my cattle.
My despised eyes here
Have darkened in eternal tears.
Will the day come, when you will return,
My only one. . . ?[97]

The horse is a most important participant of the Central Asiatic epic. As the main battle companion of the hero and as his helper in all the battle exploits the horse is frequently a hero himself. He is the *batyr's* closest and most trusted friend and is regarded with almost as much affection as is the hero's wife. The horse understands human speech, speaks with a human voice, encourages the hero, and offers him advice during battle:

Then the white steed chewed its bit,
Like a man he spoke;
"Sajn, hero, oh do not be afraid.
Do not flee because there are many of them [enemies],
Show now the power
With which God has endowed you.
If you cannot split
The enemy's rows, then it will be your fault.
But when from an arrow I let myself be hit, it will be
my fault.
I will run gayly,
I will prance gracefully, like a girl."[98]

Frequently the horse is endowed with almost supernatural powers: he may carry his wounded master at terrific speed through waterless steppes. He can jump wide rivers and always

[97] Orlov, *op. cit.,* pp. 20-21.
[98] "Sajn-batyr," Radloff, *Proben . . . ,* III, 253.

brings his master to the desired place in the shortest possible time. The horse cannot be held prisoner, and in the epos *Alpamyš-batyr* he even breaks out from an iron enclosure to help his master.

Like his heroic master, the heroic horse has a highly idealized biography which in many points parallels that of the *batyr.* The horse is born of famous and brave parents and, like the *batyr,* develops amazing strength in his earliest youth. His beauty and his excellent qualities are praised in tones similar to those used in the *batyr's* description of the beauty of his wife or beloved. When Er Targhyn believes that he is dying, he not only bids farewell to his wife[99] but also to his faithful horse Tarlan, and the song to his horse is not surpassed in tenderness and lyricism by his song to Aq-Žunus:

Oh my dearest grey-white horse
. . . .
As a one-year old filly you were still sucking
As a two-year old you were sucking
As a three-year old you were also still sucking.
When you were four I trained you.
Plaiting from silk eight colored ropes
I pulled you behind me.
. . . .
When you were seven
You stamped the earth in your trot,
The enemy's eyes were afraid
When they saw you from the front.
What woman will torture you now,
Oh you my steed, which traversed the mountain,
When your master Targhyn is dead?
You, whose hoofs are large as a campfire,
Your spine is like a hut;
When I look at your shoulders,
They look like smoothly hewn boards.
Your tail pleases me well,
It looks like a dagger pulled from the sheath.
Your mane pleases me,
It is like loosely pulled silk.
Your jaw-joint pleases me,
It is like a curvy river-bend.

[99] See *infra.*

Your ears please me,
They are like the reeds growing by the lake.
Your eyebrows please me,
They are like the brows of the evil spirit.
Your neck [slaughter-place] pleases me,
It has an Adam's apple like a ripe apple.
Your eyes please me,
They are like lights, ignited by the heat.
Your nostrils please me,
They are like bottomless milking pails.
Your neck [slaughter-place] pleases me,
It is like cotton pressed by the Sart.
Your chest pleases me,
It is like the high bank of the lake.
. . . .
Your rear pleases me,
Your thighs are black as coal.
Your ribs please me,
They are like a fortress built from stone.
Your hips please me,
They are like the smith's anvil. . . .[100]

Not only is the horse personified, but also some inanimate objects closely connected with the fighting career of the hero, such as weapons and armor, are often endowed with human qualities. When Er-Sajn moves against the Kalmyks, he is encouraged and advised not only by his horse but also by his white armor.

Then spoke his white armor:
"Be not afraid, oh hero Sajn.
Speak no other words.
If you do not destroy
The ranks of the enemy, it will be your fault.
If ninety arrows come and penetrate me,
It will be my fault.
May Heaven protect you."[101]

Oral art constituted the most important and most highly developed means of cultural expression in Kazakh society. All the varied elements of Kazakh life, the people's mores, beliefs, emotions, and ideals, found expression in their folk literature, and

[100] Radloff, *Proben* . . . , III, 178-80.
[101] *Ibid.*, III, 253.

above all, in their epos. As an art Kazakh folklore is far more than a direct reflection of Kazakh life. It is also a product of the imagination and of the artistic and aesthetic sense of the people. Kazakh folk literature is rich in imaginative pictures and symbolism and possesses considerable beauty, much of which is inevitably lost in translation. The student of modern Kazakh literature will find an examination of the folklore invaluable, for most contemporary writers have drawn from early Kazakh traditions. Furthermore, the oral art of the nineteenth century, which developed into a protest against Russian expansion as well as the expression of a new Kazakh nationalism, grew directly out of the early epic tradition which stressed the bravery and strength of the Kazakh warrior heroes who defended their peoples at all costs.

Chapter IV

FOLKLORE IN THE NINETEENTH CENTURY: REFLECTIONS OF RUSSIAN RULE

It has been noted that early Kazakh folklore followed a relatively traditional pattern and was created by *aqyns* whose names were lost to posterity. The authors of the old Kazakh oral art were, in the words of the contemporary Kazakh writer and critic Sabit Muqanov, "the collective of anonymous *aqyns* and *džyršy* who created poetry and, in the course of centuries, embellished their original variants."[1] Kazakh cultural life in the nineteenth century was characterized by two new phenomena: the appearance of oral poetic works, composed in the main by known *aqyns,* whose productions reflected a new social and national content, and, in the second half of the century, the development of a written literature and the emergence of a national intelligentsia. These new currents in Kazakh culture were stimulated by the contact of the Kazakhs with Russian culture during the period of colonization. The impact of the invader on the Kazakhs brought to the fore varying attitudes toward the new rulers. The early *aqyns* of the eighteenth century sang in their poetry of the resistance to the Russians and of the fight against all things Russian. These revolutionary poets acted as spiritual and political leaders of the people and incorporated their names into their poetry, leaving no doubt as to their authorship. But as it became clearer that the Kazakhs must accept foreign rule, the later oral poetry reflected more and more trends of resignation, submission, and bitterness. Somewhat later in the century, a native intelligentsia emerged and with it the first begin-

[1] Sabit Muqanov, "Kazakhskaya literatura XIX veka," Sobolev, ed., *Pesni* . . . , p. 215.

nings of a national written literature made their appearance. This development was encouraged by varied influences, including the effect of the Kazan Tatar *mullās,* teachers and traders who were particularly active in the steppes during the nineteenth and early twentieth centuries, the new Russian educational system, and the considerable number of Russian political exiles who spent many years in the Kazakh steppes.

Bukhar Džyrau (c. 1693-1787)

A few remarks must be made about an eighteenth-century Kazakh poet, Bukhar Džyrau, whose work anticipated the later social poetry and who departed from the traditional folklore forms and from the traditional objective attitude toward society. Bukhar was one of the first Kazakh poets whose name remained known to posterity. He was distinguished from the earlier poets, as he was not a wandering bard, but a bard with a definite and firm position in the entourage of khan Ablaj.[2] He might be described as a court poet, although one cannot speak of a Kazakh "court" in the traditional sense. By this time formal court life was somewhat more developed among the Kazakhs as the result of the influence of the sedentary societies to the south and of the gradual increase of power of local rulers. In most of his works Bukhar supported Ablaj's policies of expansion and his efforts to unite the Kazakh tribal federation (*äl*), which had been split into several hordes, in the face of the danger threatening it from Russia and China. His support was not, however, unqualified. In many respects his writings were similar to those of the didactic court poets of the Renaissance and also to the works of some of the eighteenth-century classic poets who considered it their duty to exert a pedagogic influence on the rulers or the princes. Such didactic works had been extremely popular long

[2] Ablaj (1711-1781) ruled over the Middle Horde at a time when both China and Russia were clashing in their interests over the land of the Kazakhs. Ablaj cleverly used the differences of the two powers to his own advantage, playing one against the other. At the same time, he was able to extend vastly his realm by his successful struggle against the Kirghiz and the Kalmyks and by conquests in the southern regions (Khodžent, Tashkent). He succeeded in uniting under his despotic rule not only the Middle Horde, but also the western parts of the Old Horde.

before Bukhar's writings in the sedentary societies of Central Asia, just as they had been in the Middle Ages in the West.[3] Bukhar acted as advisor to the khan and it was in this capacity that he composed most of his poetry of advice and admonition.

The works of Bukhar do not appear to be influenced to any great extent by his adherence to the Moslem faith but are primarily concerned with political and moral questions of the day and abound in concrete allusions to historical situations, such as the negative advice which Bukhar gave to Ablaj, when the latter was considering fighting the Russians:

> Do not enter battle with the Russians;
> Spare your people from war,
> Your people who guard you like a precious stone.[4]

There were instances in Bukhar's writings of sharp and bitter recriminations against the khan and even of social protest.

> Oh, Ablaj, Ablaj,
> Always victorious over the enemies,

[3] Bukhar had significant precepts for his didactic poetry written in Turkic languages, as the tradition of didactic poetry directed towards the education of the ruler was an old and extremely important one among the sedentary Turks. The most famous and significant document of this character is the long Uighur didactic poem *Qutadghu-Bilig* ("The Happiness-Bringing Knowledge"), written in approximately A.D. 1068 in Kashgar by Yūsuf from Balāsāghūn, a chancellor (*ḥājib*) at the court of the Uighur ruler Bughrā-Khan. Qutadghu-Bilig is a purely didactic work, concerned with the duties of a ruler and clad in the form of instructions given by the Vezir Ögdülmiš to his son, who was about to enter the service of the khan. Although it is a work written under, and inspired by, the influence of Islam, it is not a glorification of Mohammedanism and its religious content appears superficial and external. (For text and translation of this document, see H. Vambéry, *Uigurische Sprachdokumente und das Kudatku Bilik* [Innsbruck, 1870]; Radloff, *Das Kudatku Bilik des Jussuf Chass Hadschib aus Balasagun* [St. Peterburg, 1891-1910], 3 vols., and Abdurrašid Rahmati Arat, *Kutadghu Bilig,* Vol. I [Text] [Istanbul, 1947].) *Qutadghu-Bilig* must have been an extremely popular work and it appears to have spread all over the Turkic-speaking world. We have verses from this work which were found on a fragment of pottery as far away from Kashgar as Sarajdžik (Saraichikovskoye) at the mouth of the Ural River on the Caspian Sea. (See *Zapiski kollegii vostokovedov,* XXI, 42, quoted in Barthold *Zwölf Vorlesungen . . . ,* p. 136.) Recently, in Turkey, a work of a somewhat later date, but representing the same kind of dry didacticism, was found, entitled the *Hibat al-ḥaqa'iq.* (See J. Deny, "A propos d'un traité de morale turc en écriture ouigour," *Revue du Monde Musulman,* LX [1925], 189-234.)

[4] Bukhar-Žirau, "Obraschcheniye poeta Bukhara k khanu Ablayu," Sobolev, ed., *Pesni . . . ,* p. 225.

And still you are not satisfied.
You have squeezed the people with extortions
. . . .
You never think of the slaves of the tribe,
Must I tell you what kind of man you are?[5]

Although Bukhar's works departed in many respects from the past, the old forms of traditional folk songs were often apparent in his works. Thus his *džoqtau,* composed at the occasion of departure from the native pasture lands in the flight from the advancing Kalmyks, follows the traditional pattern.[6]

The Folklore of Revolt

By the latter part of the eighteenth century the Russians had begun their expansion into the land of the Kazakhs, and by 1858 they controlled the entire area of Kazakhstan. The Russian advance was met with fierce resistance by the population, whose pasture lands were increasingly restricted; and before the Russians could consolidate their rule over Kazakhstan they had to face a series of violent popular uprisings. Among the most important risings were the revolt in the 1790's in the western Kazakh steppes led by Srym Datov, another rising in the early 1830's led by Isataj Tajmanov and the *aqyn* Makhambet Ütemisov, one in the early forties in the central Kazakh steppes, led by Kenesary Qasymov, the revolt under the leadership of Žankhoža (1856), and the rising in the Aktyubinsk steppe led by Eset Qotybarov and Beket Serkebajev, the defeat of which in 1858 ended organized Kazakh resistance and firmly established Russian rule.

These revolts against the Russians found strong expression in the oral tradition of the period. A great number of poems and songs have been recorded which memorialize the uprisings and their leaders. Composed for the greater part by contemporary *aqyns* who were themselves often active and even leading participants in the uprisings, these songs are important not only as records of the bitter struggle, but also as significant weapons in the awakening of national consciousness. The names of

[5] *Ibid.*, p. 224.
[6] See chap. iii, *supra.*

only a few of the more important *aqyns* of this period have been preserved, e.g., Makhambet Ütemisov, Dosqoža, Nasynbaj, and Šernijaz. Their poetry, simple in style and language, was filled with a great popular energy, a feeling for the justice of the national cause, and an undying hatred of the Russians and their Kazakh collaborators. It is a poetry rooted in the tradition of the Kazakh heroic epic, with its worship of the brave hero, who was strong enough to defeat all enemies and preserve the integrity of the nation.

Among the most vivid reflections of the risings against the Russians are the songs of the *aqyn* Makhambet Ütemisov (1804-1845) about the revolt led by Isataj Tajmanov. Makhambet, who participated in this revolt as Isataj's close associate, can be regarded as the intellectual leader of the rising. As he knew Russian he was of considerable value to Isataj and carried out all of Isataj's negotiations and correspondence. Fortunately many of his songs have been preserved. They characteristically sing of the glories of the revolt and call on the people to rise to fight the invaders and their domestic helpers.

In his call for support of the people for the revolt, Makhambet described the need for merciless fight:

> We must walk in mud up to our knees
> So that we may pull ourselves out of it.
> The one-humped black camel
> Is needed by us for this.
> For this we need a hero,
> Not afraid of pain, even
> If they should break all his ribs
> One after the other.
> We cannot now take that which is ours,
> We cannot now, in great expanse,
> Camp in our own fields—
> A high-handed enemy has gripped us all around
> In a tight vise.
> Oh, men, we all are cursed
> Cursed by our unhappy life.
> Like free deer we went
> To drink from the clear spring; like the wild horse

We grazed on the plains—
And now again we are hemmed in by an enemy.[7]

He attacked in his poetry not only the national oppression of the Russians, but also the social oppression on the part of the khans and the tribal chiefs:

What good are golden thrones to the people,
What good are dashing khans to the people,
If there is no justice
For the weak and the poor?[8]

In a poem which is probably his best known, "The Address of the Hero Makhambet to Sultan Bajmagambet," he assails the tribal leaders who have betrayed their people by collaborating with the Russians:

Khans like you and fat elders
I wanted to behead,
Make them bawl like camels,
So that they—with mugs raised to the skies—
Would howl, remembering former dignity. . . .
I wanted to break into your *džurt*
With its snow-white cupolas[9]
With my ax and hack to pieces its wooden frame
Like dry brush wood;
Your fine felt I wanted
To cut up for saddle cloth,
And your wives, oh you crowned khans,
I would take for my wives by force.[10]

Not always, however, was Makhambet's poetry fiery and warlike. He could be soft and lyrical. When, in 1838, Isataj was killed in battle with a Russian punitive detachment, Makhambet's song was full of sorrow over the loss of a close friend and of a leader of the people:

[7] Makhambet Ütemisov, "Na nashem puti gryaz po koleno," Sobolev, ed., *Pesni . . .*, pp. 246-47.

[8] Ütemisov, "Chto tolku," *ibid.*, p. 249.

[9] A white *džurt* was a sign of wealth and station. The poor man's *džurt* is black.

[10] Ütemisov, "Obrashcheniye batyra Makhambeta k sultanu Baimagambetu," *loc. cit.*, p. 251.

O dismal, gloomy, dark was the day, full of grief,
The day, when a deep-hanging cloud covered up the sun.
. . . .
The day when the evil breathing of the tornado sounded from the
North,
When, in the midst of battle, the firm steel of the sword
Was broken—and lo, only the hilt remained whole;
The day, when the proud beautiful poplar
Could not withstand the blows. . . .

This song follows the traditional form of the mourning song (*džoqtau*) and the song of notification of death (*estirtû*), in which the qualities of the deceased were extolled and in which frequently the deceased is metaphorically depicted as an animal or a plant.

Under the influence of Makhambet there developed a strong tradition of patriotic poetry. Bard after bard composed songs to memorialize uprisings during Makhambet's life and after his death. The revolt under the leadership of Kenesary Qasymov was immortalized in the songs of the *aqyns* Nasynbaj and Dosqoža, and the last large-scale uprising, defeated in 1858, was celebrated in the songs of an unknown *aqyn* which were discovered and written down at the end of the last century.

Nasynbaj and Dosqoža were active participants in Kenesary's uprising and composed their verse while fighting in the ranks, as had Makhambet Ütemisov. When Kenesary, after several defeats by the advancing Russians, was forced to leave the old nomadic grazing grounds, Dosqoža, who accompanied him, composed a farewell song (*qos-tasū*) in which he sang with deep feeling of the suffering of his people and of the beauty of nature in the Kazakh steppe which they had to leave to the invader:

Farewell forever,
Cool mountain heights,
Green carpet of grass.
Never would we have left you,
But the enemy is pressing us.
. . . .
On my native isles,
Where with the stag and the wild ram
Sheep herds were grazing.

I must leave you forever to save myself,
O my summer grazing ground.

He describes the sad fate of his people:

And the drowsy forest now
Remains behind, like an orphan.
My people, who live in these woods,
Will now be tortured with fierce longing.[11]

In Nasynbaj's songs there are already anticipations of a mood of disillusionment which was to become prevalent later. In his poem *Kenesary-Nauryzbaj,*[12] Nasynbaj describes the last campaign of Kenesary's revolt and ends with a passionate mourning song, similar to the traditional *džoqtau,* in which he bemoans the death of the two revolutionary leaders:

Oh, rulers, khans, if my speech
Were only fiery:
Can the pheasant keep his feathers,
If the locusts are upon him?
And the goose, frightened by the owl,
Will he not fly high in the air, cackling?
How then can the people be strong,
Dragging their lives without a khan?
. . . .
Like the larks we used to sing
But now, the whole nation is silent.
Is not this the end, my friends?
Now a lowly *šaban*[13] talks rudely to us. . . .
Oh, my deserted people!
You have lost your power and your peace.
Oh, people, we find ourselves
In the most dire misery.[14]

The last great uprising against the Russians was memorialized by the unknown author of the forceful poem **Beket-Batyr,** dedicated to one of the leaders of the revolt. The poet tells how

[11] Doskhoža, "Pesnya spetaya pered pereseleniyem Kenesary s Kokchetava," Sobolev, ed., *Pesni* . . . , pp. 231-32.
[12] Nauryzbaj was Kenesary's brother and co-leader of the uprising. In 1847 both brothers were killed in battle.
[13] *šaban*—a herder.
[14] Nasynbaj, "Plach po Kenesary i Nauryzbayu pevtsa Nasynbaya, bezhavshevo iz kirgizskogo plena," Sobolev, ed., *Pesni* . . . , p. 226.

Beket collects a band of insurgents and attacks and kills the ruling sultan. Later he is betrayed to the Russians, captured, and sent into exile. On the road to Siberia, as the poem goes, his old mother finally reaches him to bid him farewell. She sings:

Oh my son, my stately *tulpar,*
I hurried to you, my *tulpar,*
Over the steppes, through meadows and woods.
If ever a fox would run out of the brush,
You would catch him with your hand.
And if the evil enemy would think to strike
Hotter than fire your eyes would glow,
And he would not dare approach.
And if you would choose a horse
You would always find a pacer.
O you bright falcon, my own begotten,
You have hitched a horse to your carriage
And left your mother for a distant land.
Have you no pity for your dear ones?
Be happy then, my beloved one.
But could it be that a son
Would throw over his mother and father?
O Beket, you are our only one;
Let me embrace you, my son.
Tell me where your path leads you.
O my own, my long awaited one,
My dearest, my beloved,
Come back to us soon.

. . . .

The cruel news has spread,
That a misfortune has befallen you,—
At this your family was distressed
The people became upset.
The people remember that you are stronger than all.
They know that you are braver than all.
The *aul* is an orphan without you.
I ran to you like a mare
Whose udder is full,
But whose foal was taken long ago.

And Beket spoke in answer:

O my beloved mother,
My native home is far away.

Your son was a mettlesome horse
But now Beket is in captivity.
I am in the infidels' chains.

. . . .

Farewell, beloved mother.

. . . .

I had a sword and a lance,
I had two beloved horses.
But now I am disarmed,
My hands and feet are chained.
The Lord's world is no longer dear to me.
Grief is choking me.[15]

On the way to Siberia, the poem tells us, Beket's wife, disguised as a Tatar trader, also reaches Beket and hands him a dagger with the aid of which he frees himself, returns home, kills the man who betrayed him, and continues to fight. The whole poem breathes the spirit of the heroic epos. The hero Beket is described with all the imagery and metaphoric devices which are used in the depiction of the epic *batyr*. The author of *Beket-Batyr* is only one of the many unknown *aqyns* who spread the spirit of revolt through the power of their songs. While the heroic epic was the form most commonly used as a model for the new songs, other traditional forms were also employed, as the *džoqtau* and *estirtṻ* in the song composed by Makhambet Ütemisov at the occasion of the death of Isataj.

Poetry of Resignation

The defeat of the uprising under Eset Qotybarov and Beket in 1858 ushered in a period of unbridled Russian domination. The strong economic measures taken by the Russians, as well as the political domination and the Russification policies, brought about the disintegration of much of the old patriarchal and tribal structure. With the exception of a few sporadic uprisings, Kazakh resistance remained effectively broken during this period. As the era of revolt had found its echo in the heroic songs which expressed defiance and resentment, so the period after the defeat of the resistance witnessed its reaction of complete dejection,

[15] "Beket-batyr," Sobolev, ed., *Pesni* . . . , pp. 262-64.

cynicism, and hopelessness expressed in a popular art which has been termed the poetry of the "time of lament" (*Zar zaman*). The artists of this era borrowed from the traditional songs of mourning in their descriptions of the hopeless fate of their people. Salvation was sought only in mysticism and in resignation.

This school of pessimism received its name from a poem by the chief exponent of this mood, Šortambaj Qanayev (1808-1871). Šortambaj, who had studied widely, clearly saw the changes that were taking place in Kazakh society and was probably the first Kazakh bard able to analyze the sweep of history and its effects on the people in something more than an immediate and subjective way. He sang of the destruction of the tribal patriarchal order, the introduction of mercantilism and its effects on the national traditions and on the moral fiber of the people. He sought salvation for his people in the return to the tribal patriarchal society of a past which he romanticized. In his poem *Opasyz Žalgan*[16] ("Faithless Lying") he bemoans the unhappy fate of his people:

> O unfortunate good people,
> O ill-starred times,
> God's anger, it seems, has
> Struck you, my native land.

And he sadly paints the oppression by the Russians and their local helpmates:

> Everywhere the enemy sets nets for us,
> There's no freedom, wherever you may look.

He chides the people who, as a result of the breakdown of the tribal customary law, carry their quarrels and litigations to the Russian authorities and try to gain riches by taking advantage of their own countrymen:

> Hardly have two started quarreling
> When they take to the pen
> And have recourse to the law
> And in quarreling among each other
> They come to harm at the hands
> Of the officials from the West.

[16] Šortambaj, "Obmannaya zhizn," Sobolev, ed., *Pesni . . .*, pp. 267-68.

. . . .
Unhappily my friends
The jail has made its appearance in our land.
. . . .
Alas, many more threats
Come from the tsar's officials.

Šortambaj comments on the new money economy:

Instead of herds, money. From such cattle
You can obtain no milk.
How can one put a saddle on it?[17]

He advises his people to have none of the new ways:

We had better follow our cattle
And sleep peacefully, not knowing anxieties
. . . .
Tear your souls out of the captivity of evil
And guard your blood and your home,
So that life may flow quietly again.[18]

Among the followers of Šortambaj's school were the poets Bazar, Abu-bäkir, Akhan-säri, and Murat. Perhaps one of the most colorful of the poems expressing the mood of the *zar zaman* school is Murat's poem *Three Epochs,* which reflects the feeling of bitter despondency over Russian colonization. After recalling the rich and heroic past of the Kazakhs, when men were honorable and brave and land and cattle were plentiful, the poet laments:

The soldier's bayonet has taken the steppe from us—
The tsar has thrust his hand into our pocket,
And when he took the *Džajyq*[19] from us
He gripped us by the collar.
He has realized his intentions.
The black hand of the thief
Has forever taken Uil from us
And the Mangyshlak peninsula.
Dragging his bullock cars, he advanced,
To Ürgench, Tashkent, and Bukhara,
Taking, along the road, everything for himself;
Women and men and even the children,

[17] Muqanov, "Kazakhskaya literatura . . . ," p. 219.
[18] Šortambaj, *op. cit.,* p. 267.
[19] *Džajyq*—the Ural River.

Cattle and land. If you look around,
O men—over our native land
The day of life, like an evil night, is dark.[20]

Like Šortambaj, Murat was concerned with the corruption and impoverishment of the people. He resented the adoption of any Russian customs, even that of wearing Western clothes:

He wears a suit, without sleeves,
Straight as a board. Between body and belt
You cannot even stick a finger—everything is pulled tight.[21]

For Murat there was no way out. When towards the end of the poem he asks the question, "How shall we heal this epoch?" he finds no answer.

What little written literature there was in this period continued to be concerned with religious themes (in the tradition of the earlier mentioned "book songs"). There were also a great number of translations of religious and mystical works from the Arab and Persian. It was not until the later part of the nineteenth century, when the influence of Russian culture began to be strongly felt, that there developed a Kazakh secular literature concerned with Kazakh themes and problems.

[20] Murat-aqyn, "Tri epokha," Sobolev, ed., *Pesni . . .* , p. 271.
[21] *Ibid.*, p. 272.

Chapter V

THE GROWTH OF A KAZAKH INTELLIGENTSIA AND OF A WRITTEN LITERATURE

The Nineteenth Century

By the second half of the nineteenth century strong new trends could be discerned in Kazakh cultural life. As a result of Russian contact there were opened to the Kazakhs new channels of cultural expression, and a young intelligentsia schooled in the traditions of Western culture began to emerge. The growth of this new group was greatly facilitated by the development of a limited system of education both in Russian and in Kazakh[1] and by the presence in Kazakhstan of a considerable number of Russian exiles. This distant Central Asiatic province was a favorite spot of the tsarist government for the banishment of liberals and revolutionaries. Russian exiles in Kazakhstan included members of the socialist Petrashevski circle, Butaslevich-Petrashevski himself, Durov and Dostoyevski, a number of "Populists," and such other liberal and revolutionary subjects of the empire as Korolenko, Shevchenko, Severin Gross, Dolgopolov, E. P. Mikhaelis, and others. Most of these exiles found their sympathies with the Kazakh nation. The Ukrainian poet Taras Shevchenko, who was exiled to the Kazakh region in 1847 and lived in Orenburg for a decade thereafter, wrote a number of poems and stories which clearly reflect the sympathy he felt for another oppressed nation. Shevchenko arrived in Kazakhstan at a time when the revolt under the leadership of Kenesary Qasymov had not yet been quite extinguished, and he was much impressed by what he heard about Kenesary. Indications of Shevchenko's interest in the Kazakhs and their culture can be found in many of his poems.

[1] See chap. ii, *supra*.

In "Mojï dumy" ("Song of Mine") he called on his songs, his dearest companions, to join him and stay

> With the poor and needy Kirghiz [i.e., Kazakh];
> They are really poor,
> Yes, and naked, but in freedom
> They can pray to God! . . .[2]

In another poem, also written in exile, "A Hatchet Lay behind God's Doors,"[3] he drew his subject matter from a Kazakh legend.

The most illustrious exile to Kazakhstan, Dostoyevski, who spent four years at hard labor at Omsk and five years as a soldier in a disciplinary detachment at Semipalatinsk, strongly influenced the thought of the important Kazakh writer Čoqan Valikhanov.

Kazakh thought was also greatly influenced by Russian scholars and artists who visited Kazakhstan, one of the most important of whom was G. N. Potanin, who lived in Kazakhstan for a considerable period and who knew the language well. Potanin studied at Omsk at the same time as the Kazakh ethnologist and geographer Čoqan Valikhanov, and they became close friends. In 1889 Potanin published his *Eastern Motifs in the Medieval European Epos (Vostochnyie motivy v srednevekom yevropeiskom epose),* in which much space was devoted to Kazakh folklore. Other visitors to Kazakhstan included the Russian Turkologist V. V. Radloff, whose writings include much valuable information on Kazakh culture, the Russian geographer Semyonov (Tyanshansky), and the Russian painter N. G. Khludov, who has left a number of paintings concerning the life of the Kazakhs. Finally there was Pushkin, who visited in Kazakhstan in 1833 while collecting material for his "History of Pugachev" and who became greatly interested in Kazakh folklore.

The emergence of this new Kazakh intelligentsia was marked by conflict between the Kazakh nationalist traditionalists on the

[2] Taras Shevchenko, *Selected Poems,* Clarence A. Manning, transl. (Ukrainian National Assocation, Jersey City, N. J., 1945), p. 184.

[3] "U boha za dvermy lezhala sokyra," Taras Shevchenko, *Kobzar* (Kiev, Akademiya Nauk URSR, 1939), pp. 422-24.

one hand, and the growing group of Westerners on the other—reflecting a division among Kazakh intellectuals which was not unlike that between the Russian Slavophiles and the Russian Westerners. The Kazakh nationalists, heirs of the *zar zaman* period, rejected Russian culture in its totality. They reached back to the religious mysticism of Persian, Arabic, and Čagataj literatures and to the traditional Kazakh epic folklore. The nationalists were primarily occupied with translations of the religious literature of Islam, hoping by this to counterbalance the growing influence of Western thought. It was this group of writers who acquainted the Kazakh people in their own language with many gems of Arabic literature and with such Persian writers as Firdūsī, Omar Khayyam, and others. The comparatively small amount of original poetry produced by this group was concerned primarily with religious themes.

The Western school of thought, the larger and more significant one in Kazakh cultural development, was characterized by the new attitude which looked upon the traditional Kazakh society as to some extent a hindrance in the necessary development of Kazakhstan into a modern nation. The writers of this group were unsympathetic to the survivals of the old tribal social order and urged adoption of educational measures to overcome the ignorance which was felt to be the greatest asset to the Russians. Three of the most important nineteenth-century exponents of the new school of enlightenment were Čoqan Valikhanov, Ibraj Altynsaryn, and Abaj Qunanbayev.

Čoqan Valikhanov (c. 1837-1865)

Probably the first important Kazakh representative of Westernized thought was Čoqan Valikhanov, the first Kazakh geographer, ethnographer, linguist, and historian. In his very brief life Valikhanov emerged as one of the foremost interpreters of his own culture to the Russians.

Valikhanov, born about the year 1837 (the exact date of his birth is unknown), was the grandson of Vali-khan, the last khan of the Middle Horde. His family belonged to that part of the Kazakh aristocracy which had collaborated with the Russian authorities and was in the good graces of the Russian provincial government. Several members of his family held Russian officer rank. His father, Činghiz Valiev, had been educated in the Russian cadet school at Omsk; and his uncle, Musa Čormanov, carried the rank of a Russian colonel and held the distinction of having visited the Russian capital twice.

In 1847, the then ten-year-old Čoqan was placed, as had been his father before him, in the Omsk Cadet School, and although he knew no Russian at the time of his enrollment, he rapidly mastered the language and proved a brilliant student. At this school the young Kazakh was introduced to the Russian literary journal *The Contemporary,* and through its pages Čoqan became familiar not only with contemporary Russian letters and philosophy, but also with English literature, which interested him so much that he undertook the study of English. Dickens captivated the boy, as did also the English travel writers. His interest in English literature never left Valikhanov, and in his later ethnological work on Kazakh shamanism he quotes extensively from Carlyle.[4] Already at a very young age, Valikhanov showed interest in Kazakh national culture and recorded a number of Kazakh songs which he had heard from wandering *aqyns.* He was also interested in Oriental philosophy and studied the Arabic language.

In 1853, after graduating from the cadet school, Valikhanov joined the ranks of a Siberian regiment and soon became the adjutant of the Governor-General of Western Siberia, Hasford, in which capacity he traveled throughout much of Asia. In 1856 he participated in an expedition to the Isyq-Köl (in present-day Kirghizia) under the leadership of Colonel Khomentovski, where he carried out his first serious studies of Turkic folklore and culture. He recorded fragments of the Kirghiz national epic cycle *Manas* and wrote his *Note on the Mountaineer Kirghiz* (*Zapiska o dikokamennykh Kirgizakh*), both of which were published by the Russian Geographical Society.

A great influence was exerted on Valikhanov by Russian

[4] Valikhanov, "Sledy shamanstva u kirgizov," *Sochineniya,* p. 1.

exiles, and particularly by Durov and Dostoyevski. He also knew a number of Russian scholars, including Potanin, Yadrintsev, and Semyonov (Tyanshansky). Dostoyevski, who perceived the talent of the young man, was fascinated by Valikhanov's interest in Kazakh culture, and saw Valikhanov act as something of a cross-cultural interpreter between the Kazakhs and the Russians. There is preserved an extensive correspondence between these two men, in which Dostoyevski counseled the young Kazakh on many aspects of his promising work.[5] The following letter of Dostoyevski to Valikhanov testifies to the exceptionally warm relationship which existed between these two men.

SEMIPOLATINSK [*sic*], December 14th, 1856.

. . . You write so nicely and dearly that somehow I see you in front of me again. You write me that you love me. I will tell you without ceremony that I have fallen in love with you. Never, to anybody, not even to my own brother, have I felt such attraction as I do to you, and God knows how this came about. One could say much in explanation, but why should I praise you! And you will believe in my sincerity even without proof, my dear Valikhanov. Even if one were to write ten books on this theme, one could not write it all: feeling and attraction are an inexplicable phenomenon. . . . You ask my advice. . . . I feel this way. Don't stop studying. You have much material. Write an article about the steppes. . . . It would be very good if you could succeed in writing notes about life in the steppes, about your youth here and so on. That would be a novelty which would be of interest to everybody. . . . You would arouse the interest of the Geographical Society. . . .

[He advises Valikhanov to go to Russia and then to travel in Europe for a year or two.] Is it not a great aid, a holy matter to be . . . the first to tell in Russian what the steppes are, what their significance is, and about your people . . . at the same time you could serve your country by educating the Russians about her. . . . Remember that you are the first Kirghiz completely educated in the European fashion. . . . You cannot put it off.[6]

A similar influence was exercised on Valikhanov by the Russain geographer P. P. Semyonov (Tyanshansky), who, like Dos-

[5] For a letter from Valikhanov to Dostoyevski, see Valikhanov, *Sochineniya,* pp. 526-27.

[6] F. M. Dostoyevsky, *Pis'ma,* ed. A. S. Dolinin (Moscow-Leningrad, 1928), I, 200-202.

toyevski, urged the young Kazakh to study in Petersburg. However, it was only after being ordered on an expedition to Kashgar and other parts of Eastern Turkestan, from 1858 to 1859, that Valikhanov was able to carry out his plans for academic pursuits. At the time of the Turkic revolt against the Chinese, led by Ja'qūb-Bek, the Russian authorities, interested in any anti-Chinese activities in territory which they themselves coveted, sent Valikhanov to Eastern Turkestan, disguised as a merchant, to collect intelligence for them. Valikhanov, whose Turkic background and Western upbringing well qualified him for such a position, spent one year in the Chinese Turkic province as a Russian intelligence agent, at the same time enriching his knowledge of Turkic culture. Upon his return his observations were published as an article in one of the organs of the Imperial Geographic Society. This article, which was cumbersomely entitled "Report on the Situation of the Altyšar or of the Six Eastern Cities[7] of the Chinese Province Nanlu ('Little Bukhara') from 1858-59,"[8] quickly established Valikhanov's fame in Russian academic circles. He then went to the capital to study, became a member of the Russian Geographical Society, and contributed to its publications. Here he also became acquainted with a number of leading Russian thinkers and writers, including Maikov, Nekrasov, and Chernyshevski, and with the Orientalists Beryozin, Kazim-bek, and Vasil'ev. In 1860, however, the tuberculosis which had made its first appearance while Valikhanov was still in the Cadet School forced him to leave the capital for warmer climates, and five years later he died in the *aul* of his father-in-law, near the Chinese border.

Valikhanov contributed considerably to Western knowledge of his own culture and tribal history in such works as *Ablaj* and *Arms of the Kirghiz*[9] *in Ancient Times and Their Armor, Kirghiz Genealogy, Kirghiz Migratory Routes.* His works on

[7] The six cities described by Valikhanov were Kashgar, Yangi-Hisar, Yarkand, Khotan, Aq-Su and Üč-Turfan.

[8] Valikhanov, "Otchet o sostoyanii Altyshara ili shesti vostochnykh gorodov kitaiskoi provintsii Nan-lu (Maloi Bukhary) v 1858-59 gg," *Sochineniya,* pp. 1-76.

[9] "Kirghiz" was a term erroneously applied to the Kazakhs by the Russians in the 19th century.

Chinese Central Asia, which are of a geographical character (*Report on the Situation in Alty-šar, Dzungarian Sketches*), still must be counted among the most valuable contributions to our knowledge of this inaccessible and relatively unknown region. Of considerable interest to the folklorist and anthropologist are also his extensive remarks on Kazakh shamanism, entitled *Notes on Shamanism.* It was in this work and in his writings on the folklore of the Kazakhs and that of the other Central Asiatic Turks that this early Kazakh scholar made his most valuable contribution. His recordings of Kazakh epics and tales are the first of their kind and his collection precedes by many years that of Radloff, although it is much less extensive than the latter. Valikhanov was sometimes satisfied with giving only a résumé of an epic, such as of the epic *Erkokči-Erkosaj* and *Uraq-batyr,* but he did publish a complete recording, including some samples of the text in the original Kazakh, of the epos *Edige-batyr* (*Idige*).[10] Of equal interest to the folklorist are Valikhanov's reports on Kazakh legends (*Traditional Tales and Legends of the Large Horde of the Kirghiz-Kaisaks*). Outside of his immediate cultural horizon, Valikhanov was the first to commit to paper some of the episodes of the collection of Kirghiz national epics *Manas* (*The Death of Kuko-taj Khan and His Burial*). Because his interests were not linguistic and his primary aim was to acquaint the Russian scholarly public with the traditions of his people, Valikhanov published all his folklore texts in Russian translation, with the exception of a few examples of the Kazakh text.

Valikhanov as an individual typified many attitudes among the Kazakh educated class under the influence of Russian civilization. He appeared to be highly Westernized, dressed, we are told, like a Russian dandy,[11] was strongly impressed by the rationalist views which he heard from many of his Russian friends and mentors, and quite frequently identified himself with the Russian point of view rather than with that of his tribal heritage. Russian occupation of his people's lands was viewed by him

[10] Valikhanov, *Sochineniya,* pp. 223-64.
[11] See Potanin's preface to Valikhanov, *Sochineniya,* p. xx.

sympathetically, and his frequent memoranda to Russian officials in which he advises them regarding desirable policies leave little doubt about Valikhanov's interest in the success of the Russian colonizing mission, from which he believed many cultural advantages would come to his people.

He was not, however, servile, or uncritical, and he frequently condemned what he considered high-handed attitudes towards the traditions of the Kazakhs. In several memoranda he takes exception to the lack of consideration displayed by Russian policy towards the needs of the Kazakh people and to the preference which, he felt, the Russians were giving to the advice of the tribal leaders. In this respect Valikhanov shows the influence of the Russian social thinkers, for his approach to Kazakh social problems and to the Kazakh political hierarchy was equalitarian and democratic in spirit. In one of his memoranda he expounds the idea that the interests of the tribal leaders are not always identical with those of the people; and that, while the opinions of the latter cannot always be accepted as an expression of true national needs either, that of the privileged classes "can only be regarded as a negation" of these needs. For "the interests of the titled and the rich are, even in highly civilized societies, commonly hostile to the interests of the masses, of the majority."[12]

Valikhanov's strongest criticism of Russian policies, however, was concerned with Russian policies towards the religious life of the Kazakhs.[13] He sharply attacks the Russian administrators for fostering Mohammedanism, which he considers as harmful to the cultural fabric of his people. He terms the period of Moslemization of the steppes the "Tatar Period"[14] and compares it to the Byzantine period in the history of Russia. The Byzantine influence and that of the Tatar *mullās,* he holds, have been equally pernicious to indigenous Russian and Kazakh culture, since both acted as a powerful damper on the continuance

[12] Valikhanov, "Zapiska o sudebnoi reforme," *Sochineniya,* p. 152.

[13] It is not known whether Valikhanov was officially a Mohammedan or a baptized Christian, although available evidence would favor the latter hypothesis, since he speaks of Christianity as "our" religion and quite apparently considers it a higher form of religion than Mohammedanism.

[14] Mohammedanism was spread to a large degree by Tatar *mullās.*

and development of the oral art. Just as in Russia the oral art had been supplanted with an art expressing the new religious world view, so also the Kazakh bards were now beginning to sing Moslem apocrypha adapted to the folk style, in place of the ancient epics.[15] However, while Byzantine influence brought Christianity, which is "unquestionably an enlightened influence,"[16] the Tatar-Moslem ascendancy brought no such advantages. Valikhanov urged the Russians to stimulate the conversion of the Kazakhs to Christianity and to cease supporting Mohammedanism and even to undertake repressive measures against Islam.[17] He warned that Russian support of a religion which is so alien to Kazakh culture could only increase already existent anti-Russian sentiment.

The significant position which Valikhanov holds in Kazakh cultural development is indisputable; his researches into Kazakh traditions have not only been a significant contribution to Western knowledge of the Kazakhs, but have also acted to strengthen and stimulate the development of an indigenous written national literature and to increase the awareness of the Kazakh intelligentsia of their own cultural heritage. Valikhanov's primary contribution was probably the interpretation of his own culture to the Russians. As a frequent visitor to Russia and a member of the Russian government service, he was first of all a product of Western education, and to some extent he sacrificed his own Kazakh cultural heritage to his newly adopted culture.

Ibraj Altynsaryn (1841-1899)

The first representative of the Westernized intelligentsia in Kazakhstan whose ideas successfully synthesized Western and Kazakh cultural traditions was Ibraj Altynsaryn, the first Kazakh pedagogue in the Western sense of the word, and the first author of prose. To Altynsaryn, as to so many of his group, the only road to eventual emancipation of his nation lay in the introduction of Western culture and thought through widespread secular

[15] Cf. Valikhanov, "Zapiska o sudebnoi reforme," *Socheneniya* pp. 181, 194.
[16] *Ibid.*, p. 194.
[17] *Ibid.*, pp. 197-99.

education. It was as a result of his activities that Western education was first brought to the Kazakh steppes on a relatively large scale.

Altynsaryn's pedagogical activities had their beginning when he traveled from *aul* to *aul,* teaching Kazakh children Kazakh history and disseminating the idea of study in Russian schools. In 1879 he was appointed by the Russian authorities inspector of schools in the Turgai district, after he himself had completed the course in one of the newly established Russo-Kazakh schools.[18] The schools which Altynsaryn was called upon to inspect offered only a limited curriculum, as their function was primarily the education of Kazakh cadres as aides to the Russian colonizers. Nevertheless, Altynsaryn, like most of the Western-orientated intellectuals of his time, regarded the education thus offered by the Russians as an excellent tool for preparing the Kazakh people for their eventual task of achieving independent status. He attempted by all means at his disposal to make educational opportunities available to all strata of his people and was successful, at least, in increasing considerably the network of schools in his district. In almost all his other concrete steps, however, he was less successful, partly because of political objections of the Russians, who clearly perceived the dangers to the colonial regime of popular education, and partly because of the resistance of his own people.

In 1887, Altynsaryn bravely attempted to introduce a limited program of education for women.[19] His proposal, however, which aroused great indignation among the Kazakhs and brought objections from the Russian government, resulted in failure. Altynsaryn also attempted to open an agricultural school, but again was rebuffed by Russian opposition.[20] In his fight for a wider education he finally faced attacks and polemics from the Kazakhs similar to those leveled by the Russian Slavophiles against the Russian Westerners, but they did not shake his unswerving zeal and his conviction that education was the only

[18] Abdykalykov, Pankratova, *op. cit.,* pp. 331-32.
[19] *Ibid.,* p. 332.
[20] *Ibid.*

effective answer to the question of Murat, "How shall we heal this epoch?"

Of great importance were the textbooks which Altynsaryn wrote in the Kazakh language in a Cyrillic transcription for the schools under his jurisdiction, his *Russian Primer for Kazakh Schools* and his *Kirghiz Anthology,*[21] a collection of Kazakh folk tales and proverbs.

Altynsaryn was one of the first to recognize the need for adapting a Western alphabet to the Kazakh language, which was written in the difficult and complicated Arabic script. To Altynsaryn the Arabic script served only as a cumbersome weight which hindered the spread of education and made literacy unattainable for the mass of the population. He created an alphabet based on the Russian letters, an innovation which also aroused protest from the clergy and from the tradition-conscious Kazakhs and thus made little headway.

Not only as a national pedagogue, but as a man of letters, Altynsaryn was an innovator and reformer. Like other leading Kazakh writers of the period, he was profoundly influenced by Russian writers, particularly by Tolstoy, Pushkin, and Lermontov, and by the social critics of the sixties with whom he became acquainted during his studies at the Russian school. It was through his translations of some of the Russian nineteenth-century writers that Russian literature made its first appearance in the steppe region. His outstanding contribution to creative Kazakh literature, however, was his works in prose; for prose, with the exception of religious prose, was a genre totally new to the Turkic cultures of Central Asia. Altynsaryn introduced secular prose, in the form of a number of short stories after the manner of Pushkin, many of which, like "The Rich Man's Son and the Poor Man's Son," "The Wooden Horse," and "The Džurt," were retold Kazakh folk tales.

As a poet Altynsaryn was first and foremost a didacticist and repeatedly he propounded his favorite theme of education, as in his poem "Children, Let's Study":

[21] *Bukvar russkovo yazyka dlya kazakhskoi shkoly* and *Kirgizskaya khrestomatiya.*

My child, when you start to learn,
Knowledge, brighter than a lamp,
Will light your way through darkness;
Therefore, children, let us start to learn,
And let us weave forever into our grateful memory
The bright thread of knowledge.[22]

There is no question of the considerable influence exercised upon Altynsaryn by the works of the Russian classics. This is especially noticeable in his realistic nature descriptions, which stand out in sharp contrast to the stereotyped nature descriptions of the oral art and to the prevalent mystical, ornate, Eastern-oriented poetry. In his poems "Spring" and "The River," the influence of Pushkin and Lermontov is clear.

April, filled to the brim with nature's abundance:
Flocks of geese in blue distance are cackling,
Rains, pouring, are flying from mountains like waterfalls,
And in the valleys the lakes' snowy waters are shining.
The limitless space in the dewy warmth of earthly exhalations
Begins to be covered with fresh, aromatic grass.
. . . .
And towards evening the sun descends behind mountain heights,
Coloring half the sky with golden and purple colors.
And in the night-time, praising their maker,
The hearts of lovers flow into one in happy felicity,
And the young girl, just before dawn, lets her lover
Out of her *džurt,* covering her rosy face with a cloth.[23]

Abaj Qunanbayev (1845-1904)

It was the task of the man who is regarded today as the greatest Kazakh intellectual leader of the past century, Abaj Qunanbayev, to direct his interest not only towards bringing Western education and literature to his people but also towards acquainting the Kazakh people with other aspects of Western culture. Abaj saw the need not only for education for his people, but also for broad social reforms and for a reorientation in the basic outlook of his culture. He eventually became the accepted leader of the Western-oriented intelligentsia of his generation.

[22] "Davaite, Deti, Uchitsya!," Sobolev, ed., *Pesni* . . . , p. 276.
[23] Altynsaryn, "Vesna," Sobolev, ed., *Pesni* . . . , pp. 275-76.

Abaj was the son of the chief of the nomadic tribe of the Tobyqty, a group which had accepted Russian rule shortly before Abaj's birth. He was sent to a Mohammedan school (*medrese*) in Semipalatinsk, where, under the influence of Arabic and Persian teachings, he developed an early interest in Oriental literature. Later he entered a Russian school, where he attempted his first writings of poetry. This study was interrupted by a call home in order to train as his father's successor, which brought Abaj into deep conflict with the autocratic ideas of his father, a conflict which was to have great influence on his later writings and his criticism of Kazakh society. By the age of twenty-eight Abaj had broken with his family and returned to his study of Russian culture.

Compared to the average education of even the most advanced Kazakh thinkers of the day, Abaj's was of considerable breadth and scope. He was well versed in the literature of the Orient, particularly in Arab, Persian, and Čagataj poetry. He knew such classics as Firdūsī, Nizāmī, Nawāī, Bā̦bur, and Ḥafiẓ̈, and much of his early poetry was written in imitation of these classics. He studied the historical works of Ṭabarī, Rašīd ad-Dīn, Bābur, and Abū'l Gāzī and was well versed in Islamic theology. Equally broad was his knowledge of Rusian literature and social thought. He became a close friend of such revolutionary exiles as E. P. Mikhaelis, Severin Gross, Nifont Dolgopolov, and Leont'ev, and through these friendships he received much of his inspiration to study Russian and Western culture. He read avidly the works of Pushkin, Lermontov, Krylov, Nekrasov, Saltykov-Shchedrin, and Tolstoy, as well as the socio-critical writings of Belinski, Dobrolyubov, Chernyshevski, and Herzen; and he eventually translated into his native language some of the works of Lermontov, Pushkin, and Krylov. Through Russian translations he became acquainted with the works of Goethe, Heine, and Byron, with classical Greek literature, and with Western thinkers, including Darwin, Spencer, and Spinoza. It was Abaj who first translated some of the poetry of Goethe and Byron into Kazakh from Russian translations.

From this background of Kazakh, Islamic, and Western culture Abaj took his inspiration, and in his writings he attempted to synthesize these three traditions. His significance lay not only in his liberal and enlightened attitude and in the broad sweep of his interest, but also in his faculty of penetrating criticism. His writings covered all aspects of Kazakh life and were of many shades and colors, extending from didactic prose works to lyrical and romantic poetry. No subjects of oppression, injustice, or ignorance escaped him. He was at once an educator, a humanist, and philosophical internationalist as well as a poet, prose writer, and translator. His position as the most outspoken "Westerner" of his time was the more significant since his was the period of extreme nationalism in the steppes, a nationalism which took the strong direction of pan-Islamism and pan-Turkism.

The basic philosophical bias which conditioned Abaj's life and his writings was his humanist belief in the strength of man's reason, and it is with this approach in mind that we must assess the main contributions he made to Kazakh culture.

In Abaj's early life he was strongly influenced by Persian and Arabic literature, and his early poems were marked by praise of the art of the East. In 1858 he sings about Islamic poetry:

> Just like a jewel, you are precious to our eyes,
> You glisten with your marble brow,
> And delicately pale is your face
> . . . .
> And seeing you, and once only meeting
> Your eyes, right away we must lower our glance. . . .
> We haven't the strength . . .
> We fail. . . . But why?[24]

In his mature life, however, Abaj quite frankly turned his back on his erstwhile teachers, the Islamic classics, and those Kazakh poets who, like Abaj in his early youth, had avowedly imitated Oriental poetry with its predominantly religious subject matter, its highly ornate forms, and its abundance of metaphorical language.

> I do not write a hymn to Ḥaẓret-'Alī,[25]
> Nor do I sing of beauties with a face of gold . . . . [1889][26]

[24] Abaj Qunanbayev, *Izbrannoye*, ed. L. Sobolev, (Moscow, 1945), p. 3.
[25] Ḥaẓret-'Alī, Mohammed's son-in-law and the fourth caliph of Islam.
[26] *Ibid.*, p. 83.

The mystical content of Islamic writings and the dogmatic teachings of Islam became increasingly alien to him, his only religion being the perfection of human morals. Yet he continued to value Oriental culture highly and later in his creative career he was to bring into the cultural horizon of the Kazakhs such creations of the East as the *Arabian Nights,* the Persian epos *Šāh-nāme,* as well as many Persian and Turkic folktales.

The primary influences in Abaj's thinking were his own cultural heritage and Russian and Western enlightenment, rather than Islamic culture. While he valued his own cultural heritage and did not wish to see it submerged, he was essentially a reformer and wished to incorporate Western thought into the traditions of his own culture. Yet he remained a strong critic of all Russian oppressive policies and attempts by the Russians to deprive his nation of her political and cultural independence.

In his early verse Abaj was largely preoccupied with Kazakh themes. Yet even in these works there is little evidence of the traditional oratorical style of Kazakh oral poetry or of the traditional subject matters of Kazakh folklore. In a programmatic poem, written in 1887 ("Poetry, Ruler of Speech") Abaj defines his attitude towards the songs of the *aqyns:*

> Like the old begs I do not speak in proverbs,
> [Like the *aqyn*] I do not utter words,
> Changing my mind for pay.
> I like to be short, but true in my words,
> So listen to my simple speech.[27]

Abaj not only deviated radically from the vocabulary and the traditional Kazakh system of symbols, but he also introduced problematic literature concerned with such questions as ignorance, bribery, parasitism, the position of women, and the dangers of an education limited to religion.

Abaj's great passion, which he shared with Altynsaryn, for bringing the fruits of Western enlightenment to his people by means of a broad education for all, was expressed in many of his works, particularly in his *Ghaqlija* (*Edification*), a prose work of philosophical conversations with his readers:

[27] *Ibid.,* p. 54.

The desire to learn and understand everything; to see and to study—that is a high passion of the soul.

If this desire is lost, if you no longer wish to know everything perfectly, or to find out about it at least in part, then you are no longer a human being.

If we do not strive for knowledge, then our soul is no longer a human soul, but an animal soul. [1891][28]

In his quest for education for his people, Abaj was the first poet of the Kazakh steppe to conceive of the social role of the poet. This is clearly expressed in the following lines:

Not for amusement are my lines composed,
Nor are they filled with inventions.
My verse is born for those
With eager ears and hearts and souls.
Sagacious and sensitive hearts
Will understand the thoughts in my verse.
You must approach me on a road that's straight.
My verse will then uncover all that's hidden.
You will not understand it right away
Since 'tis the first time you have heard such words.
How queer it seems to me that people who cannot understand
Immediately ask another kind of words.[29]

And elsewhere he expresses similar thoughts on the role of the poet:

I want to sow the seed of truth and put wings to the tongue,
So that the light will enter not only the eyes, but also the soul.[30]

Knowledge and learning were to be extended to all, even, as Altynsaryn had said before him, to women. Abaj wrote that only if all rid themselves of "the ignorance [which] has been drunk into the very meat and bones of the people together with the mother's milk and [which] has driven from it all aspects of humanity"[31] could the Kazakhs find the road to national salvation.

Abaj stressed to his people the possibility of, and the need for, at once incorporating into Kazakh culture the fruits of Western

[28] *Ibid.*, p. 267.
[29] *Ibid.*, p. 83.
[30] Abdykalykov, Pankratova, *op. cit.*, p. 326.
[31] Qunanbayev, *op. cit.*, p. 304.

culture and civilization and maintaining the Kazakh cultural heritage:

> It is good to teach children. But at the beginning it is necessary to teach them their native language, to read and to write and the most elementary knowledge. . . .
>
> Remember that the most important thing is to study Russian learning. Science, knowledge, prosperity, art, all this the Russians possess. In order to avoid vice and achieve good, it is indispensable to know the Russian language and Russian culture.
>
> The Russians can see the world. If you know their language, your eyes will also be opened to the world.
>
> A man who studies the culture and language of other nations becomes equal to those nations and will not live in shame . . .
>
> Study Russian culture and art; they are the key to life. When you obtain this key, your life will become lighter.[32]

Abaj was seriously troubled by the tendency of many of his people to lose sight of their own cultural heritage and to be corrupted by the Russian occupiers. He criticized the narrowness of Russian education which taught only the minimum necessary to make good interpreters and clerks for the Russian administration. He saw that often the only motive for sending children to the Russian school was the later material profit which might be gained by the parents through their children's aid in the never-ending law suits over scarce grazing grounds. In his poem "The Boarding School" (1886)[33] he describes the child who is a product of this kind of education as one who

> Knows not good from evil.
>
> . . . .
>
> He only waits, and the time of national misery
> Will present him with fat presents.

And he complains that

> Only for very few do
> Tolstoy and Saltykov exist,
> Since he who wants to obtain honor,
> Becomes a lawyer or interpreter.

Admonishing the youth to take education seriously and to maintain their self respect, he advises them:

[32] *Ibid.*, p. 286.

[33] *Ibid.*, pp. 37-39.

For great learning you must strive

. . . .

Read and do not be lazy
Do not flatter your way into a uniform
With golden epaulettes.

. . . .

Cease the empty bragging
And the raising of the eyebrows.
Do not lower yourself before the Russian administrator.

. . . .

Walk the road that has no evil
However hard this road may be.

Abaj's ire at those Kazakhs who held offices in the Russian administration and forgot the true values in life is sarcastically expressed in the following lines:

They think that now the bird of luck sits on their head, that now they have become rulers of half the earth, they can increase their herds and that everything is available to them for the price of their cattle. Thus they walk with a supercilious air. Honor, dishonor, reason, learning, all this they place lower than their cattle. They believe that by offerings of cattle they can even obtain the good will of God. For them religion is cattle, the people are cattle, knowledge is cattle, conscience is cattle.[34]

In Abaj's mature poetry there breathes a great feeling for the misery of his people. This is particularly well expressed in his poem "Oh, My Kazakhs" (1886):[35]

Oh, my Kazakhs, my poor people,
With a tough unshaved beard you have covered your lips.
On your left cheek is evil, on your right one, goodness.

. . . .

Where then lies truth? Your mind cannot discriminate.
You are good and large in number,
But what poison has penetrated your soul?
You do not listen to the good advice of the foreigner;
Your sickle-tongue cuts all without distinction.

Earlier these realizations had left the members of the *zar zaman* school helpless before the problems of their society. Abaj,

[34] *Ibid.*, p. 269.
[35] *Ibid.*, pp. 17-18.

however, calls on the Kazakhs for further action and steadfastness:

> Heal yourselves from these infirmities;
> Only then will you not be degraded a hundred times.
> How can you be calm in your soul,
> If you cannot even take the slightest hill?
> How can you be satisfied with yourself
> If you have no bravery, no hardness?

Abaj's translations of Russian works were in themselves original and valuable contributions to Kazakh culture. He frequently attempted, with varied success, to rephrase and reinterpret writings in terms of Kazakh cultural meaning. In his translations of the works of Krylov he often changed the moral teachings of the fables to facilitate their integration into Kazakh culture. His translation of Pushkin's *Eugene Onegin* is an enthusiastically retold story. By 1887 the name of Pushkin and of his hero and heroine, Onegin and Tatyana, were known all over Kazakhstan through Abaj's translations. As Abaj was not only a writer, but also a musician with deep appreciation of Kazakh music, he set many of his translations to music, and they received wide distribution through the wandering *aqyns*. The most popular of these is probably his musical translation of Tatyana's letter to Onegin. Abaj found his greatest inspiration, however, in the poetry of Lermontov. From the middle eighties onward Abaj occupied himself increasingly with translations of Lermontov's poetry. More than one half of his total translations of Russian poetry are taken from Lermontov. In addition there exists a large body of Abaj's poetry which is either a direct adaptation of Lermontovian themes or shows otherwise a strong imprint of the influence of the great Russian poet. The Kazakh edition of the collected works of Abaj[36] lists twenty-two titles of Lermontov's poems translated by the Kazakh poet, including such well-known poems as "Borodino," "I skuchno i grustno" ("Äm žabyqtym"), "Ne ver' sebe" ("Özine senbe"), "Plenny rytsar" ("Tutqyndaghy batyr"), "Duma" ("Oj"), "V al'bom" ("Al'-

[36] Qunanbayev, *Šygharmalarynyn tolyq žyjnaghy,* ed. N. T. Sauranbayev (Alma-Ata, 1945).

bomgha"), "Kinzhal," ("Qanžar"), "Vykhozhu odin ya na dorogu" ("Žolgha šyqtym"), as well as partial translations of some of Lermontov's longer poems, such as "Demon" ("Šajtan"), "Izmail-bey," and "Vadim." There are also found retranslations into Kazakh of some of Lermontov's translations into Russian of Western poetry, as fragments of Byron's "Hebrew Melodies" and Goethe's "Über allen Wipfeln ist Ruh." Abaj's translations were always relatively free. He typically took merely the basic structure from the original and injected his own ideas and thoughts into his translations. Frequently he developed and broadened a motif, only suggested by Lermontov, so that many of his translations became rather creations of his own. Generally, he attempted to retain the broad meaning and the emotional tone of the original. Thus there is the following verse of Lermontov's:

Lermontov	*Line-by-line translation*
I opjat' bezumno upivajus'	And again I revel recklessly
Jadom prežnix dnej,	In the poison of days past
I opjat' ja v mysljax polagajus'	And again I rely in my thoughts
Na slova ljudej.	On people's words.

upon which Abaj enlarges:

Abaj's translation	*Line-by-line translation*[37]
Išip teren bojlamyn	I am submerging myself deeply, feasting
Ötken kunnin ularyn	on the poison of days past
Žene šyn dep ojlajmyn	and I consider as truth
Žurttyn žalghan šularyn.	the lying saying of people.
Taghy sene bastajmyn	Again I begin to believe
künde algaghyš qulargha	the daily deceiving rogues;
Esym šyghyp kašpajmyn,	having lost my sense, I do not run [from
Men išpegenghy bar ma?	them]; is there a poison which I have not drained?

Abaj's creative writings are of varied moods. In his lyrical poems about the four seasons, which show a deep feeling for nature and zest for life as well as an ability to depict realistically

[37] Line-by-line translation in S. Akhmetov, "Novoye o perevodakh Abaya iz M. Yu. Lermontova," *Tyurkologicheski Sbornik,* I (1951), 34. Akhmetov's study is an interesting analysis of Abaj's methods of translation. For a translation of this selection into Russian, see Qunanbayev, *Izbrannoye,* p. 182.

Kazakh life, his strong ties with Pushkin and Lermontov are again revealed:

Spring

How merrily the poplars rustle in spring time.
The wind blows, chasing many-colored dust,
All that lives is caressed by the sun of the steppe,
The earth blooms, resembling a bright-colored rug.

And the young ones sing their songs and laugh away,
Even the oldsters can't be found in the *yurts*.
Even from their deathbed they will arise, awakened
By song, sun, wind and the din of the birds.

. . . .

The world is drunk with blissfully abundant joy,
Limitless is the beauty the creator bestowed on it.
Like a mother's breast the earth has fed
All that which the father-horizon has started in it through the sun.[38]

In Abaj's later writings much of his carefree spirit was lost and the unhappiness which he suffered at the failure of much of his life's work was reflected at last in his poetry. In his efforts to enlighten he frequently aroused the strong opposition of the Russians, as well as of the religious and tribal leaders of his own people, who considered the high value he placed on Western learning and culture a betrayal of the traditions of the Kazakh tribes. His close friendship with many of the revolutionary exiles worried the Russian authorities, who eventually maintained close surviellance of Abaj and of his *aul*, which served as a gathering point for liberal Russians and Kazakhs. Kazakh tribal chiefs and the clergy conspired against him and denounced him to the Russian governor as an "enemy of the white tsar." So successful were the intrigues and the gossip leveled against him that many of his trusted friends and even members of his own family withdrew from him. Towards the end of his life, Abaj, a lonely and misunderstood man, frequently expressed in his poetry his sense of isolation and bitterness at the faithlessness of his friends:

I am tortured and deceived by all around me:
Friends and enemies have betrayed me.[39]

[38] Qunanbayev, *Izbrannoye,* pp. 109-10. [39] *Ibid.,* p. 20.

When his friends and students began to leave him, he wrote in 1889:

> I have reared a dog from a puppy,
> And he bit my leg.
> I taught a lad the art of shooting,
> And he almost killed me.[40]

In spite of his disillusionment, however, Abaj continued the struggle for his ideals. The significance of his contributions to the cultural development of Kazakhstan can hardly be overestimated. It was Abaj first and foremost who laid the basis for an expansion of the formerly meager Kazakh literature, which had been of a predominantly religious character, studded with Arabisms and Persianisms, unintelligible to the broad masses of the population. Abaj introduced a written literature free of incomprehensible expressions, which expressed new and sometimes revolutionary ideas in a manner simple enough to be understood by all. He contributed a great number of formal innovations and was the first to make extensive use of prose in his philosophical writings.

Today Abaj is regarded as the most significant Kazakh writer of the last century, probably esteemed in Kazakhstan as highly as Pushkin is in Russia. His works, considered as classics in Kazakh literature, have been translated into Russian as well as into many other languages of the USSR and have brought belated recognition to his name. Novels and dramas as well as critical works have been written about him.

THE EARLY TWENTIETH CENTURY

The Emergence of a Kazakh National Press

The short-lived reforms in Russia which followed the abortive Revolution of 1905 also made themselves felt in the steppes of Kazakhstan. As the spirit of 1905 reverberated throughout Central Asia, causing increasing unrest, the Russian government found it necessary to offer certain concessions, including a relaxation of the restrictions on publishing in the Kazakh language.

[40] *Ibid.*, p. 202.

The result was a small but significant development of publications of books and periodicals in Kazakh.

Until 1905 the Russian government had prohibited the publication of periodicals in the Kazakh language. The Kazakh educator Altynsaryn had unsuccessfully sought permission to start a Kazakh newspaper. After 1905 there appeared a number of newspapers, published partly in Russian and partly in Kazakh, such as the *Turgaiskaya Gazeta,* published in Omsk,[41] but as they were bilingual and contained little independent Kazakh thought, they could hardly be classed as national Kazakh publications. The most important and influential of the new Kazakh periodicals which emerged after 1905 were the *Qazaq,* published in Orenburg,[42] *Qazaqstan,* published in Urda, *Zaman Tili* and *Alaš,* both published in Tashkent, and *Ajqap,* published in Troitsk.[43] Of these periodicals *Ajqap* could be considered the publication of the Western-orientated intelligentsia, and *Alaš* and *Qazaq,* the publications of the nationalists.

As the restrictions on Kazakh book publishing were also somewhat relaxed, a few books in the Kazakh language written in the Arabic script were published. Because of the lack of printing facilities in Kazakhstan, however, most of these books were printed outside of Kazakhstan in such cities as Kazan, Petropavlovsk, Tashkent, and Astrakhan, while only a very few were printed in Kazakhstan proper (in Omsk, Orenburg, Semipalatinsk, and Verny [Alma-Ata]).

As Kazakh book publication grew somewhat, the hitherto primarily religious character of book publishing began to be replaced by a more secular approach. Among the new publications were a few of the national epics (*Qyz-Džibek, Ajman Šolpan, Qozy Körpöš*), a number of legends, some of the works of contemporary *aqyns,* collections of poems from the pen of Abaj,[44] and some translations from the Russian (Pushkin, *The Captain's Daughter,* selected works of Tolstoy and Chekhov), from the

[41] Abdykalykov, Pankratova, *op. cit.,* p. 368.
[42] See G. W. Hunter, *Qazaq Turki Texts with English Translation* (MS) (Tihwafu, Sinkiang, 1918), pp. 52-53.
[43] Abdykalykov, Pankratova, *op. cit.,* p. 368.
[44] See *Qazaq aqyny Abaj Qunanbaj ulynyn öländeri* (St. Petersburg, 1909).

Ukrainian (*Korolenko*), as well as from the better known contemporary Tatar writers.

Growth of a National Intelligentsia

It has been seen that the influx of Western thought and literature in the nineteenth century proved a powerful stimulus to the emergence of an indigenous literature and intelligentsia. It has also been shown that the new political trends in Kazakhstan encouraged a new kind of Kazakh nationalism directed, in part at least, towards the goal of preparing the ground for eventual independence from Russian rule. Such an attitude was expressed in literature in a strong didactic trend. The people were called upon to seek education and to learn what they could from the culture of the occupying power in order to strengthen their country and prepare themselves for the assumption of a more independent role. We also noted that the nineteenth century witnessed the beginning of the development of a decisive split in the ideology of the Kazakh intelligentsia which divided the leading thinkers of the country in their attitude towards Western culture. In the early twentieth century these trends began to solidify.

With the revolution of 1905 and the comparative relaxation of restrictions on national cultural activities immediately following the revolution, the growth of a national, socially conscious intelligentsia in Kazakhstan was subtantially accelerated. The first decade and a half of the twentieth century was characterized by an intensification of the split between the views of the Westerners and of the traditionalists.

The Westerners, however, dominated the scene in the early twentieth century and consequently the demands for various kinds of reforms modeled on Western concepts were strengthened. Poets and prose writers began to oppose the traditional treatment of women and, inspired by Western poetry, they began to call for love marriages and for the obliteration of the *qalym*. Encouraged by the revolutionary events of 1905 in Russia, Kazakh writers also expressed considerably strengthened attitudes of social protest, which were particularly stimulated by the increasing land hunger in Kazakhstan, and by the introduction of some industry and the ensuing influx of Russian workers, who spread much of their social ideology among the Kazakhs. Both the nationalists and the Westerners remained influential during a considerable part of the Soviet period. The Westerners accepted some aspects of the revolution, while generally the nationalists rejected it, holding that the new order was imposed from the West and alien to the national traditions of the Kazakh people. Many of the early Soviet literary controversies in Kazakhstan and many of the problems encountered by early Kazakh Soviet writers were colored by this conflict. The most important representatives of the Westerners in the literature of the early twentieth century were Sultan Mahmud Toruajgyrov, Mašqur Žusup Qopejev, and Omar Qarašev; while the most outstanding literary representatives of the nationalists were Ahmad Bajtursunov and Žumabayev.

The Westerners

SULTAN MAHMUD TORUAJGYROV (1893-1920). Sultan Mahmud was a typical representative of the new school of writing which so clearly foreshadowed the post-revolutionary literature of Kazakhstan. While he was considered a Westerner, he did not immediately accept the revolution in Kazakhstan and joined the nationalist opposition, which, however, he forsook after a short time for the Bolsheviks, in whose praise he wrote one of his better known poems, "Socialism."

Circumstances did not allow Toruajgyrov to obtain more than a rudimentary education. Nevertheless he became a teacher, and as a journalist he contributed to the newly founded Kazakh periodical *Ajqap*. Toruajgyrov has left us a considerable collection of writings, in which he emerges as one of the first Kazakhs to express social protest in terms of twentieth-century revolutionary attitudes. He pictures the upper social strata of Kazakh society not only in the fashion of the nineteenth-century writers, as traitors to the Kazakh national cause who collaborated with the Russians, but also as class enemies, who oppress the Kazakh masses by seizing the good grazing lands not requisitioned by the Russians. His social protest is no longer clad in the traditional forms of Kazakh oral poetry and clearly shows the influence of Russian realistic poetry; yet Toruajgyrov's matter of fact style does not obscure the rather strong emotional tones employed in the depiction of the fate of the Kazakh poor with whom the poet identifies himself. The personal element in his social protest emerges clearly in one of his longest poems, the largely autobiographical "The Pauper," in which Toruajgyrov strongly attacks social injustice in the steppe and in a realistic fashion, quite unlike the folklore poetry, describes his own life and childhood:

> From the day of birth, only hunger I've known;
> Crying I would ask my mother for food,
> And stealthily taking from the table of the *baj*
> My mother would give me a bone,
> Threads of veins still hanging from it.
> "Eat quicker, eat quicker, my dear little son.
> If they see you, they'll take me to task again.
> Swallow it, oh swallow it," she would hurry me on,
> "Or someone might see you eating."
> From earliest childhood I had but one dream:
> Once only to fill my stomach with good food.
> All my life, like an ox, I have worked day and night,
> And yet this dream has remained but a dream.[45]

Particularly characteristic of Toruajgyrov's poetry is the following realistic passage which must have appeared strange indeed to the older Kazakh writers still steeped in the spirit of the traditional Kazakh poetry:

> Autumn's hand has endowed the grass with a silvery hue;
> Over the nocturnal earth clouds are floating.
> Dark is the night. I am guarding the sheep with my dog;
> Not even a little fire lights up the darkness.
> My clothes are in rags, I am almost not clad,
> And these are the only clothes I've ever had.
> . . . .
> I am cold here in the fireless steppe,
> I am eaten by lice There is not a day

[45] Sultan Mahmud Toruajgyrov, "Bednyak," Sobolev, ed., *Pesni . . .*, p. 335.

When from the rags of my clothes
These lice do not torture me.[46]

Toruajgyrov was strongly influenced by Qunanbayev's views on poetry. Like Abaj he rejected the tradition of the ornamental poetry of Arabic, Persian, and Čagataj literature and viewed the role of poetry as primarily a social one. In a programmatic poem, "What Do I Live For?," in which he calls on his people to rid themselves of the barnacles of the past and to start a new life, the life of a modern nation, he expresses this attitude most clearly.

I do not live in order to sow flowers,
And see them bloom into live beauty;
I live to help my descendants with my song,
So that their paths may be easy and simple.[47]

Toruajgyrov's realistic social poetry was a clear precursor of the later Kazakh Soviet writings. While accepting Abaj's concept of the purpose of poetry, he went beyond the latter's general philosophical didacticism and adopted a sharp and revolutionary realism.

OMAR QARAŠEV (1876-1921). Another social writer of the Western school was Omar Qarašev, who, more than most of the Western-orientated poets, drew in his writings both from the national folklore traditions of the Kazakhs and from the religious culture of Islam. As a student in the religious schools, Qarašev became acquainted with Arabic, Persian, and Čagataj as well as Tatar literatures, and after graduating he became a member of the Mohammedan clergy, as an *išan*. The outbreak of the revolution in 1905, however, caused Qarašev to change many of his attitudes and he began to propagate new ideas acquired from the Russian revolutionaries. As a result his ecclesiastic position became untenable and he was soon deprived of his clerical station.

Qarašev then devoted himself entirely to poetry, publishing his works in the Tatar papers of Kazan and Ufa and other large cities. In his poems, which like Toruajgyrov's are imbued with a considerable political and social content, he laments the national and social oppression of the Kazakhs by the Russians and by

[46] *Ibid.*, p. 334.
[47] Toruajgyrov, "Dlya chevo zhivu," Sobolev, ed., *Pesni* . . . , p. 330.

their own aristocracy. In addition to the traditional sources, Qarašev began to draw increasingly from the literature of the West and in particular from Russian social poetry, as is evident in the following lines:

> Wide lakes, flowering valleys,
> Free nomadic wandering, free pastures,
> All these you would not even dream of today.
> Today one does not even know
> What kind of freedom there once was in the steppes.
> Now there is only the sand storm,
> And on that sand
> Pushed close together
> Are now the *auls*.[48]

In the above lines, however, the ties Qarašev maintained with the traditional *aqyns* are also revealed in his stress on the past of the Kazakhs, when the hordes were not ruled by the Russians, but roamed freely on their own grazing grounds. In other poems Qarašev looks ahead optimistically and paints a bright picture of the future of a free Kazakh people. But in such cases his affinity with the epic poetry of the *aqyns* becomes even more apparent, since in his enthusiasm he frequently deviates quite strikingly from the new realistic trend in poetry and returns to the metaphorical style of the epic, as in the following lines:

> What distinguishes a *batyr?*
> When the enemy appears at the borders,
> When the battle cry resounds,
> Then, dressing in steel armour,
> Raging against the enemy,
> White as a sea-gull,
> He heats up his *tulpar*.
> Waving his jewel-like sword,
> He cuts off the enemies' heads;
> Wading knee-deep through blood,
> Pulling the tight bow,
> He sends a rain of arrows upon them.[49]

OTHER "WESTERN" WRITERS. Other writers of interest during this period who, unfortunately, have been only meagerly

[48] Abdykalykov, Pankratova, *op. cit.*, p. 366.
[49] *Ibid.*, p. 367.

translated into Russian, are Ispandiar Köbejev and Sabit Dönentajev. Köbejev is significant as the first Kazakh novelist. His novel *Qalym,* published in 1908, is concerned with the problem of the position of women, a question which became one of the most pressing ones after the revolution. In this work Köbejev not only experimented with a new genre, but also with new attitudes toward his own culture. Not only is his novel in effect a denial of the moral justification of the *qalym,* with all its implications, but it also offers support to a revolutionary attitude toward marriage since it contains a frank advocacy of marriage for love. The heroine of the novel, Ghaiša, sold to a rich *baj* by her father, decides, with the aid and advice not only of her friends but also her mother, to escape with her lover and to marry him instead. The novel is, as might be expected, rather simple, and in places even primitive. The author does not attempt to probe the motivation and psychology of the characters, and the only method of illuminating the inner struggle of the chief characters is that of expository remarks on the part of the author. In spite of the awkwardness of this first attempt, the work does contain effectively written lyrical and moving passages which clearly take their origin from the oral tradition. Thus the song which Ghaiša sings at the house of a friend, bewailing the fate which awaits her and reproaching her father for selling her, rises above much of the prose writing. This is a common phenomenon in early Kazakh prose since the young authors are often tempted when writing their most lyrical and truly creative passages to return to the more familiar and traditional form of poetry.

Sabit Dönentajev is significant as the creator of the first Kazakh satires. Dönentajev was strongly influenced by Russian literature of the nineteenth century and particularly by the poetry of Nekrasov, the prose of Saltykov-Shchedrin, and the fables of Krylov. In his fable *The Wolf Who Has Eaten Poison,* which shows the influence of Krylov clearly, Dönentajev attacks the tribal aristocracy, symbolized by the figure of the wolf who had once been an arrogant and pitiless *batyr,* but who suddenly remembers the people when times become difficult and he himself suffers from the Russians.

Thus is it written also for the tribe of wolves:
One cannot know success every day of the year.
Only yesterday, when you were successful,
You never thought that you also might come to grief.

There is no corner in the whole wide world,
Where you did not search for conquests.
For everyone that lived, and even for your friends,
You were a *batyr,* who would occasionally swallow them.

Only recently, who would have dared to even whisper,
That some day you might no longer be strong?
But all this now remains behind.
One can not retrieve former power and glory.

Hardly dragging your legs from misfortune,
Only now do you remember "your people."
Why don't you hit yourself? It was your greed
And your insatiable mouth, which led you to misery.

Thus, where's the use of robbery and theft?
You've lost again all that you ate.
You've become a stranger among your own people,
You are unhappy, and bitter is your fate.[50]

Dönentajev's ire was also directed, in many of his poems and satires, against the nationalists, whom he pictured as robbers who, under the pretense of aiding the people, were utilizing them for selfish aims.

The Nationalists: Bajtursunov

The most important representative of the nationalists was Ahmad Bajtursunov, a man who was to be of not inconsiderable influence on Kazakh literature during the early Soviet period. In many respects Bajtursunov must be considered the most important Kazakh writer of the early twentieth century. His significance lay primarily in the considerable scope and breadth of his work, for Bajtursunov was not only a poet and a translator, but also one of the first Kazakh journalists and publishers as well as a linguist who made significant contributions to the study and propagation of the Kazakh literary language.

[50] Sabit Dönentajev, "Volku, nayevshemusya yada," Sobolev, ed., *Pesni . . .*, p. 325.

As a writer his activities began with his translation into the Kazakh language of Krylov's fables.[51] He followed Abaj's example in selecting only those works which could have meaning for the Kazakh reader and which corresponded to the spirit of Kazakh culture. Not infrequently he changed the sense of the original, as had Abaj, in order to facilitate their integration into Kazakh culture.[52]

In his attitude toward the function of his original poetry Bajtursunov also followed the precepts of Abaj, for he viewed poetry as an educational weapon. He also demanded that the Kazakhs accept modern values, but, in contrast to Abaj, he saw the road for accomplishing this aim not in learning from the West, but in using the innate national cultural resources and the age-old traditions of the Kazakhs. It is not surprising, therefore, that Bajtursunov was considerably more preoccupied with the development of the Kazakh language than were his Western colleagues. Probably his most important contribution lay in his attempts to preserve and modernize the Kazakh language.

It is in Bajtursunov's journalistic writings that his philosophy and his nationalist views emerge most clearly. Bajtursunov undertook the publication of the nationalist periodical *Qazaq* in Orenburg in 1913, and, in a programmatic editorial written for this journal, he defined his views in relation to the situation in the steppes in the following way:

The Kazakh nation for a long time has inhabited a definite territory, and lived a particular kind of life. Now we see the tremendous wave of colonizers in the Kazakh steppes. What will be the fate of our nation in the future? Judging from the historical course of events, it is not difficult to guess that the new elements arising here will prove themselves culturally the stronger compared with the local population. As time goes by, the latter will be devoured by the former. On the other hand, if both prove to have cul-

[51] *Revue du Monde Musulman,* XI, No. 6 (1910), 298.

[52] M. Dulatov, "Akhmed Baitursunovich Baitursunov," *Trudy Obshchestva Izucheniya Kirgizskogo Kraya* (Orenburg), No. III (1922), p. 20. This was actually the method of Krylov himself, who borrowed a great many themes and tales from La Fontaine, but filled the formal structure of the tales with new content which he drew from his own Russian culture.

ture on the same level, then they will be able to develop independently, and they will exist in their own right, preserving their own national fate. Now, however, a rupture in the economic life of the Kazakhs is unavoidable. Peasants are settling in those regions which are suitable for agriculture; regions which are suitable for cattle breeding are taken away from us by the new colonizers. . . . In one word, by all kinds of roads foreign nationalities are entering into our midst. Thus there arises a grave question for us, the question about the independence of the Kazakh nation. In order to save our independence, we must attempt, with all the forces and means at our disposal, to rise to a state of enlightenment and general culture. For this purpose we must first of all occupy ourselves with the development of literature in the national language. We must never forget that only that nation has a right to demand an independent life, which speaks its own language and has its own literature. In this regard matters stand very badly with us. The modern Kazakh intelligentsia, having received their education in Russian schools and Tatar *medreses,* already begin to feel contempt for the Kazakh language, and begin to speak Russian or Tatar among theirselves. That is a bad sign. If it should continue further, then we shall have once and for all said goodbye to the Kazakh language and, along with it, to the Kazakh people as an independent nation. If we do not want this to happen, it is absolutely necessary to solve this question from its very root and to start right now with the perfection of the Kazakh language and literature.[53]

As a result of these convictions Bajtursunov devoted much of his life to the propagation of the use of Kazakh both as a spoken and as a written language but he realized, as did Altynsaryn, that Kazakh literature could not flourish if the Kazakhs continued to use the Arabic script in its original form. Unlike Altynsaryn, however, he rejected attempts to introduce an entirely new script based on the Cyrillic or Latin alphabets and rather attempted to reform Arabic by adapting it more closely to Kazakh phonology through such measures as the provision of symbols for the vowels which Arabic lacks.[54]

Bajtursunov's sympathies led him not only to write of the national struggles of the Kazakhs but also to participate directly in anti-Russian activities. As a result of his revolutionary activi-

[53] Quoted in Dulatov, *op. cit.,* pp. 21-22.

[54] Ilya Omarov, "Uchennaya deyatelnost' A. B. Baitursunova," *Trudy O-va Izuch. Kirg. Kraya,* No. III (1922), 9.

ties he was jailed by the Russian authorities in 1909 and remained in jail until 1910.[55]

It was primarily Bajtursunov who prepared the ground in Kazakhstan for the powerful movement, during the Soviet period, of the anti-Russian nationalists. Since Bajtursunov's nationalist and anti-Russian convictions would not allow him to accept the position of Kazakhstan as a part of the USSR, he joined the nationalist group *Alaš,* a group with strong pan-Turkic coloration which advocated complete national independence of Kazakhstan. By March, 1919, however, Bajtursunov had left the *Alaš* and joined forces with the Bolsheviks, who accepted him in spite of misgivings since, as one of the most popular figures in Kazakhstan, his change in allegiance was of great educational and propagandistic value. As a Bolshevik, Bajtursunov rapidly rose to a position of importance as a professor in the newly organized Kazakh Institute, as chairman of the Commission of Science and Literature of the Commissariat of Education, and as honorary chairman of the Society for the Study of the Kirghiz (i.e., Kazakh) Region (*Obshchestvo izucheniya kirgizskogo kraya*). His nationalist tendencies, however, continued to irritate the new Communist writers and critics, and, as criticism of both his works and his attitude increased, Bajtursunov's influence began to wane, and he finally lost his position of literary leadership.

Concluding Remarks

The harsh events of the nineteenth and early twentieth centuries, the battles against colonial rule, the suffering under subjection, combined with the infiltration of Russian and Western thought, formulated and solidified trends of Kazakh thought. While the majority of the Kazakh people continued their traditional way of life, a small but coherent and vociferous intelligentsia was formed, and took a leading position in developing Kazakh literature from a simple oral art to a more sophisticated written literature which was strongly influenced by Russian culture but was not entirely absorbed by it.

[55] Dulatov, *op. cit.,* p. 20.

The period of the early twentieth century provided, in many respects, a link between nineteenth-century literature and thought and the literature of the Soviet period. Not only did the early twentieth century see the strengthening of both the Westerners and the nationalists, but also many new developments took place: the introduction of a number of new genres—the novel, satire, and journalistic prose—and the infiltration of new attitudes of social thought and protest into the literature of the Westerners. The small concessions which the Russian government gave to the steppes after the 1905 revolution acted to encourage the further growth of the still small local intelligentsia, which was rapidly becoming more influential.

CHAPTER VI

CULTURAL DEVELOPMENT OF SOVIET KAZAKHSTAN

Historical Background

Conditions in Central Asia had changed considerably by the beginning of the twentieth century as a result of the transformation of this region into an adjunct of the economy of the Russian empire. The ever-increasing land appropriations by the Russian government had led to a sharp decrease in nomadism. The traditional home production in the *auls* had been gradually displaced by the imposition of a mercantile economy. There had even been effected, on a limited scale, some industrialization, utilizing the huge natural resources of Kazakhstan. Industrialization as well as land confiscation brought increased economic impoverishment to the Kazakhs, driving many former herders into ill-paid industries and into agricultural pursuits, and caused further destruction of the tribal order. Russification policies and political subjection heightened the nationalist feelings which had already grown to considerable strength by the end of the nineteenth century. Nationalism of all shades was further strengthened by the 1905 revolution in Russia, which introduced to the steppes a new kind of revolutionary thought. Under the influence of revolutionary events in Russia and of Russian workers in Central Asia there occurred, after 1905, a number of serious strikes, already clearly motivated by political and national, rather than by purely economic, aims.

The outbreak of the First World War affected Russian Central Asia relatively little, because the local population, for obvious reasons, was not subject to call to military duty. In 1916, however, the entire region was shaken violently by an uprising which was once again to weld the people of Central Asia together in armed struggle against the Russians. On June 25, 1916, the Russian government issued a decree "requisitioning" all Kazakh, Uzbek, Kirghiz, Türkmen, Uighur, and T'ungan males from the ages to 19 to 43 for labor duties in the rear of the Russian armies. The reaction to this mobilization decree was immediate and spontaneous and by July discontent had spread into a full-blown uprising against the Russians all through Central Asia. By September of the same year the Russians had succeeded in quelling the uprising, but guerilla activities continued to harass Russian supply lines.

The outbreak of the February and later the October revolution presented the nations of Central Asia with a new and far more complicated situation. Soviets were formed in all major centers of the steppes. The civil war was particularly bloody in Central Asia, where the pan-Turkic nationalists united with the forces of the Whites against the revolutionaries. In Kazakhstan the nationalists formed the *Alaš-orda,* a political party which stood for complete political autonomy of the Kazakh steppes and gave its support to the Whites under Kolchak. In December, 1917, *Alaš-orda* supporters formed an autonomous regional government and established their own national Kazakh militia. Only in 1920 did the Red Army defeat the forces of Kolchak and Dutov, at which time Soviet power was established over most of the Central Asian nations with the exception of the khanates of Bukhara and Khiva, which for some time retained a special and privileged position in the Soviet federation.

Shortly after assuming power in Central Asia, the Soviet authorities put into effect a new delimitation of national frontiers in Central Asia. Under this new system the majority of the Central Asian nationalities were united in individual republics to form in the south the Uzbek Soviet Socialist Republic[1] and the Turkmen SSR and in the north the Kazakh[2] and the Kirghiz-Autonomous Soviet Socialist Republics. The latter two northern

[1] The Uzbek republic included, until 1931, as an autonomous unit, the Tadzhik Autonomous Soviet Socialist Republic.

[2] In 1925 the name of the republic was officially changed from "Kirghiz" to Kazakh ASSR.

republics were elevated to the status of full Union Republics only in 1936.

The Bolsheviks faced problems in Kazakhstan and in the rest of Central Asia which were considerably more complex than those which they faced in gaining the allegiance of the population in the Russian-speaking areas. The Russification policies and the disastrous land policies of the Russian colonial administrators of the nineteenth century had left their mark in a suspicious and frequently openly hostile attitude on the part of the Kazakhs toward any innovations which were considered to be of Russian origin. The Bolsheviks attempted to gain the support of the Kazakh people by applying the basic principles of the policies on the national minorities which had been outlined in detail by Joseph Stalin in a series of articles before the Bolshevik assumption of power,[3] which included the principles of equal treatment for all nationalities inhabiting the territory of the former tsarist empire, the right of a qualified autonomy for the larger nationalities, and the raising of the cultural and economic levels of backward regions through education, industrialization, and the settling of nomads. The Bolsheviks encouraged the Kazakhs to express what they considered to be Kazakh traditional culture within the framework of the new society.

Under the Communist regime the life of the Kazakhs experienced a transformation which was of considerably more far-reaching proportions than any changes which the area had undergone as a result of the Russian penetration in the nineteenth century. In the economic field these changes involved a prolonged, and initially quite unsuccessful, attempt to settle the nomadic cattle breeders, and to introduce modern agricultural methods and, in the 1930's, collective and state farms. These efforts were made against the hard and tenacious opposition by the nomads to any attempt to change their traditional economy and involved a series of harsh and forceful measures on the part of the Bolsheviks. It was only in the mid-thirties, after many struggles and mass slaughter of cattle by the protesting nomads,

[3] See Joseph Stalin, *Marxism and the National Question,* Eng. ed. publ. by International Publishers (New York, 1942).

that Soviet sources could claim anything resembling success in their fateful campaign, with the assertion that 98 per cent of all cattle had been turned over to collective farms,[4] and that 90 per cent of all agricultural pursuits were now centered in collective or state farms.[5] In addition, the Soviet government put into execution a program of rapid industrialization of the region with the apparent twofold aim of utilizing the large and almost untouched natural resources of the area and of dealing a double-barreled blow at the traditional culture of the Kazakhs. Through industrialization, it was hoped, there would be created a Kazakh proletariat which would support the aims of the Soviet government and form the cadres from which future political administrators of Kazakhstan could be chosen. Consequently, the Soviet government poured quantities of capital into Kazakhstan, as also into the other Central Asian republics, in order to create an industry which today allows favorable comparison with that of Central Russia. By 1936 it was reported that over 120 new industrial enterprises had arisen in the republic. The largest enterprises are the Karaganda coal mines, which are among the largest mines in the USSR; the extensive lead mines, which produce the bulk of Soviet lead output; and the oil fields in Emba, which today are second only to those in Baku. In addition, rubber production, sugar refining, fish and meat canning, and chemical industries all combine to make Kazakhstan today one of the most significant industrial bases of the Soviet Union.

An indication of the new economic developments in Kazakhstan is the growth of cities. Before the revolution Kazakhstan had not one major city. But between the years 1926 and 1939, there was hardly a city which had not doubled its size. Alma-Ata, the capital, had multiplied five times to a population of over 230,000 in 1939 and Karaganda, an entirely new city, had grown to a population of 166,000 by 1939.[6] It is probable that with the mass-scale war evacuations and the increased in-

[4] N. I. Gusev, ed., *Kazakhstan* (Moscow, 1936), p. 135.

[5] *Ibid.*, p. 152.

[6] *Bolshaya Sovetskaya Entsiklopediya,* USSR supplementary volume (Moscow, 1947), p. 1843.

dustrialization of the area during and since the war these cities have again grown greatly. It is also quite evident that there has been a considerable influx of Russian technicians and skilled workers into the area.

As a result of these changes there is today in Central Asia a strange mixture of the new and the old. Thus one contemporary Russian writer describes Kazakhstan:

> In the conditions of life in Kazakhstan one meets amazing mixtures, as for instance: side by side with the old nomadic economy with the patriarchal traditions, there exists a huge socialist factory, where everything is built according to the latest technique. The task [remaining now] is to wipe out these differences.[7]

"Crimes Based on Customs"

The Kazakhs, just like the other Turkic nationalities in Central Asia, still maintained in the Soviet period many age-old customs, such as that of the traditional *vendetta* (*qūn alma*), robbing expeditions against neighboring tribes (*barymta*), as well as customs engendered by early shamanism and Islamic law.

The most important traditions which hindered the development of the region, since they ruled against the participation of approximately half of the population in the public life of the nation, were those which related to the role of women: the traditions of polygamy, compulsory marriage, and bride buying.

Almost immediately after taking over power in Kazakhstan, the local Bolsheviks attempted to do away with these traditions by declaring the equality of women before the law and by prohibiting polygamy, the *qalym* (bride price), forced marriage, and other customs which were stamped with the epithet of "crimes based on customs" (*bytovyie prestupleniya*).

Similar decrees were passed by other Central Asiatic republics, but there was at first no uniformity among the various regions in dealing with these problems. It was only in 1924 that the federal government itself entered the battle and attempted to unify the law by promulgating, on October 16, 1924, a decree

[7] S. Dimanshtein, "K 15-ti letiyu Kazakhstana," *Revolyutsiya i Nation-al'nosti,* No. 10 (1935), p. 32.

entitled: "Decree about the struggle against crimes based on customs" (*Postanovleniye o bor'be s bytovymi prestupleniyami*),[8] which was submitted to the member republics for ratification. The discussion in the Central Asiatic republics was violent, with considerable opposition, particularly from the clergy, who considered this proposed law a stringent interference with the traditions of Islam. Just as the introduction of the new alphabet was to become a struggle over religious issues, so also the struggle for women's equality became a fight over basic questions of religion. It was not until April, 1928, that the decree was ratified by all the republics concerned and became law. The new law prohibited the *qalym,* compulsory and child marriages, polygamy, and the levirate, in addition to other "traditional crimes," such as the *barymta,* the assumption of judicial power by the Mohammedan *šerī'at* courts and compulsory religious taxation.

It is not surprising, however, that such deeply ingrained practices could not be abolished by the mere passage of a decree. Not only was opposition to the law formidable before passage, but in the early years of the new law its provisions were by-passed with amazing tenacity. It became necessary to establish special courts all over Central Asia equipped to consider only cases involving transgression of this law, and the number of offenders haled before these courts bears witness to the difficulties involved in eradicating old practices and beliefs. It was clear that greater than the need for a law was the need for a long and patient educational process. So deep rooted was the tradition of marriage by *qalym* that opposition emanated not only from the tradition-minded and from the clergy, but also, in some instances, from quite unexpected quarters such as the local Communists. In many cases transgression against the law by Communists was a result of misunderstanding of the meaning of the decree, testifying to the difficulty of assimilating so radical an innovation as the abolition of bride buying.[9]

[8] S. Akopov, "Bor'ba s bytovmi prestupleniyami," *Revolyutsiya i Nation-al'nosti,* Nos. 4-5 (1930), p. 60.

[9] A rather colorful example of this problem is reported by Fannina Halle concerning the case of the mountain republic of Daghestan, where, it appears,

Despite the early difficulties, the Soviet attempts to alter the position of women met, after a period of years, with considerable success. Women began to be accepted as equals and to play a growing role in the public life of their republic as teachers, lawyers, deputies, collective farm chairmen, and party officials. Judging from the later literature of Central Asian authors, the equality of womanhood is regarded by the new generation as something quite natural. There are a great number of modern Kazakh novels in which the heroine is a factory or collective farm director, a scientist, or a Communist party official. But cases concerning traditional treatment of women continue to be tried, though with decreasing frequency, by Soviet courts.

Education and the New Alphabet

In many respects the most ambitious program the Bolsheviks undertook in Central Asia was the initiation of a program of mass education which, at its very inception, met with what appeared to be insurmountable obstacles. The task of mass education was particularly difficult to carry out because of the lack of native teachers and educational facilities of any proportions and also because the new government had inherited the results of the tsarist Russification policies, one of the characteristics of which had been lack of instruction in the local languages. Soviet theorists took upon themselves the task of formulating new policies on which to base the new educational program. Soviet policy in relation to the education of the non-Russian nationalities had been outlined by Stalin on several occasions. In his theses for the tenth congress of the Russian Communist party in March, 1921, Stalin included in his enumeration of the "im-

---

the local Communists were incapable of imagining that so ancient and sacred an institution as that of bride buying could be the cause of objection. Rather, they interpreted the new law as a move of the Soviet government to promote social justice and do away with profiteering on the "wives' market," and they proceeded to publish a list of "price ceilings" for wives of different "quality":

1. Girl, quite young, pretty, of well-to-do family..300 rubles
2. Girl of poor family, or orphan..................150 rubles
3. Young widow or divorcee......................100 rubles
4. Middle-aged widow or divorcee................ 50 rubles

(Fannina W. Halle, *Woman in the Soviet East* [New York, 1938], p. 133.)

mediate tasks of the Russian Communist party in relation to the national question" the recommendation that the party should help the backward regions "to develop their own press, schools, theaters, clubs, and cultural and educational institutions generally, functioning in the native language."[10]

Stalin enlarged on this theme two years later, when he outlined the following steps needed to raise the cultural level of the local population:

a. The establishment of (non-party) clubs and other educational institutions in the local languages.
b. The expansion of the network of all degrees of educational institutions in the local languages.
c. The attraction to work in the schools of more or less loyal teachers of local origin.
d. The creation of a network of societies for the spread of literacy in the local languages.
e. The extension of publishing.[11]

It was clear, however, that an educational program in Turkic Central Asia would not be feasible without a solution of the complex problems of linguistic reform in this area. Some of the Central Asiatic nations did not even possess written languages, and those nationalities which did possess a script employed the ill-suited and complicated Arabic script. This script, characterized by a great variety of forms in which one and the same sound can be represented according to its position in the word and by the absence of symbols for vowels, is not only poorly adapted to the Turkic languages, particularly to those which have preserved the principle of vowel harmony, but is so difficult to learn that it is ill-suited as a mass medium.

It was evident that alphabets had to be literally "created" for such preliterate nations as the Kirghiz, and the cumbersome Arabic script had to be replaced in all cases where it was in use. This was achieved by the initiation, not only in Central

[10] Stalin, *Sochineniya* (Moscow, 1947), V, 24.
[11] *Ibid.*, p. 298.

Asia but among all peoples using the Arabic script, of a complex and long-term program which had as its aim the conversion of all peoples who used Arabic to the use of a graphic system based on the Latin.[12] The Latinized script was introduced in the late 1920's,[13] after a vigorous battle not only against obvious technical and linguistic difficulties, but against a tenacious opposition emanating from part of the intelligentsia and from the Mohammedan clergy, who saw in the abolition of Arabic an abrogation of their hegemony in educational matters and a cutting of an important link with other Moslem cultures. The Latin script was changed to one based on the Cyrillic alphabet towards the end of the 1930's. By 1936 all the Soviet nationalities, not only those in Central Asia, but also the preliterate Palaeoasiatic peoples in the north, had received an alphabetic script.[14] Of the hundred

[12] A similar program, it will be remembered, was also carried out in Turkey. The problem of transition to a Latin-based script in the Soviet East is of particular importance today, as it may provide some useful glimpses of the problems of the new China, where the government finds itself faced with a quite similar problem and where discussions over latinization have been going on for many years. Here also a beginning in the same direction seems to have been made with the provision of the Latin-based script for the Yi minority in Sikang and of a Cyrillic-based script for the Mongols of Inner Mongolia. (See John de Francis, "National and Minority Policies," *Report on China, Annals of the American Academy of Political and Social Science,* CCLXXVII [September, 1951], 153-54. For background material on this problem, see de Francis, *Nationalism and Language Reform in China* [Princeton, 1950].) For a detailed account of the new alphabet, see T. G. Winner, "Problems of Alphabetic Reform among the Turkic Peoples of Soviet Central Asia, 1920-41," *Slavonic and East European Review* (London), XXXI, No. 76 (Dec. 1952), 133-147.

[13] Latin was not the only basis for a new script which was being considered in the 1920's. A number of non-Islamic and smaller national groups based their new written languages on the Cyrillic system, notably the Minusinsk Tartars (Khakass), Oirats, Shors, Chuvash, Altai, and the East Finnic and Permian peoples—the Mordvins, Mari (Cheremiss), Komi, Permyaks, Votyaks (Udmurts), as well as two nationalities with no definite territorial base, the Gypsies and the Aisors (*aisoriytsy, novo-siriytsy*) (see Ye. D. Polivanov, "Osnovnye formy graficheskoy revolyutsii v turetskikh pis'mennostyakh SSSR," *Novy Vostok,* Nos. 23-24 [1928], pp. 317, 318, 319, 322 and *passim*). Among these nationalities which had been under relatively stronger Russian cultural influence, Cyrillic scripts seem to have developed more or less spontaneously on the basis of earlier missionary transcriptions. This, however, seems to have been regarded by the language reformers as an unavoidable evil rather than a desirable development (see *Stenograficheski otchot pervogo plenuma VTsK NTA* [Moscow, 1927], p. 29).

[14] Most of the scripts of the Palaeoasiatic peoples were based initially on the Cyrillic system rather than on the Latin.

and more Soviet nationalities, more than sixty have acquired a script since the Russian revolution.[15]

The Anti-Illiteracy Program

Closely connected with the creation of a new alphabet was the struggle against illiteracy. Vigorous campaigns were initiated to urge the population to learn to read and write. Individuals were hurriedly trained in the essentials of reading and writing in mass intensive courses and were then sent throughout the country in order to instruct the population. "Red caravans" and "red *džurts*" on the model of the Russian "red clubs" became the centers for the anti-illiteracy campaign, or, as it was officially called, "liquidation of illiteracy" (*Likbez*). The process of eliminating illiteracy was extremely slow and laborious, particularly before the general introduction of the new alphabet. Literacy among women was, for reasons of their special position in the society, even lower than that of males. The following figures, which were obtained in the All-Soviet census of 1926, show clearly not only the slow progress in the eradication of illiteracy in comparison with the progress in the Russian-speaking regions of the USSR, but also the lag of women, many of whom still held back from visiting the *Likbez* centers by their husbands, by communal prejudice, and by their own timidity.

PERCENTAGE OF LITERACY (1926)[16]

Nationality	TOTAL POPULATION			CITY POPULATION			RURAL POPULATION		
	male	fem.	total	male	fem.	total	male	fem.	total
Russians	57.6	33.9	45	74.4	60.2	67	53	26.9	39.9
USSR average	50.8	29.2	39.6	70.7	56.7	63.5	46.5	23.3	34.4
Kazakhs	12.5	1.0	7.1	37.0	9.2	25.4	11.9	0.9	6.7
Kirghiz	8.4	0.3	4.6	39.7	9.1	27.7	7.9	0.2	4.2
Uzbeks	6.4	1.0	3.8	20.0	4.1	12.5	3.2	0.3	1.9
Turkmens	4.2	0.2	2.3	35.3	5.0	24.3	3.6	0.2	2.0

[15] G. Musabekov, "Pobedy novogo alfavita," *Literaturnaya Gazeta* (Moscow), Jan. 26, 1936, p. 2.

[16] *Nationalnaya politika VKP (b) v tsyfrakh* (Moscow, 1930), pp. 271-72; also *Bolshaya Sovetskaya Entsiklopediya* (Moscow, 1947), XVIII, 789. These figures must be viewed with some reservations, since it is difficult to understand how the Kirghiz, who before the revolution were almost pre-

During the years of the first Five-Year Plan measures to eradicate illiteracy began to be more successful and by 1935 Soviet statistics claimed that 61 per cent of the total population of the Kazakh republic were literate,[17] while by 1939 the literacy figure had been raised, according to official statistics, to 76.3 per cent as compared to an average of 81.2 per cent of the USSR as a whole.[18]

With illiteracy on the wane, the huge task of constructing a system of mass education, both adult and juvenile, could be seriously undertaken; and during the 1930's a network of primary and secondary schools was created all over the republic, with instruction in the local language. In 1930, 8,834 primary schools were counted in Kazakhstan, of which 3,454 were Kazakh schools, 2,135 schools of the various non-Kazakh minorities in Kazakhstan, exclusive of the Russians, and the rest Russian schools. By 1930 there was also a considerable increase in the number of secondary schools and there were even established some specialized institutions of higher education—two workers faculties (*rabfak*), four *tekhnikums,* and seventy-five trade and factory schools.[19] In 1934, there were in Kazakhstan, according to a Kazakh source, 5,000 primary and secondary schools, ninety *tekhnikums,* and eight higher educational institutions (VUZ). In the same year, the first university, the Kazakh State University, was opened.[20] By the academic year of 1935-36, according to the chairman of the Central Executive Committee (TsIK) of the KSSR, there were the following number of schools in Kazakhstan:[21] 7,113 grammar schools, 788 incomplete secondary

---

literate, should, in so short a time, have outstripped the sedentary Uzbeks, who had a considerable literary tradition before the revolution. The only possible explanation for this apparent discrepancy could be the fact that the NTA took a much less rapid hold on the cultures in which there had been a higher degree of literacy in the Arabic script.

[17] Gusev, *op. cit.*, p. 174.

[18] *Kul'turnoye stroitel'stvo SSSR, statisticheski sbornik* (Moscow, 1940), p. 7, table 5.

[19] A. Rysakoff, *The National Policy of the Soviet Union* (London, 1932), pp. 59-60.

[20] T. Zhurgenev, "Boyevyie voprosy kultstroitelstva v Kazakstane," *Prosveshcheniye Natsionalnostei,* No. 1 (1934), p. 17.

[21] U. Kulumbetov, "Kazakhstan nakanune preobrazovaniya v soyuznuyu respubliku," *Revol. i Natsion.,* No. 11 (1936), p. 45.

and secondary schools, sixteen VUZ, and eighty-three *tekhnikum* schools. In the same year some 640,000 Kazakh children were reported as attending schools.[22]

A very special problem in Kazakhstan, particularly in the early years when there were still a large number of nomadic peoples, was the inclusion of the children of nomads in the educational system. Even after settling there was the problem of schools for the children in *auls* which were too small to warrant separate schools and which were isolated from neighboring *auls*. In order to provide such young people with an education, the Kazakh government established a series of boarding schools (*internaty*), in which young people could receive a primary and secondary education. In 1936 there were two hundred such boarding schools in which there were enrolled approximately 22,000 Kazakh children.[23]

A most significant development was the new and unprecedented participation of women in the educational program. By the academic year 1938-39 official Soviet statistics claimed the following figures: of the total number of students in the seven- and ten-year schools, women accounted for 42.7 per cent in Uzbekistan, 43.8 per cent in Turkmenistan, 45.2 per cent in Kazakhstan, and 43.6 in Kirghizstan.[24]

It need not be stressed that in such areas as Central Asia the attainment of a network of higher educational institutions was a far more difficult task than the attainment of a system of primary and secondary education. The attainment of a firm primary and secondary basis was a *sine qua non* for the establishment of higher educational facilities in which instruction would be offered in the native language and in which at least the major proportion of the faculty could be composed of nationals of the republics. We have noted that it was only in 1934 that the first large-scale attempt at higher education was made in Kazakhstan with the creation of the Kazakh State University, which at that time was limited to the faculties of history and

[22] "Postanovleniye Presidiuma TsIK SSSR: O sovetskom khozyaistvennom i kul'turnom stroitelstve KASSR za 15 let," *Revol. i Natsion.*, No. 1 (1936), p. 82.

[23] Gusev, *op. cit.*, p. 174.

[24] *Kul't. stroit. . .*, p. 65.

economics, literature and linguistics, physics and mathematics, chemistry and biology.[25] By 1947, however, the network of higher educational institutions in Kazakhstan had grown to ninety *tekhnikums* and twenty-three institutions of higher learning, including the Kazakh State University, the Molotov Medical Institute, the Abaj Kazakh Pedagogical Institute, a mining and metallurgical institute, and an agricultural school. In the academic year of 1947, 5,200 students were accepted in these higher institutes.[26] Numerous new departments had by this time been added to the Kazakh State University, including a Department of Journalism and a Department of Psychology and Philosophy.[27] In 1948, the student body in the State University was roughly two thousand, half of whom were Kazakhs, the rest belonging to the various minorities in Kazakhstan, including the Russians.[28] In addition, there were founded in Kazakhstan several branches of federal higher educational institutions, such as the Kazakh branch of the All-Union Lenin Agricultural Academy, the Kazakh branch of the Marx-Engels Institute, and the Kazakh branch of the Academy of Sciences of the USSR.[29] In June, 1946, the Kazakh branch of the Academy of Sciences gained regional autonomy and was reformed as the Academy of Sciences of the Kazakh SSR (ANKazSSR). In 1948 the ANKazSSR had 1,200 scientific collaborators, of whom 85 held doctoral degrees; however, even at this late date, only 260 of this total number were Kazakhs, with 14 doctoral degrees. In 1948 a total of 20 doctoral dissertations were defended, of which, however, again only one-third were by Kazakhs.[30]

Instruction is, wherever possible, in the national language, either Kazakh, or in the languages of the minorities of the KazSSR; however, in the higher educational institutions, a great amount of instruction is carried on in Russian, partly because of the still low number of trained Kazakh scholars.

[25] Zhurgenev, *op. cit.*, p. 21.

[26] *Kazakhstanskaya Pravda,* Oct. 5, 1947, p. 1.

[27] Statement by Kh. Ibrashev, prorector of the University, in *Kaz. Prav.,* Sept. 2, 1947, p. 3.

[28] *Kaz. Prav.,* June 29, 1948, p. 3.

[29] Abdykalykov, Pankratova, *op. cit.*, p. 586.

[30] See *Kaz. Prav.,* Oct. 24, 1947; K. Satpayev, "Dva goda Akademii Nauk Kaz. SSR.," *Kaz. Prav.,* June 1, 1948.

Chapter VII

KAZAKH SOVIET ORAL ART

Oral Art on the Eve of the Revolution

Study of the oral art of the period immediately preceding the revolution does not present as many difficulties as study of the earlier folklore, as a considerably large proportion of the more recent creations have been preserved and the names of many of the contemporary *aqyns* are known. It has been noted that after the defeat of the initial resistance against the Russian invader much of Kazakh folk singing became dominated by the expressions of dejection, pessimism, and cynicism of a defeated people. By the end of the last century there could be noted a striking contrast between the new positive, secular literature of the young intelligentsia and the more traditional oral art of the Kazakhs. By the revolution of 1905, however, two new trends in Kazakh oral art could be observed: first, some of the earlier spirit of national revolt was regained; and, second, the beginning of expression of social protest began to be injected in increasing measure in the oral art. It was not until the year 1916, however, that these trends of social and national protest began to issue forth more boldly. In June, 1916, when the imperial government issued a decree calling for the mobilization of the Central Asian population for nonmilitary work at the front, the decree was met by a storm of protest among the Kazakhs, who had never known forced military service. Rising discontent rapidly blossomed into a full-blown revolt, which shook all of Russian Central Asia.[1]

The revolt and its leaders were echoed and re-echoed in a

[1] For a detailed treatment of the 1916 revolt, see Edward D. Sokol, *The Revolt of 1916 in Russian Central Asia,* "The Johns Hopkins University Studies in Historical and Political Science," Series LXXI (1953), No. 1.

vast store of oral creations including revolutionary songs in the old epic spirit, in which battles were celebrated, leaders of the uprising praised, and resistance urged, as well as less militant songs reflecting the more tragic aspects of this era, the lyrical songs, and the weeping songs over the death of heroes.

As in the revolutionary period of the nineteenth century, the new heroes of the anti-Russian struggle took their place in the folk tradition alongside the old *batyrs.* Again the *aqyns* became not only active participants in the struggle, but also leaders and propagandizers, wandering from *aul* to *aul* calling on the people to rise. One of the most outstanding *aqyns* of this period of whom we have definite knowledge was Byzaubaq (Bzaubaq), who composed many stirring appeals to the population in which we find the traditional hyperbolic epical style and the note of national protest of the nineteenth century, combined with a new sense of social consciousness. Here is one of Byzaubaq's songs:

Tsar Nikolai is perplexed and upset:
The enemies' armies are drawing close from all sides.
There are also not a few internal enemies,
Enemies are everywhere, and he's in despair.
And the miserable courtiers cry,
Give him advice, but it's all in vain.
They want to take all our youth,
Since they've not enough soldiers of their own.
But even if we give in to them now,
And send our men far to strange shores,
What will it matter—the tsar will continue to oppress,
Even if we offer our lives for him.
Much suffering is now in store for you, oh my people,
Your forehead is already covered with cold sweat . . . .
But if, as one, we rise against them,
They will not be able to destroy us all, my people!
No, a tsar's heart knows no compassion.
Kazakhs, give now your answer to the tsar!
Is it worth while to live the life of a slave,
Only to reach a good ripe age?
Listen to what the *aqyn* sings to you:
Misery awaits you from the tsar's hands
Even if you offer your son to him.

Go then, my people,
Go then, in war against the tsar!

. . . .

Where are now the *aqsaqals* and the wise leaders?
Or do we no longer have strength in our hands? Oh look!
They are leading your most beautiful ones to the tsar!
Why are you silent? Is there no heart in your breast?

. . . .

Oh youth! You are the beauty of our land!
The time has come! Just listen to the thunder of the storm!
To horse then, and let your steel shine in the sun,
Like a deadly scythe in your hands!
The day of sharp suffering has dawned . . . .
Oh come you all! Close your ranks my people!
Oh place no faith in cowards who speak sweetly to the foe.
To arms! Our land is calling to us!
Oh my people! You are so proud, so strong, so much alive!
Oh listen to my battle cry, to my fiery call!
You will be happy after bloody fight,
After defeating the enemies of your liberty.[2]

The new more realistic trend emerges more clearly in another song, by the *aqyn* Qulbaš, which also appeals to the people to take up arms. This song, presented in the form of a letter to the *aqyn's* brother, is couched in surprisingly simple language with far less recourse to standard folklore devices and metaphors than is found in the poem of Byzaubaq. The *aqyn* asks his brother if he has seen the tsar's manifesto and then describes the preparations for the uprising and the growing revolutionary mood in the steppe.

The times have become evil,
Under the heaviness of the tsar's hand.
What can we expect from the authorities,
Since for them we are but beasts of burden?
Hearts have become inflamed in anger against them,
The *džigits* are eagerly awaiting the rising.
They will not submit to the decree,
But are going into battle.[3]

[2] Bzaubak, "Prizyv akyna Bzaubaka k vosstaniyu," Sobolev, ed., *Pesni* . . . , pp. 343-44.

[3] Qulbaš, "Pis'mo Abdrakhmanu i ego otvet," Sobolev, ed., *Pesni* . . . , p. 340.

In a song of unknown origin entitled "Hangmen" the fury of the Kazakhs at the treatment by the Russians is most impressively expressed.

Rumors are flying across the steppe,
Rumors about human misery.
Ajtkhoža dies under the whip,
And Uzakh under the bayonet.
Above the blue waves of the Issyq-qul
A hot battle took place,
And from the deadly bullet of the tsar,
Many a *džigit* laid down his life.
And in the bloody Qaraqol
Over their captive victims
The authorities have revenged themselves
Behind the steel of prison doors:
Submissively here soldiers were shooting
In prisons, among stone walls,
And our delegates were falling,
Washing the courtyards with their blood.
By night the prison had almost emptied;
They rolled the bodies into ditches and
Ending this bloody business,
The enemy raced towards our *auls*.[4]

While a considerable number of the revolutionary songs had begun to deviate somewhat from the early tradition in their new brevity and acuteness and in their growing realism and relative poverty of traditional epic clichés, many songs of this period remained primarily expressions of the national folklore tradition. These more traditional folksongs, similar to the songs of sad news (*estirtŭ*) and weeping songs (*džoqtau*), were frequently concerned with expressions of grief over the added sufferings of the Kazakhs, who now met death not only on the battlefield, but also in Russian prisons. One of the most well known of the modern mourning songs is the *džoqtau* about the death of the leader of the 1916 uprising, Amangeldy Imanov.[5] Here we find all the metaphoric variety of the old epic songs. Amangeldy's wife calls on the *džigits* to listen to her because "your falcon has

[4] "Palachi," Sobolev, ed., *Pesni* . . . , pp. 337-38.
[5] "Plach zheny Amangeldy," Sobolev, ed., *Pesni* . . . , p. 346.

forsaken its nest." The death of the hero is compared to that of a horse which has tired itself by running and the hero himself is depicted as a "bright mirage, which at noon passed before the people, and then disappeared from sight." When the widow turns her ire against the enemy, the murderers of Amangeldy, her thoughts are expressed in a typical passage eulogizing the deceased and branding the enemies.

May the enemies' eyes be blinded forever,
May their lying mouths become dumb.
How dared they shoot into the heart of our hero,
Whose name was the hope of all the people,
Who from his youth was known as good
Even among foreign peoples,
Who had become eternal friends with
The Tatar, the Russian, the Kazakh, and Uzbek,
Who equaled a sultan in greatness,
Never afraid of the enemies,
Though he did not love fighting,
Whose words were heard and understood
By any man, be he a Tatar, a Russian, a Kazakh or Uzbek?
. . . .
What can the people do now, but compose a song
When there is nothing more for which to live,
When they have lost their leader,
When they mourn the death of their hero,
Who was the master of this peaceful house,
Who was the horse for the horseless,
The warm fur for the unclothed,
Who loved the poor, like a father himself,
Whose house was open for you day and night?

THE SOVIET PERIOD

Attitudes towards the Oral Tradition

The ancient tradition of oral art has continued to play a most vital part in the cultural life of contemporary Kazakhstan; and many of the ancient Kazakh epics, legends, and other oral forms have been recorded and printed and have even been translated into other languages of the USSR.

Soviet attitudes, however, towards the traditional oral art

have undergone constant and considerable revision and change and show conflict and uncertainty concerning the value to Soviet society of expressions of early Kazakh culture. In the early Soviet period attitudes among some Kazakh groups towards their own traditions paralleled the attitude of those Soviet Russian writers who attempted to reject all tradition. There were groups in the twenties in Kazakhstan who seriously disputed the idea that the traditional art should be revived and could become an integral part of the new culture. Such extreme left groups expressed fear lest the glorification and romanticization of the past in the traditional epics evoke a renewed nostalgia for the old order of nomadic life. Thus this frequently dominant group of Kazakh Bolsheviks adopted a rigid and uncompromising attitude towards the national heritage and even went so far as to prohibit the recital of a number of ancient epics such as *Ajman Šolpan* and *Qyz-Džibek*. Such attempts to overcome national traditions through eradication of the folklore heritage were also frequently accompanied by attempts to change the substance of the old epics and folk songs and to inject into them new elements in order that they might express ideas of the new society. Thus old folk melodies and songs were frequently forbidden or performed in an utterly changed form.[6]

In the 1930's, however, as attitudes toward the arts were relaxed all over the Soviet Union in the wake of the successful conclusion of the first Five-Year Plan, and as conditions became somewhat eased in Soviet Kazakhstan, this unyielding attitude towards the traditional oral art began to give way to a more tolerant one and eventually to an attitude quite opposed to that of the earlier Kazakh Bolshevik critics. During the thirties and through the period of the Second World War, it became a generally accepted principle that the old folk art should be revived and widely distributed, and that the oral traditions of the Kazakhs should be valued as an important aspect of the Kazakh cultural heritage. The outward impetus toward the new acceptance of past traditions was very possibly Gorky's famous speech at the first All-Union Congress of Soviet Writers in 1934, in

[6] See T. Zhurgenev, *op. cit.*, p. 19.

which he stressed the importance and value of the study of the oral folklore. This new attitude acted as a powerful stimulus to the recording of the art of the past; teams of folklorists traveled throughout Kazakhstan, recording well-known and half-forgotten epics and other folklore productions, frequently directly from the recitations of the elder *aqyns*. A special organization, the Institute of National Culture, was founded in Alma-Ata in 1934, with the express purpose of preserving the old heritage. A special folklore section in the Kazakh branch of the Soviet Academy of Sciences (KazFAN) was also organized to facilitate the study of the oral tradition. As part of the efforts of this new establishment, exhaustive research on questions of Kazakh folklore was carried out by such Kazakh writers and critics as Sejfullin, Džansugurov, Muqanov, Togžanov, Turmanžanov, and Džoldybajev, as well as by a number of Russian writers and critics as Leonid Sobolev, Academician A. S. Orlov, Mark Tarlovski, and others. By the beginning of the war, the study of Kazakh folklore had become an established science. The Kazakh Academy of Sciences (ANKazSSR) had established an Institute of Language and Literature, with the avowed aim of inaugurating scholarly collections of folklore; and the first volume of the History of Kazakh Literature was published, under the editorship of M. Auezov, devoted entirely to the study and analysis of the popular traditions of oral art. During this time there also appeared the first Kazakh monographs on this subject, as well as the first doctoral dissertations on folklore.

In the period immediately following the Second World War the prevailing attitudes towards the Kazakh folk tradition in general, and some of the heroic epics in particular, fell victim to the rigid and frequently doctrinaire attitudes which have characterized Soviet policy on questions of the arts since the historic decree of the Central Committee of the All-Union Communist party regarding the literary journals *Zvezda* and *Leningrad* in 1946 and the attack by Zhdanov on the Russian writers Akhmatova and Zoshchenko. The views expressed in the party decree were to be of far-reaching effect also in Kazakhstan.

The first official Kazakh echo of the 1946 decree on literature came in the beginning of 1947 in a supplementary decree of the Central Committee of the Kazakh Communist party.[7] This decree, although officially directed at the work of the Institute of Language and Literature of the Kazakh Academy of Sciences, went far beyond this framework and set standards for the writer, critic, and historian of literature and folklore which were destined to set the tone of official and unofficial criticism for many years to come.

In the field of folklore studies, the decree criticized the work of the Institute in the strongest language. The first volume of a projected four-volume history of Kazakh literature, which had appeared under the editorship of the well-known author and literary critic Mukhtar Auezov, came in for specific attacks. This work, which was devoted in its entirety to the epic tradition, was attacked for what was called a "mistaken relationship to the past," for an idealization of feudal traditions, for overlooking the essential note of social conflict in the heroic epos, as well as for certain nationalistic overtones. While the decree was couched in general language, in subsequent articles the new attitude was outlined in more detail and thus the ground was laid for at least a partial rejection of the epic.

The attacks on certain Kazakh epics took two principal forms. Epics were attacked for presenting socially undesirable materials and for nationalist coloration. These attacks were, however, not new. In 1945 one of the standard histories of Kazakhstan, Abdykalykov and Pankratova's *History of the Kazakh SSR,* which was itself a product of the Academy of Sciences, had been attacked for failing to view the past, in the spirit of historical materialism, as a history primarily of class struggle and for having presented Kazakh history rather from the point of view of the struggle for national independence. This, according to the reviewers, had led the authors of the *History* into the pitfalls of

[7] V TsK KP (b) Kaz., "O grubykh politicheskikh oshibkakh v rabote Instituta yazyka i literatury Akademii Nauk Kazakhskoi SSR," *Vestnik Akademii Nauk Kazakhskoi SSR, Nos.* 1-2, Jan.-Feb., 1947 (Alma-Ata), pp. 9-11.

glorifying feudal heroes and of taking a "one-sided view" of the joining of Kazakhstan to the Russian empire.[8]

It was pointed out, as an example, that the authors had glorified such "feudal heroes" as Edige, a Turkic hero who lived in the end of the fourteenth and the beginning of the fifteenth centuries who is the central figure in epics of many Turkic nationalities. Edige had come under attack before.[9]

The Kazakh version of the epic about Edige was condemned again by so high placed a personage as B. N. Stepanov, second director of the propaganda section of the Central Committee of the Kazakh Communist party, in an article[10] which outlined in detail the 1947 decree of the Kazakh party and criticized Kazakh scholars for paying excessive attention to the traditional epos, while ignoring Soviet folklore. The epics *Edige* and *Alpamyš* have since continued to be attacked in the Soviet press for showing a positive attitude towards the khans, for lack of consideration for the common popular masses, and for a glorification of aggressive warfare, carried out for the sake of the conversion of the Oirats to Islam.[11]

While criticism of these epics has been directed chiefly at their "harmful" social content and religious coloration, attacks on other epics and on some of the non-epic oral productions of the eighteenth and ninteenth centuries have been of a

[8] Views regarding the accession of Kazakhstan by the Russian Empire in the nineteenth century had been considerably revised after the Second World War, in line with the general stress on the leadership of the Russian people among the multi-national populations of the USSR. The hitherto prevalent view, which had also found expression on Abdykalykov and Pankratova's *History*, that the joining of the area to Russia had been the result of armed occupation by a colonial power was now partially rejected and the event was pictured as a "voluntary" adhesion which provided the Kazakhs with protection against further aggression from the East. Considerably more stress has been laid since then on the cultural advantages gained by the Kazakhs as a result of the contact with Russian culture.

[9] The Tatar variant of this epic had come under scrutiny as early as 1944 in a decree of the Central Committee of the All-Union Communist party concerned with political shortcomings in the Tatar Autonomous Soviet Republic, and had been labeled an idealization of the feudal period of the khans.

[10] B. N. Stepanov, "Za vysokuyu partiinost' v obshchestvennoi nauke Kazakhstana," *Vestnik Akad. Nauk KSSR*, Nos. 1-2, 1947, pp. 11-25.

[11] See *Pravda Vostoka*, Jan. 29, 1952; *Lit. Gaz.*, Feb. 14, 1952 (on *Edige*), and M. Bogdanova, "Ob epose 'Manas'," *Lit. Gaz.*, May 27, 1952 (on *Alpamyš*).

more fundamental character. The works criticized have been primarily those which celebrated the struggle against the Russians in the preceding century. When Stalin, in 1946, proposed his now famous toast to the Russian people, in which he stressed the primacy of Russian leadership in relation to the other nationalities in the Soviet Union, he set in motion a wave of Russian nationalist feeling. This trend found expression not only in the frequently advanced claims of Russian primacy in the scientific advances of the world, but also in a Russian attitude of superiority vis-à-vis many of the non-Russian nationalities of the USSR, in relation to whom the Russians were considered as "older brothers" and leaders toward progress. In accordance with this attitude, there could be heard, in the years following Stalin's pronouncement, sharp criticisms of works appearing among the non-Russian peoples of the USSR for failing to give proper credit to the role played by the Russians in the cultural development of the minorities. Artists who failed to heed this new line and who continued to write works critical of the Russian administration of the nineteenth century were condemned as "bourgeois nationalists" for having failed to point out what was called the dual effect of the Russian occupation: the negative one of the political and social measures taken by tsarist officials, and the positive one of contact with Russian culture and with Russian revolutionary and democratic thinkers. The assault against these "bourgeois-nationalist" tendencies in the non-Russian literatures was launched, as is so common, by *Pravda* in a leading article in which the Ukrainian poet Sosyura was taken to task for what was called the nationalist tone of one of his poems. Soon after the *Pravda* assault on Sosyura, the Central Committee of the Kazakh Communist party promulgated a decree (August 14, 1951) "Against Ideological Mistakes in Kazakh Literature." In the wake of this decree there appeared in the Kazakh and Russian press numerous articles critical of contemporary Kazakh writers for their lack of stress on the positive aspects of Russian occupation in the nineteenth century and for overly sympathetic attitudes towards the heroes of the Kazakh anti-Russian struggle of the preceding century. There emerged a distinct revision of official attitudes towards the leaders of the nineteenth-century anti-Russian struggle, such as Tajmanov, Serkebayev, and Kenesary Qasymov, as well as towards the oral creations which had arisen about these men and towards the *aqyns* who had sung about them. Kenesary, who heretofore had been celebrated as a national figure of great stature, was reduced to the position of "a leader of the feudal-monarchist movement of the nineteenth century"; and the *aqyns* Dosqoža and Nasynbaj, who sang about him, were now termed no longer truly national creators, but were rather condemned as "court *aqyns,*" servile to the desires of the feudal aristocracy and inimical to the needs of the popular masses.[12]

Despite the new condemnatory attitude towards many of the folklore productions of the past, research in the oral traditions continues as evidenced by the large number of publications of old epics and by the increased number of dissertations on the subject not only of the older folk art, but also on the subject of the disputed *aqyns* of the eighteenth and nineteenth centuries.

Modern Oral Creations

Side by side with the research in, and the rediscovery of, the folklore heritage and the printing and collecting of the ancient songs and epics, there has emerged another trend in Soviet Kazakhstan: the growth of modern oral art. The student of literature and oral art, however, finds himself somewhat at a loss in characterizing these creations. While what we most commonly call folklore is generally considered the quasi anonymous and practically unconscious creation of a people in reflection of their general culture and the most striking events in their lives, in a modern society these qualities of oral art are frequently lost. Modern Kazakh oral art is neither anonymous, nor truly spontaneous. Insofar as modern Kazakh oral art serves primarily as a propaganda function, it is more of interest to the sociologist than the student of literature and oral art. But inso-

[12] See "Do kontsa iskorenit' ideologicheskiye izvrashcheniya v kazakhskoi literature," *Lit. Gaz.,* Sept. 6, 1951; K. Nurmakhanov, "Poema razoblachayushchaya khana Kenesary," *Lit. Gaz.,* Feb. 16, 1951.

far as the modern oral art also developed from the true Kazakh traditional folk art, it can also boast of some literary merit. We might perhaps consider the position of Soviet Kazakh oral poetry as between what is conventionally termed folklore and modern written poetry, and as embodying a propaganda value which is a peculiar characteristic of the arts in the modern Soviet state.

Kazakh Soviet oral art is composed of many new Soviet epics, songs, legends, and tales, which are performed by a multitude of new singers. The vigor of this tradition can be explained not only by the historical heritage of oral art and by the prevalence of social elements in much of the pre-Soviet tradition of oral art, but also by Soviet policies of encouragement to modern *aqyns*. The *aqyns* are given special consideration by the regime and are encouraged to sing and create and to train new generations of singers who will not only be versed in the old heritage, but who will also express the ideas of a new society. Such a folk art, singing of collectivization instead of the nomadic wandering, of Stakhanovites instead of the traditional brave *batyr,* could, it is clear, act as a powerful asset for the political and cultural reorientation of Soviet Kazakhstan.

The *aqyn's* role today is that of a living newspaper and news commentator combined with that of a political agitator. The poetry of the *aqyns* which touched on contemporaneous happenings was of particularly great importance during the first decade of the existence of the Soviet regime in Kazakhstan, when lack of communications and printing facilities and the low general level of literacy so greatly limited channels of communication between the authorities and the masses of the population that, save for the bards, there was no way to reach the inhabitants of far-flung *auls*. In these years, and in many respects also today, the *aqyns'* creations appear to have been largely inspired by official pressures and social attitudes. Not only did the *aqyns* spread news, but they also frequently acted as the propaganda arm of the new government, in which capacity they are still fulfilling a most significant function today.

There are today throughout Kazakhstan a large number of modern *aqyns*. Although it is difficult to ascertain their total number, since many of the *aqyns* are active in relatively inaccessible places, crude estimates range from one hundred[13] to two hundred,[14] and it must be assumed that the number of actual performers is considerably higher since there are innumerable semi-professional *aqyns* in each district, on each collective or state farm, and even in the major industrial enterprises, which are not included in the above estimates. Many of the contemporary *aqyns* are old men who have kept alive the art of Kazakh singing from the past. Probably the most famous of the older *aqyns* is Džambul Džabajev (1846?-1945). Džambul is today heralded as the most significant Soviet *aqyn,* celebrated not only in Kazakhstan but throughout the entire Soviet Union. His work is not only published in Kazakh, but is widely translated into Russian and the other languages of the USSR. Yet this celebrated Soviet *aqyn* can probably best serve as an example of the difficulties encountered by the researcher, whose material is limited to published Soviet sources, in any attempt at arriving at a sober and objective viewpoint concerning the spontaneity of these modern oral creations and the application of the term "popular" to them. There is no doubt that Džambul was an exceedingly gifted bard, for we possess a number of his pre-Soviet works which testify to a high degree of versatility and poetic skill. Yet much of Džambul's work produced during the Soviet period causes one to wonder how much was created spontaneously and how many of his numerous songs about Soviet leaders and other common Soviet themes were written under the pressure of social circumstance. There is some indication, which has come to this author from Kazakh and Russian informants now outside the Soviet Union, that not all the works attributed to him were created by Džambul and that songs of his have been altered by those who have recorded or translated them. A number of younger *aqyns* also have attained fame, such as Sajadil Kerimbe-

[13] K. Altaiski, "Akyn Dzhambul," *Literaturny Kritik,* No. 12 (1936), p. 211.

[14] M. Ritman, "Literatura sovetskogo Kazakhstana," Sobolev, ed., *Pesni* . . . , p. 352.

kov, Ötep Öngarbajev, Gali Ormanov, Qazangan Bajbolov, Tuleubaj Urqumbajev, Kenen Azerbajev, to name only a few of the best known younger bards.

General Characteristics of the New Oral Art

The most traditional group of Soviet Kazakh folk songs are those which celebrate the new Soviet *batyrs.* No longer is the *batyr* a legendary or historical Kazakh hero who leads his people in battle against a superior enemy. The new *batyr* may be an outstanding Civil War leader or a Party leader. He may belong to any of the many nations of the USSR and he characteristically represents the new life of the people. There have been created innumerable songs and legends about Soviet leaders and in particular about Lenin and Stalin. The Soviet leader, be he Stalin, Lenin, or a local Kazakh leader, is often compared in typical epic fashion to a falcon, to a strong young horse, or to a tiger, who is superior not only in strength, but also in wit, before whom all enemies tremble. He is characterized, as were the legendary heroes, as the benefactor of the collective, who leads it, or attempts to lead it, to a better life. There are also maintained many of the other characteristics of the traditional epic style, the frequently high-flown hyperbolism, the characteristic epic repetition and slow movement, and the ever-present typical epithets and symbols used for both friend and foe.

A typical epic treatment of the *batyr* is given in a song by an unknown *aqyn* about the Civil War leader Frunze. From a formalistic point of view many of the passages could easily have been taken directly from any of the older epical descriptions of the hero. There is the characteristic poverty of descriptive material concerning the physical characteristics of the hero, instead of which there are the typical clichés. The hero is depicted as an almost mystical personage whose origin is unknown and who astounds everyone by his tremendous forcefulness and leadership:

He rode through the marshlands, he rode through the grass,
He rode through the yellow dunes of sand.
Behind him in dense blueness,

Thousands of bright bayonets were swinging.
And in the *auls* much talk was aroused
About his strength and bravery, like that of a lion.
"Who is this?" the wind would ask the grass.
"Frunze!"—whispered the grass to the wind.
He appeared as a dream,
His fame carried him on.
"Whence comes he?" the wind would ask the grass.
"Stalin has sent him."[15]

It is not surprising that the image of Lenin and Stalin which has been created should lend itself so easily to an adaptation to traditional treatment in the manner of the old *batyrs,* complete with the miraculous circumstances surrounding the heroes' birth and death and the common heroic metaphors and similes. A typical example is the following song about Stalin by the contemporary *aqyn* Bek:

He is great, his speech
Is stronger than the mountain's base.
He has gathered in himself the tears of the ages,
He has gathered in himself the grief of the ages,
He has gathered in himself the gladness of the ages,
He has gathered in himself the happiness of the ages,
He has gathered in himself the wisdom of the ages,
He has gathered in himself the strength of the ages.
His life is great and simple,
It is unbounded like a dream,
And he, like the morning, arises over the world.
Stalin is the name which the whole world gives him.[16]

Or the following:

Bold, beautiful and strong is the *džolbars,*[17]
The striped hero of the steppe,
But many times stronger,
Many times braver than the *džolbars*—are you!

Sharp-sighted is the falcon, and the eagle of the steppe,
Looking o'er the earth from soaring heights;
But it is you who have brought the people these heights,
More far-sighted than the falcon—are you!

[15] In K. Altaiski, "Zhivyie rodniki Kazakhstana," *Izvestiya,* March 1, 1938.
[16] "Vozrozhdyonny narod," *Lit. Gaz.,* May 15, 1936, p. 1.
[17] *džolbars*—"tiger."

The people know much wisdom,
Having come to the sun from darkness.
But the people follow you, for
Wiser than all on earth,—are you![18]

In addition to epic songs, there are also the modern mourning songs or *džoqtau* bemoaning the death of a leader or popular public figure. This folk poetry follows closely the traditional mourning song repertoire with the characteristic lyrical and mournful tone and the standardized eulogies to the deceased and the personified participation of nature on the fate of the *batyr*. A most common theme of the modern *džoqtau* is the death of Lenin. There is hardly a Kazakh *aqyn* who has not, at one time or another, composed a song in commemoration of the first Soviet leader. A typical example is the song of the *aqyn* Alibek, commemorating Lenin's death and praising Lenin's lifetime activities and achievements.

Like a granite rock you used to stand,
Like a precious diamond you used to shine,
Like a nugget of gold you used to be, Lenin,
The prophet of sickle and hammer you used to be.
Your right judgment was merciless,
With one blow you shattered
The three-hundred-year-old house of the Romanovs.
You have dug up all the roots of evil,
You've burned out the nest of violence from the very root,
Anger and fear are shaking Capital,
To the tsars and *bajs* you were horror,
The cedar bent like a rod.
You have helped us to become people,
You have helped us to breathe freely,
You gave courage to the timid,
You gave us liberty and happiness.

. . . .

Why did you die so much before your time?
Your death has taken a father from us.
Bitter is the weeping of the Soviet people,
Bitter is the weeping of the whole toiling world.
Lenin-*batyr* died before his time;
Oh, may he have eternal peace.

[18] Rakhhim Qulbajev, "Asqan-dana," *Pravda*, May 16, 1936, p. 4.

May his dust rest in peace undisturbed!
In his glory, with great sadness,
In bitter tears, I sing my *džyr*.

In the village of Gorki, which is near Moscow,
Death stood behind his head.
The white snow was darkened by a black shadow,
The sun and the moon were darkened that day,
The whole world was clad in mourning that day,
And in this village, once unknown,
There died my leader, my golden one!
But the mourning will not deprive us of our manliness.
We weep, and yet we march ahead.
Our faith, as steel so blue,
Just like your work, will never die.
Be not afraid, oh father, we, your children,
Shall never deviate from the road you trod;
As before, your guiding star is leading us on,
And your glory will never darken.[19]

In this song there is exemplified a common Soviet theme, the picturing of Lenin as a personal friend whose loss is an individual loss to each Soviet citizen. This tendency is not foreign to the traditional Kazakh epics in which the loss of a leader was often mourned as that of a saviour and father of all the people. The new note is the positive attitude, so common in Soviet literature, with which the song ends, in contrast to traditional note of dejection and sadness which is found in the traditional *džoqtau*.

This new mood is even more marked in the folk songs which are primarily concerned with picturing modern Soviet life. One group of such might be called "songs of contrast." In such songs, particularly characteristic of the *aqyns* Doskej and Nurpejs Bajganin, the past and present fate of the Kazakh people is counterposed. The initial mournful section in which the past of the Kazakhs is depicted in sombre colors is generally followed by a section in which the new life is invariably depicted in gay and hopeful tones. These songs are also rich in the typical colorful metaphorical language of the early folklore. An example of these songs of contrast is the following poem by the contemporary *aqyn* Doskej:

[19] Alibek, "Nash otets," *Lit. Gaz.*, No. 28, May 15, 1936, p. 1.

Between the Altaj and the Irtysh,
Across the steppes Doskej used to wander.
About the great national misery
His songs would sound forth sadly.
For, did not in olden times the greedy *baj,*
The powerful tsar, rule over our people.
Like a pumpkin their bellies
Would grow fat from the people's misery.
The title of *aqyn* Doskej could not obtain then.
He used to drive the cattle over the steppe,
With his melancholy song.

Only at the end of my years,
When I became old and grey,
Like the moon, so silvery white,
Suddenly the falcon of luck came flying
From heaven and sat down in my head.
And standing at the very gates of heaven,

. . . .

Doskej has arisen as an *aqyn.*
Who has caused this, that the old man would start
To sing, when he was already ninety years old?
Who is he?
He is Stalin! Stalin alone
Has prompted the *aqyn* to sing.
For Stalin—is the sun of men!
For Stalin—is the heart of men![20]

One of the most common subjects of the modern Soviet Kazakh songs is that of the settling of the nomads in collective farms and the introduction of agriculture. In the published sources this is depicted as a most happy event which brings to the Kazakh, whether a farmer or a cattle breeder, security from the inclemencies of nature and enables him to augment his cattle holding by scientific breeding. The many songs about collective agriculture are of particular interest in the light of the traditional attitude of contempt for agricultural pursuits, which had been prevalent in Kazakh society.

In springtime, when the earth was awakening,
Messengers brought us a decree from the Kremlin.

[20] Doskej, "Genii mira," A. Drozdov, M. Zenkevich, A. Tazhibaev, eds., *Sbornik sovremennoi kazakhskoi literatury* (Moscow, 1941), p. 26.

And we, like the cranes, flying in the sky,
Crowded together in our fields.

We plowed the land. Our blood was boiling.
In the blue spring we turned the virgin soil—
With the brown tractors, powerful like the black *tulpar,*
And obedient to the rein.

The work was gay, the work was hard,
But our land became soft and black,
And in torrents we poured, like a rich shining rainfall,
The grain, like liquid amber.

. . . .

If now a wanderer from far away lands,
Should ask us, what shines there like sun in the distance?
We should answer that the large patches of gold
Grow from the abundant *kolkhoz* land.[21]

Complementing the songs on the new settled economy are those which depict the introduction of industry, which has doubtless been of the greatest influence in the transformation of Kazakh society. There are innumerable songs which are directly devoted to the development of the oil, coal, and other industries. But the industrial event which has been most often sung about is the introduction of the railroad to the steppes, which was heralded with the building of the Turksib railroad line. This event, which for the first time brought the Kazakh steppe into closer contact with the rest of the country, is depicted in innumerable songs, legends, and epics, many of which are written in the old traditional manner, as is illustrated in the following selection:

A group of scouts has come,
But this time the Kazakhs welcome them.
Like the legendary horse,
The Turksib will be met and greeted by all the land,
And it will warm our hearts with joy.[22]

In many of the songs of the new industrialization, particularly in those depicting the new technical achievements of the

[21] Džambul, "Pesnya o zerne," *Zemlya rodnaya* (*sbornik*) (Moscow-Leningrad, 1939), p. 69.
[22] Abdykalykov, Pankratova, *op. cit.*, p. 522.

country, there can be observed a new trend of realism, which, however, is still strongly tempered by the old folklore formulae:

> Those who used to be slaves and serfs,
> Have now been made heroes by the Turksib.
> The simple shepherd, tempered by work,
> Has now become dispatcher of the train,
> And has thus gained *batyr*-like power.
> He used to herd the sheep, and beat them with the whip,
> But now with steady hand,
> He draws the diagram of railroad traffic.[23]

Frequently these Kazakh oral creations are concerned with propaganda against the old way of life and particularly with attacks against Islam and against the Mohammedan clergy. Islam is pictured as not only the enemy of Soviet power, but also as the enemy of all progress of mankind. This attitude is not only a reflection of the new ideology but was also born out of the struggle of the nineteenth-century intelligentsia to bring to the Kazakh people Western thought and such reforms as universal education and later a new script, all of which measures were opposed by the religious hierarchy. Much of the anticlerical folklore is satirical and light in character, picturing the weaknesses of the clergy and accentuating well-known characteristics. Some of the anticlerical folklore is also concerned with the clash of Mohammedan beliefs and traditional superstitions with modern scientific thought. The following is a typical legend which attempts to combat the traditional myth of the healing qualities of certain Mohammedan saints and members of the clergy:

A long time ago on the river Chu, there was the grave of a saint, and many pilgrimages were made to this grave. An old dervish was living there and, in the name of the saint, this dervish would heal the sick and tell fortunes. I was his assistant. One day I decided to make a pilgrimage to Mecca and set off on an old donkey which the dervish had given me for the trip. On the seventh day of the trip my donkey fell down and died. I sat down near him and began to cry, as I was fearful of the difficulties of the long trip without my donkey.

Suddenly I saw riders approaching on the road. Fearful lest they might accuse me of having killed my donkey by carelessness,

[23] *Ibid.*, p. 524.

I quickly buried him in the ground at the side of the road. When the riders saw from my dress that I was a dervish, they asked me about the reason for my tears.

I answered them: "With my best friend I had started out to the town of the prophet. But my friend died right here, and I am now bitterly crying over his grave."

"Your friend must have led a virtuous life, if you weep so sadly over him," said the riders, who threw me some gold and rode on.

However, I had hardly been able to rest from this experience when I saw from the distance a great mass of people approaching me. These were inhabitants of the near-by town. It seems that the riders had spread the news in town that a saint had died near by. Now the inhabitants had come to beg me to stay and live near the grave of my friend, promising to pay me well for this. It seems that in this town there had never been a grave of a saint.

I thought for a while and decided that the dust of the dead ass might yet be useful to me and agreed to stay. From then on I had plenty of presents and the number of pilgrims multiplied year by year.

One day my former teacher looked me up. He had heard so much about the glory of my saint that he wanted to find out how matters really stood. When I told my former teacher the whole story I thought he would be very angry, but the old dervish began to laugh and to slap me on my shoulder. Then I finally decided to ask the old dervish the question which I had never dared before to ask him. "Tell me, my teacher," I asked, "who was the saint on whose grave you yourself live?"

"That was the mother of the saint on whose grave you now live," my teacher answered laughing.[24]

The outbreak of the war encouraged anew the activities of the *aqyns,* who became again the chroniclers of the battles of their people and who were now utilized directly for purposes of morale building. During the war years there could be noted in the literature of the entire USSR a return to, and romanticization of, the national traditions, even of those of imperial Russia, if they coincided with the goals of the national war struggle. Thus past Russian military heroes were glorified, even those who had previously been condemned for their propinquity to the interests of the monarchy. Generals like Suvorov and Kutuzov were again celebrated in the rapidly growing number of histori-

[24] As told by the horse keeper Bajmurat Nurazov of the *sovkhoz* "Pakhta-Aral," in *Izvestiya,* May 17, 1936, p. 3.

cal novels concerned with previous wars in the defense of Russia. There was a conscious revival of certain folk traditions, as exemplified in Tvardovski's poem about the Soviet warrior *Vassili Tyorkin.* The same tendencies, in a far more accentuated form, can be noted in Kazakhstan. Kazakh *aqyns,* encouraged by official propaganda which stressed the ties between the hero of the ancient epics and the modern Kazakh warrior-*batyr* who fought against the Germans in the front lines or on the assembly lines, began to create an increasing number of songs in the traditional epic style. They returned to many of the epic formulae and the formal characteristics of the epics, mourning and farewell songs, many of which had been gradually abandoned in favor of more contemporary forms and language during the years of industrialization and collectivization.

Typical of such epic works is a poem by one of the older *aqyns,* Nurpejs Bajganin (died 1945), entitled "The Twenty-five."[25] This poem tells of the famed Panfilov Division, which fought in the defense of Moscow and in the ranks of which there were many Kazakh soldiers. The story is told, in general, in the traditional heroic style, with many typical epic images and formulae. The poem is concerned with the defense of Moscow, symbolizing here the Soviet Union as a whole. The poem, in contrast to the epic tradition, centers upon not one but two *batyrs.* One, Tölegen Tokhtar-uly, is a Kazakh steel worker, turned soldier. While he fights in traditional *batyr* fashion, his superiority in battle is caused not by a mysterious supernatural quality, but by motivation of twentieth-century patriotism. Consequently he is not, like his epic forebears, invulnerable and he dies in battle. The other *batyr* is not even a Kazakh, but a Russian: General Panfilov himself.

With the exceptions of the position of the *dramatis personae* and the setting of the poem in modern industrialized Kazakhstan, the poem comes closer to the epic tradition than any other modern work. Tölegen is a typical *batyr* and is compared to the famed *batyr* of ancient times Qoblandy. When he goes to battle, he goes with his faithful lance

[25] *Kaz. Prav.,* December 5, 1943, p. 3 (fragment).

which flew from the rock
Like the eagle, its ancestor.

When Tölegen rides against the enemy, he rides so fast that he has no time to stop for sustenance and so, like the legendary heroes, he bends down in full gallop and plucks the magic root *boryq,* which gives him strength. He rides, like the legendary heroes,

Stubbornly, faster than the birds
He guides his horse straight across the steppe.
And, becoming one with his horse, terrible of sight, winged,
Tölegen races after his detachment.
Look at the *batyr,* my sons!
He shines with the bright light of a full moon.
Who can be his equal? What giant
Can defeat him in hand-to-hand battle?
Who will dare to battle him in bloody struggle?
. . . .
Three days and three nights he flies through the steppe,
He spurs on his steed, straight through the steppe
And completes a six months' trip in three days. . . .

Panfilov, whose stature as a hero is even greater than that of Tölegen, is also a famed *batyr* in the tradition of the epical figures:

Panfilov's glance is like a ray of light, like a golden arrow,
His voice, like the beautiful voice of the eagle.
With his breath he brings fear and death
To the enemy on the battlefield;
His sword hews bloody furrows,
Deadly is the swirling of his lance.
. . . .
When he shouts, the earth trembles all around . . . .

The depiction of Tölegen's battle against the Germans is almost an epic description of an ancient battle scene:

When an eagle arises in the hills,
Let the Volga lands tremble
And the ducks hurry to hide:
The hero's soul knows no obstacles!
Like an eagle, 'midst mountain crags

Powerful in his fighting flight,
So Tölegen, like a storm of the steppes
Flew, circled, blinded,
And left on the field of battle
The thief, now a spiritless corpse.
Like cane on the riverbank in the storm
The enemy trembles and bends to the ground.
Remember: as long as the battle lasts
The *batyr* will not tremble in the saddle!
Hundreds of Germans lie in the field. . . .
Tölegen, the crag, Tölegen the giant
Is equal to hundreds of enemies:
"My anger will answer for me!"

The episode of Tölegen ends with the hero's death at the hand of the Germans, after he has run out of ammunition. His faithful friend sings a traditional mourning song, drawing, in traditional fashion, comparisons to the world of nature, to indicate the magnitude of the loss and the permanence of the memory of the deceased:

When a steed gallops by, a deep track is left behind,
Which hundreds of years cannot smooth out of memory;
When the eagles depart; the craggy mountain heights
remain behind,
When rains have passed, the earth retains its rich attire
And the fields remain covered, like a green rug
. . . .
Poets leave noble words to the people,
The coward leaves behind but accursed shame,
But the hero lives for ages in immortal glory.

Many shorter war songs were composed by established *aqyns* and by new *aqyns* who emerged only during the war years, such as Toleu Qobdyqov, Sapargali Alymbetov, Nurlybek Bajmuratov, Nartaj Bekežanov, many of whom were soldiers at the front. The war songs are varied and numerous. There are short appeals to the soldiers to fight bravely and to live up to the memory of the legendary *batyrs,* songs glorifying specific battles, songs of mourning, as well as a great number of short songs celebrating the *aqyns* as continuing in the ancient traditions of fighting with their words side by side with the people.[26]

One of the most significant traditional forms of singing, the *ajtys,* the singing competition, has taken a particularly popular turn since the war years, and is today being used quite frankly as an important means of propaganda and of mobilizing the population behind government decrees in the economic drives which are continually taking place in Soviet Kazakhstan as they are in the rest of the USSR. *Aqyns* are being increasingly organized, not only in the ranks of the Kazakh branch of the Union of Soviet Writers, of which many are members, but also in the frequent regional *aqyn* conferences, at which singing competitions take place and, it may be assumed, policy as to suitable subject matter is discussed. The first large-scale *aqyn* congress, to which bards from all over the republic were invited, took place in Alma-Ata in May, 1938, in honor of the seventy-fifth anniversary of Džambul's career.[27] One year later, the first of a series of all-Kazakh *ajtys* was held,[28] inaugurating a period of increased attention to this form of singing by the Kazakh government and party. Officials of government and party began, with increasing frequency and frankness, to stress the significance of the *ajtys* as a propaganda device. The Semipalatinsk party secretary for propaganda, B. Bleubajev, stated at the occasion of the All-Kazakh *ajtys* of 1943:

> The *ajtys* is a popular and easily accessible form of political mass work. We are using it broadly for an even higher mobilization of the working people of our district for a speedier destruction of our enemy.[29]

The organ of the Central Committee of the Kazakh Communist party declared in the same year:

> It is clear that it [the *ajtys*] is one of the methods of artistic and political education of the workers. The circle of *ajtys* themes can be

[26] E. G. Toleu Qobdyqov, "Vse dvesti millionov . . . ," *Kaz. Prav.,* December 5, 1943, p. 3; Sapargali Alymbetov, "Akyn Džambul . . . ," *ibid.,* Nurlybek Bajmuratov, "Ya, akyn," *ibid.*

[27] *Lit. Gaz.,* May 15, 1938.

[28] M. Ritman-Fetisov, in *Kaz. Prav.,* September 6, 1947, p. 3.

[29] *Kaz. Prav.,* December 5, 1943, p. 3.

broadened considerably if the *aqyns* will sing not only about events of local importance, but about events all over our country and abroad.[30]

In 1943 the press reported suggestions on the part of the Communist party to use the *ajtys* extensively to encourage the spirit of socialist rivalry in all parts of the national economy; and in October of the same year this suggestion was given official status by a resolution of the Central Committee of the Kazakh party, establishing regular district and republican *ajtys* gatherings.[31] As a result of this attitude, there have been held all over the republic numerous singing competitions in which the rival singers represent different industrial, agricultural, or cattle-breeding institutions which have entered into socialist competition with each other. They may be representatives of individual mines of the Karaganda coal district,[32] or representatives of two major industries, such as the *ajtys* between representatives of the coal and copper industries held in August, 1943,[33] or representatives of different Kazakh geographical regions vying with each other.[34]

These modern "agitational" *ajtys,* which are reported in great detail in the Kazakh daily press, represent a strong mixture, indeed, of the traditional form and the new socialist content. How these modern *Meistersinger* compete in emulating, in song, their industrial or agricultural enterprise, can best be illustrated by a description, taken from the Kazakh daily press,[35] of an *ajtys* between the copper and coal industries. This *ajtys* was held in the coal city of Karaganda. There had been considerable preparation on the part of the participating *aqyns,* who had spent much time at the rival industry to acquaint themselves with the conditions present there. The *ajtys* was held on the stage of the Karaganda municipal theater, against a backdrop which represented the stage as a large *džurt,* with panoramic views of the coal mines in Karaganda and the copper mines

[30] *Ibid.,* August 27, 1943, p. 2.

[31] "Vozrozhdyonnyj ajtys—moshchnoye oruzhiye v arsenale politicheskoi agitatsii," *ibid.,* December 4, 1943, p. 1.

[32] As for instance in an *ajtys* reported in *Kaz. Prav.,* June 22, 1943, p. 4.

[33] *Ibid.,* December 12, 1943, p. 3.

[34] *Ibid.,* November 16, 1943, p. 4.

[35] *Kaz. Prav.* December 5, 1943, p. 3.

of Balkhaš respectively at the wings. The *aqyns* were seated against the panorama of their respective industry. Political leaders of both districts also had been given seats inside the *"džurt."* The *ajtys* began with the traditional treat of *qumys*, which was poured by Kazakh girls. Representing Karaganda was the coal miner-turned-*aqyn* Qošen Eleulov, while the copper miner Šašubaj Qošqarbajev represented the Balkhaš district. The latter opened the *ajtys,* singing the praises of the Balkaš heroes of labor and criticizing the shortcomings in the coal production. Qošen then answered Šašubaj's criticism, singing about the heroes in the coal industry and criticizing, in turn, the copper industries. The audience participated actively in the *ajtys,* as was the custom in the traditional competitions, by interjecting calls and general heckling or signs of approval. While traditionally the outcome of the *ajtys* was left in the balance, until one of the two opponents acknowledged defeat, the results of this particular *ajtys* was not determined, it appears, by the relative artistic prowess of the *aqyns,* but seems to have been a foregone conclusion which depended on the relative production figures of the vying industries. And, the report states, since both industries were working equally well, the *ajtys* ended in a tie.

It is quite apparent that while oral art plays a part in Kazakh life even today, it is primarily the forms of the traditional art which are employed, while the content is a new one, determined by Soviet society and political thinking. Such an unspontaneous and political art can hardly be considered as genuine folklore in the traditional sense of the word. Rather, an old and once spontaneous and rich art is now being consciously fostered and used for educational and political propagandistic goals. This phenomenon, however, which can be understood only in terms of Soviet attitudes towards the role of art in society, is not entirely foreign to the spirit of the traditional oral art, which, particularly in the nineteenth century, had strong didactic and patriotic tendencies. It is this characteristic of much of Kazakh oral art which has facilitated the adaptation of this ancient art to modern purposes.

CHAPTER VIII

EARLY SOVIET KAZAKH LITERATURE

DURING THE 1920's Kazakh literature was still almost entirely dominated by the already familiar genre of poetry, inherited from the rich tradition of oral art, and the few attempts to produce prose and drama were limited indeed. Not only did early Kazakh literature suffer from the inevitable problems which must be met in the infancy of any art, but creative activity also suffered under the many theoretical conflicts concerning the character of the new literature. Contributing to these difficulties was the deep ideological split among Kazakh intellectuals over attitudes towards the new regime and toward the new literature. After the Communist Party Resolution on Literature in 1932, which called for a revision of some policies towards literature and urged a greatly increased program of translations from the Central Asiatic literatures, Kazakh writers began to show more independent activity. Thus the history of Kazakh Soviet literature may be conveniently divided in two periods: that preceding 1932 and that following 1932. The literature produced before 1932 can best be considered in relation to the main historical trends within Kazakhstan: first the period of revolution and War Communism, then the period of the New Economic Policy, and, lastly, the period of the first Five-Year Plan, since in these early years Kazakh literature was particularly vulnerable to the political pressures of the day and since no stability had yet been achieved in the creative activities of the young Kazakh writers.

Kazakh Literature and Cultural Considerations

There are particular problems involved in the evaluation of literatures of recently literate nations, whose historical development has been outside of the main stream of the development of the older world civilizations. In this regard it might be useful to pause here to analyze our approach to the new and growing literature of the Kazakhs.

The first point must be the fairly obvious one that the literary productions of such peoples as the Kazakhs cannot be measured by standards of Western literature alone. We must always take into account the particular Kazakh cultural heritage from which the modern literature emanates. We must also attempt to maintain a developmental perspective, for it is clear that the new and frequently primitive literary efforts of such groups as the Kazakhs would mean comparatively little in the stream of world literature unless continually measured against the short literary heritage these people possess. Finally, no picture of Kazakh literature can be complete without a consideration of those aspects of Soviet theory and practice which have affected, and altered, Kazakh culture and which, therefore, have profoundly influenced the development of the literary arts in Kazakhstan.

Soviety policy in relation to the literatures of the non-Russian nationalities as well as the policy towards the oral art reflected the social approach of the Marxists, who see literature as a social force in the revolutionary process. As literary policy was first formulated, it was based on the slogan that art should be "national in form and socialist in content." In its application to literature, "national in form" referred to three basic elements: language, the historical and literary tradition of a given culture, and so-called "realia." The first element, language, needs little explanation, as it refers merely to the self-evident fact that each literature is written in the national language of the people whose product it is. The second element refers to the historical totality of styles, genres, and imagery which are characteristic of a national literary tradition. By "realia" Marxist theoreticians have understood not merely ethnographic material, but the artistic reflection of national history in the broadest sense, the reflection of society, personality, mores, customs, as well as geographic specifics of a given national culture. However, for the Marxist the term historical concreteness does not imply a reflection of the cultural past alone. Quite to the contrary, the "entire historical process" is understood as not only that of the past, but also, and mainly, the present. According to one Marxist theoretician, these historical "realia" are composed of "all that is alive, revolutionary, and progressive in this process."[1] "Socialist in content" implies the expression, in a "positive" fashion, of the reality and consciousness of the Soviet citizen. Literature is to become "a weapon of society for the education and advancement of all the people along the road to socialism." Thus the new literature should, according to Soviet theory, move towards a synthesis of national traditions and the modern ideology, expressing the aspirations of Soviet policies.

During the period of the formulation of Soviet policies, there were extremist theoreticians who wished not only to reinterpret the past in terms of modern Marxist theory, but who wished to go further and abandon the past entirely. But gradually this position lost favor to the more common approach which held that cultural expressions must not only be socialist in content, but also national in form. However, as will be demonstrated later, the term "national in form" was usually interpreted in such a fashion that many national "formal" manifestations could be suppressed, or at least criticized, for not being in harmony with the "socialist content." Conflicts over ideological interpretations, which were characterized by considerable bitterness and confusion, continued until the thirties, when a somewhat broader approach to Soviet literature, that of Socialist Realism, was formulated, an approach which resolved some of the earlier difficulties but did not prevent the development of later, and somewhat different, problems of interpretation.

Growth of Kazakh Literature

In accordance with the general Soviet attitude toward the literatures of the national minorities, there gradually developed in Kazakhstan, as in the other non-Russian regions, a twofold literary program. There could be observed an increasing trend

[1] A. Sh. Gurshtein, "Sotsialisticheskoye soderzhaniye i natsional'naya forma sovetskoi literatury," *Sovetskaya Nauka,* No. 9 (1940), p. 20.

toward the revival of the national literary and folklore traditions, as well as toward the popularization of the classics of Russian and world literature in translation. At the same time, the development of a modern literature which would reflect the new conditions of Soviet society was also encouraged.

In spite of many obstacles, Kazakh literature actually went through centuries of growth in the space of a few decades. Today the Kazakh people possess a literature, rich in genres, which has been translated into many of the Soviet languages. They have developed their own publishing houses, their own national press, their own network of libraries, and their own writers association, which is an affiliate of the Union of Soviet Writers.

After the acceptance of the new Latin alphabet journalism began to develop on a considerable scale. In 1920, the first Kazakh Communist newspaper was founded, the *Enbekši Qazaq,* "The Kazakh Toiler," which became the official organ of the regional committee of the Communist party.[2] In the same year, only two other central Kazakh newspapers were published in the region.[3] But by 1925, according to Soviet sources, the total number of newspapers published in Kazakhstan had reached thirteen, with a total circulation of 15,000 in January of that year and of 34,000 in May of the same year.[4] The most rapid strides, however, were made after the acceptance of the Latinized alphabet. Soviet statistics tell us that the number of Kazakh language periodicals in Soviet Kazakhstan rose to a total of 100 in 1934[5] and to 119 in 1935[6]. By 1947 Kazakh sources report the publication of 272 daily papers, of which 130 are in the Russian language, 128 in Kazakh, while the rest are in the languages of other minorities in Kazakhstan, such as Uzbek, Uigur, and Korean.[7]

[2] I. Kuramysov, *Za leninskuyu natsionalnuyu politiku v Kazakstane* (Alma-Ata, 1932), p. 95.

[3] Ryskulov, "Sovremennyj Kazakhstan," p. 120.

[4] *Ibid.*

[5] Akademiya Nauk, otdeleniye literatury i yazyka, *Izvestiya,* Moscow, IV, 6 (1945), p. 236.

[6] Dimanshtein, *op. cit.,* p. 32.

[7] *Kaz. Prav.,* October 24, 1947, p. 1.

A similar rise is reported in the field of book publishing. The stress laid by the Soviets on publications of the non-Russian languages can be gauged from Soviet statistics which claim that while in pre-Soviet times books were published in Russia in forty-nine languages, by 1949 the number of languages in which books were published in the USSR had risen to one hundred and nineteen.[8] The rapid rise which book publishing experienced in Kazakhstan after the Soviet revolution and the decisive role which the acceptance of the new alphabet played in this development can be gleaned from the following Soviet figures:

Year	*No. of titles*	*No. of copies printed*
1922	52	18,400
1924	62	183,000
1925	46	408,000
1926	56	434,590
1927	49	420,400
1928	127	1,054,500
1929	129	1,862,730[9]

The above table would indicate that the year 1928, when the new alphabet was completely accepted, was a turning point in the field of national publishing as, according to these figures, both the number of titles published and the number of copies distributed increased by more than 100 per cent. In 1938, as reported in an official Soviet source, there were 266 titles published in Kazakhstan[10] with a total of 6,177,000 copies printed.[11] When evaluating these figures it must be remembered that many of these titles include textbooks and technical materials which were greatly in demand with the sudden rise of education and industrialization. Moreover, we do not know how many of these titles are materials written in the Kazakh language. However, Soviet sources indicate that a not inconsiderable part of the total figures include old and new Kazakh writings, as well

[8] "Izdaniya proizvedenii Pushkina na yazykakh narodov SSSR. (Po dannym Vsesoyuznoi Knizhnoi Palaty)," *Druzhba Narodov* (almanakh khudozhestvennoi literatury), No. 3 (Moscow, 1949), p. 183.

[9] K. S. Pavlov, ed., *Desyat' let Kazakhstana* (*1920-1930*) (Alma-Ata, 1930), pp. 325-26.

[10] *Pechat' strany sotsializma* (Moscow, 1939), p. 39.

[11] *Ibid.*, p. 35.

as classical and modern Russian works. By 1936 the Union of Soviet Writers included seventy members of Kazakh nationality, who had written four hundred published works since the assumption of power by the Soviets.[12] A number of Kazakh writers, as well as several of the most famous *aqyns,* have won the much coveted Stalin Prize in literature. By 1946 the work of the master of Kazakh prerevolutionary literature, Abaj Qunanbajev, had been published in fourteen different editions and had been translated into four other languages of the USSR.[13]

Revolution and War Communism (1918-1922)

INTELLECTUAL CURRENTS. The small amount of literature which appeared during the period of revolution and War Communism was overshadowed by increasingly bitter conflicts between the nationalists and the Westerners. The nationalist poets were still attempting to perpetuate their ideas of pan-Turkism and pan-Islamism while some of the poets of the new era had begun to repudiate much of the past. Nor was this struggle limited to the literary world alone. In its political aspects it became a conflict between those whom the Soviets termed the "bourgois nationalists," and the new "proletarian" writers. In this general struggle, the nationalist movement found its spiritual leader in the Kazakh writer Ahmad Bajtursunov, who attempted to accentuate the past traditions of his people and thus drew, in his writings, primarily from the national but not the social aspect of the folklore tradition.

This ideological dilemma concerning the attitudes towards the past not only caused bitter struggles between the "right wing" nationalists and the Bolsheviks and their sympathizers, but it also divided the Bolsheviks. In their desire to defeat the nationalist traditionalists, the left wing cultural leaders rejected many works of classical Kazakh and Russian literature, includ-

[12] Gusev, *op. cit.,* p. 182.

[13] N. Matsuyev, Ya. Yeletski, F. Fedoseyev, "Ob izdaniyakh khudozhestvennoi literatury v SSSR za tritdsat' let (1917-1947)," *Znamya,* No. 11 (November, 1947), p. 189.

ing works of Abaj and Pushkin, as inappropriate and "counter-revolutionary."[14]

While attitudes of intolerance to the national folklore tradition of Kazakhstan were not popular for long, many radical critics continued, throughout the twenties, to attack the use, in modern Kazakh literature, of elements taken from Kazakh folklore and Kazakh classical literature. This was particularly true of the Kazakh adherents of the Russian literary group "On Literary Guard" (*Na literaturnom postu*), which, under the leadership of the critic Averbakh, was composed of the extremists of the older intransigent "On Guard" group (*Na postu*), who had refused to adhere to the resolution of the Communist party of May, 1924, and had insisted on a continuation of this uncompromising position of war on all nonproletarian manifestations in the world of art. Thus, Mustafa Kaip-Nazarov, one of the Kazakh adherents of Averbakh and On-Literary-Guardism, in an article written as late as 1932, in the official organ of the "On Literary Guard" group, accused Kazakh writers of imitating the old folklore and the writings of such prerevolutionary writers as Abaj Qunanbajev and assured his readers that such preoccupation with the past was merely a method of furthering the aims of the Kazakh nationalists. As Nazarov exclaimed: "We must fight against this rotten idealism in relation to the classics. We must study them, but must not take them as an

[14] This intolerant attitude towards the heritage of the past was found throughout the USSR. One of the outstanding characteristics of much of early Soviet Russian literature was its iconoclastic attitude towards the literary past. This is perhaps best illustrated in the poetry of the Russian futurists, whose most outstanding representative, Vladimir Mayakovski, called in many of his poems for the destruction of the heritage of not only Russia, but of world culture:

> 'Tis time
> with bullets
> to tattoo museum walls,
> Shoot at the old rubbish from hundred-inch maws!
> You are sowing death in the enemy camp.
> . . . .
> But why isn't Pushkin attacked?
> And other
> classic generals?

In Alexander Kaun, *Soviet Poets and Poetry* (Berkeley-Los Angeles, 1943), p. 40 n.

example."[15] It was particularly the philosophy of Abaj Qunanbajev, the most significant writer of the Kazakh past, which came under critical, and frequently hostile, scrutiny during these early years. Many Kazakh and Russian critics and literary historians continued to call his work "harmful" to the new society, because it was, as one writer put it, "a conglomeration of various kinds of bourgeois idealism and theology, against which the party and government must use their influence."[16] More moderate thinkers, however, called rather for a "critical absorption" of the cultural heritage, and acceptance of those aspects of the cultural heritage which were not in direct contradiction to the new society.[17] This attitude of selective borrowing from the traditional writers was further developed, in later years, and became one of the tenets of Socialist Realism.

LITERARY TRENDS DURING THE PERIOD OF REVOLUTION AND WAR COMMUNISM. Among the group of young and talented poets who emerged shortly after the revolution was Sabit Muqanov, one of the most important Kazakh revolutionary poets, who was later to make significant contributions to Kazakh prose, literary criticism, and literary history. Other outstanding revolutionary writers of the period were Saripov, Syzdyqov, Solpan Imambajeva, Bekenov, Tiläp-bergenov, and Sejfullin. The poetry in this period was filled all too frequently with political slogans and clichés and it appeared that at times material was borrowed almost directly from political propaganda posters or newspaper editorials. The new literature often appeared to have been a not too happy combination of the formal folklore tradition and fairly crude attempts to create something new that would correspond to the aspirations of the new society. The main themes follow essentially those of the early revolutionary poetry of the modern Russian poets and are thus primarily concerned with contemporary political actuality, with the Civil War, with pictures of

[15] Mustafa Kaip-Nazarov, "Kazakhskaya proletarskaya literatura," *Na literaturnom postu,* No. 6 (Moscow, February, 1932), pp. 43-44.

[16] See Il'yas Qabulov, "Filosofiya kazakhskogo poéta Abaja i ego kritika," *Sovetskaya Step',* No. 174 (Kzyl Orda, 1928).

[17] See A. Arsharuni, "Zametki o khudozhestvennoi literature Srednei Azii," *Novy Vostok,* No. 26-27 (1929), p. 362.

Stalin and Lenin and other Soviet leaders. Other themes were concerned with the specific political, social, and educational questions in Kazakhstan in the tradition laid by Abaj, and there are in this early poetry a multitude of reflections on the vast changes in the lives of the Kazakhs such as the land and water reforms, the new position of women, and the new upsurge in learning created by the introduction of the new Latin alphabet.

In general, the literature of these early years reflected the ideological confusion which reigned in Kazakhstan during the first years of Soviet power. We find writings not only of nationalists but also of outspoken supporters of the new regime which reveal considerable misunderstanding concerning the issues of the day. For example Sakin Sejfullin, the first Kazakh proletarian poet, who had joined the Communist party as early as 1918, published a number of poems in a collection entitled *Asau Tulpar*[18] (*The Wild Horse*), which show a strange combination of pan-Islamism, pan-Asianism and misconstrued Marxist theories. Thus in a poem, entitled *"Ajt"* ("Holiday"), Sejfullin writes:

> Today is *ajt,* a glorious day
> For all celebrating Islam.
> . . . .
> Today the doors of paradise have opened,
> And true believers reverently made obeisance.[18]

In the poem "Asia," in which the author was clearly influenced by a somewhat confused reading of Alexander Blok's *The Scythians,* the poet warns Europe to keep her hands off the Soviet Union in the following words:

> Treacherous Europe, land of violence, of exploitation and
> cruelty . . .
> Many times have I directed you to the road of truth,
> Many intelligent minds have I sent you. . . .
> I sent my Huns, my Magyars, Bulgars, Moors and Arabs.
> You saw my Tatars and my Turks and Mongols. . .
> Days, years went by: you still have not forsaken evil.
> . . . .

[18] Sakin Sejfullin, *Asau Tulpar* (Orenburg, 1922), p. 15.

To purify the earth from dirt,
I also sent you my Semites
Headed by Karl Marx
Woe, woe, to Europe, if she does not listen
To the voice of justice, to the voice of Asia.[19]

In Sejfullin's career we find typified many of the problems faced by the early Kazakh poets. Sejfullin was born in 1894, the son of a Kazakh cattle-breeding family. He received a rudimentary education at the Russian teachers seminar in Omsk, from which he graduated in 1917 on the eve of the revolution. He then began a rather short-lived career as a teacher in a Kazakh *aul,* which was soon interrupted by the revolution and the civil war. It was as an *aul* teacher that Sejfullin began to write poetry. His first collection, entitled *Ötkön Kündör* (*Years Past*), was published in 1919.

Sejfullin was one of the first Kazakh poets to proclaim his wholehearted acceptance of the revolution, and this fact, probably more than his actual writings, accounted for his great early success as a writer and as a political figure. After joining the Bolshevik party he participated enthusiastically in political work and organized the first Soviets of Workers Deputies in Akmolinsk. With the establishment of the Kazakh Autonomous Soviet Socialist Republic, Sejfullin became the chairman of its Council of Peoples Commissars. Sejfullin's preoccupation with revolutionary activities is revealed by the titles of his early poems, as for example "To The Workers," "Comrades," "The Marseillaise of a Young Kazakh." Unfortunately by the time the program of translating Kazakh works into Russian had taken on significant proportions, Sejfullin's position was no longer secure since he was soon attacked for what was termed his failure to rid himself of his nationalist and pan-Turkic tendencies, and therefore few of his works have been translated.

In general, Sejfullin has had a rather checkered career both as a writer and as a Communist, and the attitude of both Kazakh and Russian critics towards him has varied considerably. His importance, however, for Kazakh Soviet literature cannot be

[19] *Ibid.*, p. 98.

overlooked, since he was the first Kazakh proletarian writer. He was also one of the earliest organizers of Kazakh literary activity, having been one of the prime movers in the organization of the Kazakh Association of Proletarian Writers. In addition to his contributions as a poet, he also distinguished himself in research and in the collection of Kazakh folklore. In the course of his studies, he published two large volumes of collections of Kazakh folk songs, legends, and proverbs. Finally, Sejfullin was the first Soviet writer to leave the confines of poetry and to devote himself also to drama and prose as well as to criticism.

The most important poet of this period, Sabit Muqanov, began his life, like so many of the young Kazakh Soviet artists, as a herder. In 1936 he was elected chairman of the Kazakh Union of Soviet Writers, a position which he has held ever since, and today he is doubtless one of the most important Kazakh poets and prose writers. After the revolution, the twenty-year-old herder "liquidated his illiteracy" and began to study in one of the workers' facilities (*rabfak*) which had been established throughout the country. It was as a student at the Orenburg *rabfak* that Muqanov began to write his first long poem, *The Poor Man of Yesterday and Today,* which depicts the Kazakh herdsman, Qozybaqa, and contrasts his poverty-stricken and traditional life before the revolution with his new role after the revolution as he begins to participate in the establishment of the new political order.

While the contributions to Kazakh literature during this period were not yet of great significance, there did appear new genres: drama, unknown in pre-Soviet Kazakhstan, and prose, which had been only meagerly represented in pre-Soviet Kazakhstan.

The absence of a dramatic tradition in Kazakhstan was partly caused by Mohammedan prohibitions. No doubt other factors which discouraged the development of pre-Soviet Kazakh drama were the constant mobility of the tribal group and the lack of any significant urban population. Dramatic elements were of course important in the oral art in the presentations of the *aqyns,* but formal dramatic art as we know it was not known.

With the establishment of Soviet power, the dramatic arts slowly began to emerge, and by the early thirties drama had become a relatively significant aspect of Kazakh literature. Kazakh drama in its infancy was concerned with two main themes: (1) the revolution and the Civil War and (2) the historic past of the Kazakh people. In the latter case themes were commonly taken directly from the Kazakh epos and historical legend and adapted to stage production. An example of the first type is Sejfullin's *Red Falcons* (*Qyzyl sunqalar*), the first Kazakh Soviet drama of significance. The play is concerned with the Civil War in which the author was an active participant. Sejfullin, like so many of the early Soviet Russian writers, was particularly impressed with the romantic and heroic aspect of these battles. During the early periods, however, it appears that the historic theme and the folklore adaptations were still predominant. The man who contributed most towards the development of the Kazakh folk drama and who became one of the most significant Kazakh dramatists and prose writers during his later creative period was Mukhtar Auezov. He is today most noted for his epic novel *Abaj* and for his contributions to the history of Kazakh literature and folklore.

Mukhtar Auezov was born in 1897, the son of a herding family in eastern Kazakhstan. His education was wide and variegated. Before the revolution, he attended the *medrese* and a Russian teachers seminary and after the revolution he attended the University of Leningrad and later the Central Asian State University in Tashkent, where he obtained a degree in Oriental literatures. By the age of fifteen, the young Auezov had begun his study of literature and had read widely in Arab and Kazakh classics, both of which sources strongly influenced his earliest literary attempts. In general his literary development is typical of the rapid growth of the new Kazakh intelligentsia. By 1918 his first dramas, *Bajbiše Toqal* and *Äl Aghasy,* had appeared in print; and in 1921 the young author wrote his first Soviet play, *Änlik and Kebek,* which is still one of the most popular and frequently produced Kazakh plays. The play is concerned with a well-established folklore theme, the struggle of young love against the marriage restrictions of society. The protagonists of the play, Änlik and Kebek, are unable to consummate their love since Änlik has, according to ancient tribal customs, been sold for a *qalym* to a neighboring tribe and is thus the property of her future husband and his tribe.[20] *Änlik and Kebek* evoked considerable criticism and opinions as to its literary and political merit were sharply divided. In one of the earliest reviews, which appeared in 1923, the play was praised as a real and moving tragedy revealing considerable insight into the Kazakh folk tradition.[21] However, the reviewer brings up a typical shortcoming of early Kazakh drama, its excessive and obvious didacticism. While in 1923 the adherence of this play to the traditions of the past and to Kazakh folk literature was praised as one of its chief merits, a later discussion[22] points to just this element as its greatest fault and as further proof of the contention of Russian and Kazakh critics that Auezov, in the early revolutionary years, had been overly influenced by the nationalist ideas of the *Alaš-Orda* and consequently expressed, at times, a clearly anti-Soviet position.[23] In the early thirties, when campaigns against what was termed "nationalism" in Kazakh literature were at their height, Auezov was publicly accused of a nationalist past which, it was said, was reflected in his earlier works such as his dramas *Änlik and Kebek, Qaraköz,* and *Ajman Šolpan,* all of which were rooted in the Kazakh epic tradition, and in 1933 Auezov publicly admitted to past "nationalist" tendencies.[24] Since then critics have generally acclaimed his later works and have shown a more sympathetic attitude towards his earlier ones. Thus, in 1940, *Änlik and Kebek* was again praised as a realistic play about the past of the Kazakhs in which the author's realism "remains victorious over the tendentious falsification and falsely subjective representation of past as well as present."[25]

[20] The best example of a genuine folklore source in which this theme occurs is the lyrical epos *Qozy-Körpöš and Bajan Sulū.*

[21] T. Sedel'nikov, "Auezov: Änlik i Kebek," *Zhizn' Nats.,* Nos. 3-4 (1923).

[22] Sabit Muqanov and N. Sidorenko, "Literatura Kazakhstana," *Revolyutsiya i Natsional'nosti,* No. 7 (1934), p. 65.

[23] Ritman, *op. cit.,* p. 356.

[24] See Muqanov, Sidorenko, *op. cit.,* p. 65.

[25] Ritman, *op. cit.,* p. 356.

The first beginnings of Soviet prose writings could be noted with the appearance of the first Kazakh novel, Sejfullin's *Difficult Roads,* the theme of which is the author's imprisonment by the Annenkov forces during the Civil War. There also appeared a number of short stories including Sejfullin's *Diggers of the Earth* and *Asia* and Auezov's *Defenseless Woman.*

The Reconstruction and NEP Period (1923-1927)

With the relaxing of the stringent restrictions which had characterized the period of Civil War and of War Communism after the victory of Bolshevik arms on the battle fronts, and with the adoption of the less severe New Economic Policy in 1924, the character of the Kazakh literary productions underwent considerable change. The sloganistic mannerisms of the early poetry were less obvious and a number of writers entered the literary scene who were neither of working class origin nor Communists by conviction. Such writers, who may be compared to the Russian group dubbed by Trotsky the "fellow travelers," including Majlin, Džansugurov, Davletbajev, and Dönentajev, who were characterized by their desire to create more freely, unhampered by party line, discipline, and political demands on literature. Most of the Kazakh "fellow travelers" with the exeception of Dönentajev followed a similar course to that of many of the comparable Russian groups, that of eventual acceptance of the regime to which they had originally maintained a critical attitude.

While the folklore element remained important in the literature of the NEP period, we can frequently note more critical attitudes towards the traditions of the past. An excellent example of the new approach to the Kazakh folk tradition is Sejfullin's long poem *Kokša-Tau,* a simple quasi-folk legend concerned with the well-known theme of the struggle of khan Ablaj against the Kalmyks. In contrast to the traditional songs which characteristically celebrated Ablaj as the leader of the Kazakhs against the infidel Kalmyks, Sejfullin's poem pictures Ablaj as a cruel expansionist and sharply attacks the national tribal leaders. Sejfullin's hero is no longer Ablaj, but rather a simple soldier by the name of Adaq, who is able by superior sportsmanship to win a beautiful Kalmyk captive girl from all the *bajs* and sultans. Particularly striking are Sejfullin's realistic and frequently gruesome battle descriptions and pictures of wanton slaughter, clearly indicating the author's social approach to the traditionally acclaimed victory of Ablaj over the Kalmyks. The following picture is given of the victory orgy of the Kazakhs, a picture which has little in common with schematized victory scenes of the old epic:

> The young ones they tie to their saddles,
> But they hack off the old ones' heads without much ado. . . .
> They are like howling wolves.
> They run into the *yurts*
> And in attacks of bestial fury
> They rip open the bellies of pregnant women
> And pull the young ones from the womb.[26]

A very similar treatment of the past is given by Sabit Muqanov in his poem *Sulušaš* (*Beautiful Hair*) a novel in verse, the first of its kind in Kazakh literature, modeled after Pushkin's *Eugene Onegin.* In this poem also the past is viewed critically and, like Auezov's earlier play *Änlik and Kebek,* the poem is particularly concerned with the evils of the *qalym* and the subordinate position of women in general. Of special interest is the rather incongruous mixture of the traditional form and content with modern political ideology. The story follows in many respects that of the traditional love poem *Qozy Körpöš and Bajan Sulū,* but it ends with a moral, which sounds entirely new. The theme—the unhappy love of Sulušaš, the daughter of a rich *baj,* and Altaj, the son of a slave—is based on an old legend which Muqanov heard in his youth from the *aqyn* Gabdulla, to whom he acknowledges his debt in his autobiographical *My School Years.* Aside from the bare theme, however, the poem has little in common with the legend. Sulušaš is sold for a large *qalym* to the son of another rich *baj,* Rysty, despite her love for Altaj. The unhappy Altaj decides to kidnap his love with the aid of a friend. He enters Rysty's *aul* in disguise, frees Sulušaš,

[26] In N. Dmitriyev, "Kokche-Tau," *Lit. Gaz.* (July 15, 1936), p. 2.

and escapes with her. The poem ends in general disaster: Altaj's friend Qajsar is killed during the escape; Sulušaš herself is wounded by a tiger and commits suicide, and Altaj, having come to the conclusion that private happiness can never be achieved under a social system which allows for economic exploitation, and finding that he should have fought for a new order, rather than for his own narrow happiness, stabs himself.[27]

Among the new political and social themes common in the literature of the NEP period were the position of women, land and water reforms, and the problems involved in the propagation for, and final acceptance of the Latin alphabet. An interesting example of the preoccupation with problems of the day is a polemic poem written by Sabit Muqanov on the occasion of the official translation of Kazakhstan to the new alphabet. The poem, entitled "Complaint of the Arabist," satirizes those who opposed the introduction of the new script, especially the nationalist writer Bajtursunov, who had attempted to introduce his own reformed Arabic script instead of the new Latin alphabet. Muqanov mockingly quotes Bajtursunov as complaining:

> He said—I've given a script
> To my country, just like Mohammed.
> And therefore, I must rule the Kazakhs.
>
> but
>
> The Bolsheviks' strength began to grow,
> The poor themselves took over power.
> Now our alphabet[28] lies in its grave
> And soon we must lie in it too.[29]

There were produced, during the NEP period, a number of anti-NEP poems which reflected the influence of the extremist Kazakh leftist groups, comparable to the Russian "On Guard." Many of these expressed disappointment with the compromise economic solutions and attacked the more tolerant political atmosphere of the times. NEP policies were criticized as bringing

[27] Muqanov, *Sulušaš,* trans. into Russian by N. Sidorenko (Moscow, 1935).
[28] I.e., the reformed Arabic script.
[29] In Fatuyev, "Novy alfavit i poeziya narodov SSSR," *Revol. Natsion.,* No. 3 (1935), p. 85.

about, in effect, the gradual restoration of the power of the old ruling groups. A poem reflecting this attitude is Sejfullin's "Second Class Coach," in which the poet gives vent to his indignation against the NEP policies which he feels will bring about the rebirth of the old order. He bitterly depicts an incident in which a Soviet invalid, riding on a second-class railroad car without a ticket, is pulled from the train by a member of the bourgeoisie.

The period of the mid-twenties marked a milestone in the development of Kazakh literature, for it saw the emergence of a number of poets who grew to considerable importance, e.g., Asqar Toqmagambetov, Abdylda Tadžybajev, Tahir Džaruqov, Qalmaqan Abdyqadyrov, and Galim Maldajev. As the new alphabet was gradually accepted, conditions encouraged the development of a more flourishing literature. One of the most important literary developments of this period was the increase in prose writing. Among the early prose works are Sabit Muqanov's short stories, as well as the first works of the important Kazakh prose writer Gabit Musrypov.

The new developments in Kazakh literature were expressed, in the year 1925, in the formation of the first Kazakh professional writers organization, the "Kazakh Association of Proletarian Writers" (KazAPP), a group which might be compared to the "Russian Association of Proletarian Writers" (RAPP) formed after the dissolution of the "On Guard" group. The nationalists were the only literary group which did not join the KazAPP. They formed instead their own writers organization, which they named *Alqa.* Although the Kazakh writers association and the Russian RAPP were the most powerful literary organizations in their respective countries, in other respects these two organizations differed considerably. The Russian organization (RAPP) was only one of many writers groups in Russia. Others, such as the "On-Literary-Guardists" and the "Serapion Brotherhood" also existed. The KazAPP, on the other hand, was, with the exception of the nationalist group *Alqa,* the only writers organization, and thus included groups of writers of various political shades from the "fellow travelers" to the communist writers. For this reason, there cannot be observed in the KazAPP any unified ideology, or firm platform of literary philosophy uniting all its members, as was the case in the RAPP.

Literary Trends during the Period of the First Five-Year Plan (1928-1932)

The development of Kazakh literature during the period of the first Five-Year Plan paralleled, in many instances, literary developments in Russia proper. In Kazakhstan as well as in Russia, the Plan demanded of each individual all his energy. In the field of literature the Plan demanded once again the sharpening of political lines and the liquidation of attitudes of compromise towards nonpolitical writers which had been adopted after the notable Party resolution of 1924. Writers were urged to dedicate their works to the Plan and to collectivization and to bring, in their writings, inspiration and encouragement to the builders of the new society. By a resolution of the Kazakh Regional Committee of the Communist party the KazAPP, which hitherto had adhered to no strict political formula, was called upon to increase its vigilance in relation to the class struggle and to guide literature to a more thorough Marxist point of view. Among other things it was stated in the resolution that:

> The "Kazakh Association of Proletarian Writers" must spread its activities far and wide. It must strengthen the group struggle among its members and carry on a straight class line in its work among the proletarian writers, working as much as possible to achieve a revolutionary Marxist point of view among the proletarian writers.[30]

Under the pressure of these new demands and the exigencies of the construction efforts, a number of writers who had previously been hostile or indifferent to the regime now began to support the government and its activities. Unfortunately as a result of the scarcity of Plan literature available, we can only make some generalized judgements about the quality of the literature of this period. From the titles of published works during the years 1928-1932 it is apparent that the industrial theme pre-

[30] Resolution of Plenary session of the Kazakh Regional Committee of the All-Union Communist party, December, 1929, in Pavlov, ed., *op. cit.*, p. 321.

dominates.[31] It appears also that with the introduction of modern economic techniques, scientific methods, and industrialization, and with the complementary influx of Russian technicians, engineers, agronomists, veterinarians, physicians, Russian influence in literature was greatly increased. It was actually not until this period that Soviet Russian literature exercised a truly decisive influence on Kazakh literature. It will be remembered that during the nineteenth century Russian literature, particularly the writings of Pushkin, exerted a most significant influence on the creations of such Kazakh writers as Abaj Qunanbajev. This influence seems to have been relatively superficial during the early days of Soviet Kazakhstan when writers were more preoccupied with the recreation of the traditional folk art and with the immediate political problems of the day. During the first Five-Year Plan, however, as the Kazakhs began to be faced with problems increasingly similar to those of the Russians, there can be noted in Kazakh literature not only many themes paralleling those employed in the Russian Plan literature but also the clearly defined influence of some of the foremost modern Russian writers on their Kazakh compatriots. As Kazakh literature of this period is still characterized by the prevalence of poetry over other genres, it is not surprising that the influence of Soviet Russian poets was particularly strong. It was Vladimir Mayakovski, the outstanding Russian bard of the revolution, who seemed to have the most to offer to the young Kazakh writers. Not only did many of the foremost Kazakh writers accept and follow Mayakovski's doctrine of "social command" and lend their muse to agitational purposes, but also Mayakovski's penetratingly declarative verse with its shortened, broken, declamatory lines and its contempt for traditional verse forms began to find its way into Kazakh poetry. The new Russian influence, however, brought its own new problems, for "influence" often took the form of sheer imitation rather than integration. One of the earliest examples of Mayakovski's influence is a work of Muqanov which sings the praise of the newly constructed Turksib railroad:

[31] E.g., such titles as Abdyqadyrov's collection of poems, *Tempo,* and his poem *The Miner.* Syzdyqov's collection of poems entitled *The Fruit of Labor* (1929) and *Achievement* (1931) would tend to bear out this assumption.

For centuries
silently,
for centuries
unhearingly
the steppe
was dozing
from border
to border. . . .
But suddenly
there stretched
into sand-blown
distance—
from border
to border
a road made from steel:
like a mighty
heart
the Turksib
was pulsing.[32]

Concluding Remarks

The newness of formal literature in Kazakhstan and the frequently unhappy effects of political guidance and ideological conflicts all contributed to an early period of confusion in Kazakh literary development. With the exception of the early nationalist writers who rejected the new regime completely, most of the new writers attempted to express the new times; but political didacticism appeared often to be more important than perfection of form. There was not attained during this period any general agreement concerning the role of traditional folklore in the new literature. After the first short-lived attempts on the part of some of the extreme Bolshevik critics to reject the past, most, although not all, of the Soviet Kazakh writers arrived at a qualified acceptance of folklore as the core of the new literature. But in the NEP period many writers again adopted a more stringent attitude toward the folk art. Finally in the Five-Year Plan period many writers began to look increasingly to Soviet Russian poetry for inspiration rather than to the old folklore. It would seem that far too many Kazakh writers during the Plan period assiduously avoided the tradition of oral art and instead attempted, rather prematurely, to create a somewhat forced new poetry. Other writers who remained closer to the national folklore were more successful during this formative period in Kazakh literature, although even they had great difficulties in expressing in their writings a true synthesis of the spirit of the modern times and of the old oral art.

[32] Quoted in Abdykalykov, Pankratova, *op. cit.*, p. 526.

Chapter IX

KAZAKH POETRY AFTER 1932

General Trends

The most significant literary developments in Kazakhstan, as well as in the entire USSR, occurred after the resolution of the All-Union Communist party on literature of April 23, 1932, which called for the dissolution of the RAPP and for the grouping of all Soviet writers, regardless of their political tendencies, into one Soviet writers organization, the Union of Soviet Writers (SSP), with national branches in the various Union Republics. The Kazakh branch (KazSSP) was established in 1932 under the initial chairmanship of the Kazakh literary critic and historian G. Togžanov. This notable resolution meant an important break with many literary trends of the era of the first Five-Year Plan, since policies emphasizing sharp restrictions and the "social command" were now superseded by broader criteria which were less vulnerable to the fluctuations of the political issues of the day.

Critics now began to emphasize the shortcomings of the literature of the minorities as well as the Russians, and the need for a broad program of cultural exchange and for widespread discussion throughout the USSR concerning all aspects of literature was now stressed repeatedly. Two of the stated aims which bear particular relation to the literature of the minorities were the following: (1) a closer amalgamation of the literatures of the various nationalities and increased exchange of ideas between various national writers groups, and (2) an increased effort to revive the literary and folklore heritage as well as encouragement of the development of new forms.

In order to achieve these aims the Union of Soviet Writers

outlined a broad program of action, which included the organization of interrepublican writers conferences and interrepublican writers courses. Russian writers were urged to participate in the work of the new writers organizations of the national republics and there were established in almost all republican writers organizations Russian sections, the journals of which were to publish both Russian literary works translated into the native languages and literary works of the national minorities translated into Russian. Plans were made to publish, in Kazakhstan, the Russian journal *Literatura i iskusstvo Kazakhstana* (*Literature and Art of Kazakhstan*). During the following years there were increasing calls for the development of translation projects. At the First Soviet Writers Congress of August, 1934, serious complaints had been voiced concerning the inadequacy of the translation program of both Russian and world literature into the languages of the national minorities.[1] In 1936, at the meeting of the Presidium of the Union of Soviet Writers, the translation program was held to be too meager and of poor quality. The Presidium called for a "broadening of the work of translations by attracting the best masters of poetry, prose, and drama"[2] to aid in the new effort. As a result of these efforts there could be noted the gradual appearance of a considerable number of works of Russian and a few of world literature in Kazakh translation. In a report in 1937, the following works are listed as having been translated into Kazakh between 1934 and 1937: Gogol's *Dead Souls* and *Inspector General,* Tolstoy's *Resurrection,* Goncharov's *Oblomov,* Turgenev's *Fathers and Sons* and *Rudin,* Korolenko's *Tongueless* (*Bez yazyka*) and *The Blind Musician* (*Slepoi muzykant*), Chekhov's *Selected Short Stories,* Gorki's *My University Days* (*Moi universitety*) (and other works not specified in this source), Demyan Bedny's *Selected Verses,* Serafimovich's *The Iron Flood,* Fadeyev's *The Nineteen* and *Rebellion,* Furmanov's *Chapayev,* Sholokhov's *The Silent Don* and *Virgin Soil Upturned,* Sobolev's *Complete Overhaul* (*Kapitalny*

[1] Speech by K. I. Chukovski; cf. Akademiya Nauk, Otdeleniye literatury i yazka, *Izvestiya,* IV, 6, p. 237.

[2] See Sangurski, "Ob izdaniyakh tvorchestva narodov SSSR," *Revol. i Natsion.,* No. 5 (1936), p. 7.

remont), Yasenski's *A Man Changes His Skin* (*Chelovek menyayet kozhu*),[3] as well as a great number of works by Pushkin.[4] Of non-Russian literature the following titles are given: Defoe's *Robinson Crusoe,* an unidentified work by Jules Verne, *The Arabian Nights,* etc.[5]

By 1936 we can also see evidence of the growth of a program of translation of Kazakh literature into Russian. Kazakh works, translated by some of the foremost Russian writers, began to appear regularly on the pages of the Russian literary journals.

Soviet cultural festivals were another means adopted to increase cultural exchange. In May, 1936, there was held in Moscow a ten-day festival (*dekada*) of Kazakh art. More than three hundred Kazakh artists are reported to have participated in the festival, including the members of the Kazakh State Theater and the Kazakh State Philharmonic Orchestra, as well as a great number of *aqyns.* In preparation for the festival, Russian newspapers and journals devoted considerable space to discussions of Kazakh art, literature, and folklore. A number of literary evenings were given over to Kazakh literature and folklore, and the famous Moscow theaters were opened to Kazakh actors. The Kazakh musical dramas *Qyz-Džibek* by Musrypov, based on the old epic tradition, and Bejimbet Majlin's *Džalbyr,* also based on folklore material, were performed; and the Bolshoi Theater included in its program a series of Kazakh ballets and a Kazakh concert program in which the Kazakh national philharmonic orchestra, a Kazakh choir, and a great number of *aqyns* participated.

One notable concomitant of the initiation of cultural exchange was the re-examination of the Soviet theoretical approach to literature. The earlier slogan "national in form and socialist in content" was now considered inadequate and was replaced by the newly formulated theory of Socialist Realism. Socialist Realism was interpreted as the new guiding literary theory which called for a portrayal of the present and the past realistically,

[3] Sejfullin, "Pisateli Kazakhstana" (Speech at Fourth Plenary Session of SSP), *Lit. Gaz.* (March 10, 1937), p. 4.
[4] "Izd. proiz. A. S. Puskina . . . ," pp. 184-85.
[5] Sejfullin, "Pisateli Kazakhstana."

but with a direction which would appear to offer a message of optimism. Such a message, however, was not to be confused with romantic utopianism. The success of socialism was to be presented as inevitable, yet to be won only through the constant efforts of the people. The unrealistic and romantic attitude, expressed by certain groups, that the past had no further value would be abandoned; but, on the other hand, the past was not to be viewed uncritically since it was to be considered from the perspective of the socialist present and the communist future. The aim was the creation of a new synthesis of the old culture and modern values, and the role of the Socialist Realist artist was to depict and probe this new process. The artist would concern himself not only with the social problems of the new era, but also with the problems of the individual in the new society, and would, in effect, bring society closer to the people.

In relation to Kazakh literature, Socialist Realism implied, among other things, a more conscious, but qualified, utilization of the oral tradition. But with the new stimulus to a partial return to the traditional forms came also the repeated warning concerning the writers' duty in the battle for socialism. As the Russian critic Selivanovski put it:

> . . . closeness to folklore does not exclude but, on the contrary, presupposes the overcoming of narrowly local themes as well as of conservative traditionalist forms.[6]

The new theories, new organizations, and increased cultural exchange altered some problems, but also created many new ones. Considerable resentment was felt by local writers towards the Russian writers who were accused of overlooking the literary talent in the non-Russian regions. Kazakh writers frequently complained bitterly that their organization was treated as a stepchild by Russian writers, that they rarely, if ever, visited Kazakhstan. Thus, in 1937, the Kazakh writer Sakin Sejfullin, speaking at the fourth plenary session of the SSP, decried what he considered the unco-operative spirit of most Russian writers

[6] A. Selivanovski, "Zametki o kazakhskoi literature," *Lit. Gaz.*, May 1, 1936, p. 5.

who were said to ignore Kazakh literature.[7] Similar grievances were voiced at this session by other non-Russian writers groups.

On the other hand, many Russians were critical of the members of the non-Russian writers organizations. Kazakh writers were told that their writings did not sufficiently reflect Soviet problems and that too many writers had remained indifferent to what were termed "hostile elements" in the literary world of Kazakhstan. Such elements were said to include extreme left groups which still maintained an intransigent attitude towards the national heritage, and nationalist groups, which were held to constitute the greatest danger. Thus one writer stated:

> At a time when the literary public of the country is mobilizing to destroy and root out Averbakhism . . . and to fight against bourgeois nationalism, the leadership of the Kazakh Writers Union passes these questions by completely. . . . We wonder whether in reality it would not behoove the leadership of the SSP of Kazakhstan to start their activities of unmasking [hostile elements] within their very midst. Take for example the chairman of the SSP of Kazakhstan, Sabit Muqanov. Sabit Muqanov . . . in his words speaks against hostile class elements . . . in literature. But his actions belie his words.[8]

In general the year 1937 represented a period of sharpest attack against what were considered the two main "deviations" in the national republics, nationalism and leftism (Averbakhism). We find similar statements concerned also with other Central Asiatic literatures, particularly that of Kirghizia[9] and of Uzbekistan.[10]

After the resolution of 1932 certain new trends gradually began to develop in Kazakh literature, reflecting the new literary approach which had been urged on the writers. Kazakh writers began to concern themselves in increasing measure with broad

[7] Sejfullin, "Pisateli Kazakhstana."

[8] Anur, "V soyuze pisatelei Kazakhstana," *Lit. Gaz.*, September 26, 1937, p. 3.

[9] Anur, "Razoblachit natsionalistov do kontsa! V soyuze pisatelei Kirgizii," *Lit. Gaz.*, September 15, 1937, p. 5.

[10] "Aktivno pomoch bratskim literaturam," *Lit. Gaz.*, September 20, 1937, p. 1.

contemporary problems and with pan-Soviet themes. There was organized, for example, a special Kazakh competition to encourage writers to use the theme of the Chelyuskin polar expedition in which Muqanov obtained first prize for his poem *The White Bear*. Other Soviet subjects which were treated in the literature during the early years after the first Writers Congress included Kirov's death and the anti-Trotsky campaign. Increased attention also began to be paid to the Russian classics as well as to modern Russian literature. This period marked the beginning of a new growth in the literatures of the Soviet Central Asiatic peoples. There can also be noted the more forceful emergence of the new genres, prose, drama and even criticism, although poetry was still to remain the dominant form of the new Kazakh literature.

The general strictures which were impressed upon the arts in the USSR after the Second World War,[11] and which have already been noted in relation to the oral art of the Kazakhs, sharply affected literature also. The strong demands for more ideological content (*partijnost'*) and for a revised attitude towards the Russians have had far-reaching effects on much of the postwar writing in Kazakhstan. Many of the foremost Kazakh writers have become, as a result of this new line, victims of the campaign against "bourgeois nationalism," which has been renewed with increased vigor. Another result of the recent pronouncements has been official criticism[12] of the literary section of the Kazakh Academy of Sciences for neglect of Soviet letters in Kazakh literary scholarship and for a "mistaken" interpretation of the cultural heritage.

POETRY

The literary scene in the 1930's was marked by the emergence of many younger poets, such as Asqar Toqmagambetov, Abdylda

[11] See the Party decree on literature of August 14, 1946, *Pravda*, August 21, 1946.

[12] See V TsK KP (b) Kaz., "O grubykh oshibkakh. . ."; Stepanov, *op. cit.*, S. K. Kenesbayev, "O realizatsii Postanovleniya TsK KP(b)K 'O grubykh politicheskikh oshibkakh v rabote Instituta yazyka i literatury AN KazSSR,'" *Vestnik ANKazSSR*, no. 3, 1947, pp. 13-16.

Tadžybajev, Tahir Džaruqov, Qapan Satybaldin, Džumagali Sajn, and others who flourished under the more permissive climate of the times.

It has been noted that many of the critical debates of the thirties were concerned with the problem of synthesizing the ancient traditions and the modern socialist culture, in line with the dictum that art should be national in form and socialist in content. In the twenties there had been relatively little success in this direction, and poetry frequently impressed the reader as being propelled in opposite directions. Poets who drew most directly and immediately from the oral traditions rarely succeeded in imparting a new spirit and a new content; on the other hand, many poets who were concerned with the new forms life had taken disregarded the formal traditions of oral poetry and succeeded merely in creating a poetry which sounded artificial and stilted.

In the thirties we again find Kazakh writers adopting two divergent approaches. The first, and most common, approach, and clearly the more natural one in the context of Kazakh culture, sought to integrate folklore traditions into modern poetry. While we still find many of the metaphors and epithets typical of the old folklore in this poetry, these techniques are increasingly employed in a purely formal, almost automatic, fashion, and the development, on the part of these poets, of a new characteristic form and style can be observed, a style which moves somewhat closer to the desired synthesis of the formal aspects of the folk tradition, the philosophical and intellectual aspects of nineteenth-century Kazakh and Russian poetry and Soviet Russian poetry with its new content.

The second, and as yet the more rare, approach depended for inspiration almost entirely on postrevolutionary Russian poetry. A considerable body of Kazakh poetry, particularly of late, shows the immediate influence of the flamboyant revolutionary style of the Russian poet Mayakovsky. The most significant follower of Mayakovsky in Kazakh poetry is doubtless Sabit Muqanov, whose earlier poem on the Turksib railroad has already been mentioned. The following is a selection from a more recent programmatic poem by Muqanov dedicated to Mayakovsky. It is entitled "Marshal of Poetry":[13]

Warmed by Stalin's thought
and heart,
In firm hands
we gripped our pens.
We love
and proclaim
our country,
Crushing our enemies
like a furious storm.
Engineers of souls
justly
Calls us
Stalin
the great.

The poem ends with a typically Mayakovskian phrase addressed directly to Mayakovsky:

I finished my verse;
you have the floor;
Marshal of Soviet poetry!

The poem represents a report to the Russian poet concerning the new themes of Kazakh poetry, and the new adherence to Mayakovsky's dictum of the "social command."[14]

[13] In Dmitri Moldavski, "Mayakovski i poeziya sovetskogo Vostoka," *Zvezda,* No. 4 (April, 1949), p. 167.

[14] The literatures of other Central Asiatic nationalities also show the influence of Mayakovsky, both in form and in ideas. One of the most typical and probably also one of the most significant of these Mayakovskian poems is a poem by the Kirgiz poet Džusup Turušbekov, entitled "Listen, World!"

Universe, listen! Listen, entire world!
Shanghai! Paris!
To you the poet calls!
Hear, entire world,
that which has happened
in fifteen years
of our great victories! (*Ibid.*, p. 170.)

The poetry of the Uzbek poet Gafur Gulyam also reveals typically Mayakovskian language. His poem "Standard Bearer" shows the direct influence of Mayakovsky's poem *"Vo ves' golos"* ("With All My Voice"):

I, in battle
and in terrible sieges
am only
a nameless private
giving his all to the struggle. (*Ibid.*, p. 168.)

The Older Generation of Poets

SABIT MUQANOV. Muqanov, one of the first Kazakh poets to answer the call of the revolution, was until 1928 primarily concerned with treating the Kazakh past. But with the initiation of the first Five-Year Plan, Muqanov's writings began to show the influence of modern Russian poets, particularly Mayakovsky. The influence of Soviet Russian form and content became even more pronounced after 1932 when Muqanov went to study at the Institute of Red Professors (*Institut krasnoi professury*). In close contact with Russian fellow-students, he came to know Russia and, through Russia, the world beyond her boundaries. His poetry began to lose its close ties with the epic tradition as he began to write increasingly on pan-Soviet themes, as is indicated by the titles of many of his poems of the thirties: "Welcome, May!," "Bolshevik Autumn," "Parade," "The Great Gardener" (Stalin), and "Marshal of Poetry" (Mayakovsky). Though elements of the Kazakh oral tradition never disappear completely from his verse, Muqanov, as the first significant Kazakh poet to lessen his dependence on traditional forms and to experiment with new techniques, was in many ways the initiator of a new approach which was to make itself felt most pronouncedly in the poetry of the younger Kazakh poets. In addition to the great influence of Mayakovsky, Muqanov was also strongly influenced by Pushkin. Actually, few Kazakh poets of the Soviet period have drawn as much inspiration from Russian classical poetry as did Muqanov. The dual influence of the warm, lyrical, and yet incisively realistic poetry of Pushkin and the exuberant, flamboyant verse of Mayakovsky is apparent in one of Muqanov's first poems of the later period: "Welcome, May!"[15]

The poem begins in a fashion quite untypical of traditional Kazakh poetry, as the poet greets the month of May as the symbol of awakening spring. The enthusiastic nature portrayals and the close, almost pantheistic relationship of nature to man vividly recalls the vibrant nature poetry of Pushkin.

[15] Muqanov, "Zdravstvui mai," Sobolev, ed., *Pesni. . . .*, pp. 473-74.

Welcome, May, my long-time comrade,
Gay fellow of my youthful days!
The apples and the cherries hail your welcome,
The lark devotes his song to you.

I sing the song which
Walked, with man, the forest of the ages,
As he warmed glaciers and mountains
As well as the woods and pastures of the native
land with his tune.

Remember, May, how on slanting slopes
I used to plow the furrows patterned like
Astrakhan fur,
So that, in green whisks, the oats
Could celebrate the month of May.

In sandy wastes—I dug *aryqs* for you
So that from border to border fields would lie
As on a chessboard. Oh, my sunny comrade,
For you—my pick-axe, my labor, and my harvest.

The earth's surface has become bright and gay,
So much like a Persian rug.
Accept, my friend, my simple present.
Who can say that this present is not fine?

Here I am singing on your birthday,
And celebrating you with my songs,
Loving your walk, the very beating of your heart
And your youth.

Be welcome then! Roar in the hearts and in
the birchtrees,
Sound forth in rivers, bend the grass,
Grow in the shops, in mines, and in *kolkhozes!*
Be welcome, for you're the earth's best guest.

But in the second part of the poem Muqanov leaves his quietly flowing and enthusiastic nature lyricism and turns to a depiction of the role of the poet. Here sound not only the views of Abaj, but also, and much more forcefully, the conception of Mayakovsky of the poet as an important cog in the gigantic machine of socialist construction and as a soldier in the army of revolutionaries:

I can't sit still, I dig and search,
Under the clouds and in the earth,
For my melodious songs I find my food,
My mind is keen, I know no fear.

In battle dust I bend like a metal spring,
So that my sword may beat upon the enemy's chest.
I am but part of a machine; and my machine bears
The trade-name "Marx and Lenin." Just look:

On one sixth of the great wide earth
We have erected a factory for this machine.
We are storming forward under a strong commander—
Comrade Stalin leads us on!

Regiments of workers are streaming from all sides,
And I, like a banner, have raised my song;
I am a son of the earth and I am its master,
Poet and stonemason march side by side.

Then, after depicting in rather conventional colors the difficulties and hardships of the past and, much in the manner of the Soviet *aqyns,* contrasting it to the new life, Muqanov finishes by celebrating May First, the holiday of the workers, the day when "in the collective farms, in the cities, we tighten our workers' ranks." Again the poem echoes typically Mayakovskian accents:

Comrade May, into the ranks of the workers' army
I have been called together with my fighting song.
I am a standard bearer, a Bolshevik, a shock-brigader,
I am a bugler, calling to battle.

This poem is in the strongest contrast to traditional Kazakh poetics. It lacks almost completely the hitherto prevalent metaphoric language derived from the ancient epics. In only one instance, when the old *bajs* are compared to tigers, does Muqanov return directly, though in a purely formal fashion, to tradition.

The same mixture of lyrical nature contemplation and new realism can be observed in a poem which was written in 1936, "The Day of the *Kolkhoz Aul*."[16] The author depicts, through the reactions of an old *kolkhoz* watchman who is observing an

[16] Muqanov, "Den' kolkhoznogo aula," Drozdov *et al.*, eds., *Sbornik,* p. 236.

average day on his collective farm, the problems and aspirations of the new Kazakhstan and the Soviet Union as a whole. In realistic colors, totally unlike earlier Kazakh writing, the poet tells of harvest time on the collective farm. There is no mention of the old *batyrs* and little use of epic metaphors and imagery, although some similes utilizing the animals of the old nomadic herding culture are still found. No longer do the inventions of modern technology appear as something supernatural to the poet which should be depicted in terms of the traditional mythos.

> The warm earth resounds.
> There, leaving the trace of his iron hoofs,
> Runs, snorting like a horse, the powerful tractor,
> And the tractor is guided by a *džigit*.
>
> Behind the tractor the combine follows
> On the golden roadless field.
> The grain rustles with its heavy ears,
> Though hardly a wind stirs it.
>
> As an icecutter breaking the ice with its bow,
> The combine is breaking a road for itself
> And cuts the grain, as one cuts the wool of a sheep.
> . . . .
>
> Like a mountain stream the grain is flowing,
> Heaps of fresh straw are growing.
> The five-ton truck is loaded with wheat
> And takes it to the *kolkhoz* village.

This realistic description of a harvest scene is followed by a lyrical, musical depiction of the evening after work is over and harvesting completed. These stanzas again recall Abaj's nature poetry and the lyricism of Pushkin and Lermontov. Here again the ancient oral tradition, with its poverty of lyrical nature scenes, is forsaken:

> Now in Stakhanovite fashion the day is ended,
> And a lilac shade is settling all around.
> The swans are swimming on the lake,
> Too lazy to move their wings.
>
> Above the lake the air is tranquil,
> The reeds, as charmed, stand still and silent,

The velvet grass stands calm and quiet.
Oh, stillness, you are nature's own.

Trunks of birches, silver covered, stand,
Foliage hangs like a tent of green,
The willow tree lifts its heavy branches
Over the dreamy swans' lake.

Dreamy sounds the water's splashing,
Gardens fill the air with the aroma of fruit.
Drink in, like *qumys,* this heady air,
As your best reward for your toil!

Although Muqanov does not usually employ the more obvious folklore metaphors, his poems frequently abound in metaphorical language, but his imagery is taken from the new conditions of life and technology. Thus in another poem, "The Great Gardener,"[17] dedicated to Stalin and the Soviet Constitution of 1936, the poet employs the traditional device of picturing himself flying above the earth and reporting what he sees. But where in olden times he would have compared himself to a sharp-sighted eagle or hunting falcon, and his pen with their wings and eyes, he now writes:

My pen—my steel wings—
Never tires. Freely and without effort
I fly high above the earth.

Occasionally, however, we find, interwoven with the realistic depictions, modern imagery or lyrical reflections, traces of the ancient epic language. We are told that the old watchman is as untiring in talking as the legendary *dželmaj*[18] is in running. The tracks of the tractor are compared to "steel hoofs," while the tractor itself is represented as a snorting horse. These instances, however, generally constitute but fleeting remembrances from which the poet rapidly passes on to more modern pictures. There are times, however, when the use of folklore language is particularly striking. This is especially true in a poem, written

[17] Muqanov, "Veliki Sadovod," Sobolev, ed., *Pesni . . .* , p. 470.

[18] *dželmaj* (*džel-maja*)—a legendary camel which, according to folk tradition is "as large as a haystack and as fast as the wind." Radloff, *Opyt slovarya . . .* , IV, 81.

in 1935, entitled "The Two Eagles."[19] The eagle, the horse, and the falcon were, it will be remembered, the most popular folk figures employed to characterize the *batyr*. In this poem the two eagles are Lenin and Stalin. The poem begins with a description of their first meeting in 1905 in Tammerfors. The poem itself harks back to the folklore style, glossing over details, giving few external descriptions of the heroes, and simply recording their heroic, almost supernatural, actions:

> That memorable night, the storms were howling
> And the mountains of the Caucasus were trembling,
> And over Mount Elbrus, on frozen wings
> An eagle flew against the wind.
>
> This eagle was Stalin. The wind against him
> Beat at his eyes, but knowing storms,
> The eagle flew where the stars were shining
> O'er Tammerfors, a Finnish town.
>
> O'er woods and plains
> He had heard the older eagle's call:
> "My bold brother, leave for a while your mountains,
> And fly to me as fast as your wings allow!
>
> From now on we must fly together—further . . ."
> And through the storm
> Our eagle flew to the far away lake region,
> Following Lenin's voice.

The two eagles meet and flying together break the dark clouds of night to bring light and sunshine to the people. But the older eagle dies from the bullet of the enemy who, well knowing for whom to prepare the bullet, had long lain in wait "like a snake." Now the younger eagle, Stalin, must complete Lenin's work.

While there can be noted some traces of the formal techniques of folk art in Muqanov's poems, he never returns to traditional subject matter. His concern is partly with lyrical depictions of nature, but primarily it is with problems of the new society, its new heroes, the laboring people, technicians, engineers, and explorers. He writes poems about the Kazakh poor before

[19] Muqanov, "Dva orla," Sobolev, ed., *Pesni. . .* , p. 472.

the revolution ("The Poor Man"), about the revolutionary days in Kazakhstan ("October Crossings"), about socialist construction and the Five-Year Plans ("Turksib," "The Corner," "Communism"), and about outstanding citizens of the USSR ("Marshal of Poetry," "The Great Gardener").

OTHER POETS OF THE OLDER GENERATIONS. One of the more significant of the older poets is Džahan Syzdyqov, whose lyrical and musical writings reveal a mature and sensitive perception of nature. Delicate and subdued shades of colors make Syzdyqov's poems particularly effective:

> Evening time, ruled by silence,
> And a dream—beautiful as a legend! . . .
> I see the cold glitter of the wave,
> And hear the proud breathing of the Irtysh.
>
> I see wisps of white foam,—
> And winding, like a snake in the sand,
> The river carries it triumphantly
> When the moon pours out its smile.
>
> My Irtysh! Cold like mica,
> He is not always speechless;
> And sometimes near the Elk Mountain
> One hears the roaring rustle of eagles' wings.
>
> In the roaring of the waves I hear the eagles calling,
> The waves run faster than an arrow.
> My Irtysh sings a song that is bold,
> And terribly he beats on the old rock.[20]

Poets of the older generation who did not move so far from folklore in this second decade include Sakin Sejfullin. Though his works no longer reveal nationalist sentiments, they are still steeped to a considerable degree in the old folklore tradition, and this trait remains one of the outstanding characteristics of Sejfullin's writings. But even Sejfullin, who was decorated with the Order of the Red Banner of Labor in 1936,[21] is concerned almost entirely with modern subjects. His long poem *Red Horse* is concerned with the problem of collective horsebreeding farms and with the social enmities in the *aul*. His poem *Albatros*

[20] Džahan Syzdyqov, "Tainy gor," Sobolev, ed., *Pesni. . .* , p. 517.
[21] *Lit. Gaz.,* May 30, 1936, p. 1.

describes in large outlines the birth and growth of Soviet Kazakhstan. Titles of his many smaller poems such as "In Stalin We See You, Oh Lenin!" also indicate his concern with modern political themes.

Another poet who composed poems particularly reminiscent of the older folklore is Mukhtar Auezov, about whom more will be said in the section on prose writings. In his prose poem, "I, the Kazakh Song, Am Singing," there are considerable allusions to the folk tradition. The form of this work is interesting since the lyrical, reflective prose writing employed in this work was hitherto unknown in Kazakh literature. The musical quality of this poem and the vibrant sentiment easily reveal the considerable talent of Auezov, who combines, probably more successfully than any other Kazakh writer, the two genres of prose and poetry. The lyric is an imaginary soliloquy of a Kazakh song personified and while the form is an innovation, the content is based on the now traditional counterposition of the past and present Kazakhstan. At times the enchanting pictures are reminiscent of the warm and full-colored pictures given to us by Gogol, and then again they recall the more delicate pastel shades of Turgenev's nature pictures:

> The winds were chasing the grassy steppes to the mountain heights. Little gurgling streams were meeting these steppes. Over these steppes the song was wandering like a nomad. . . . Listen to it, listen, as closely as you can to this olden song of the Kazakh.
>
> I used to sing in olden times when, raising dust up to the skies and drinking the rivers dry, innumerable hordes of the tribal confederations were wandering. The sultans used to smile, caressing beautiful captive girls as well as the wives of my people, who could be considered little more than prisoners. And the people, hungry, suffering and tired, looked up into the full sky. Sadly I sang then!
>
> I sang when metal guns, looking for conquest . . . , roared with deadly thunder, desiring to tear out my throat. Mournfully I sang when, wandering on sandy hillocks, undulating like my thoughts, I went far away into the high rocks which were filled with clouds. I hid in the mountains.
>
> It was cold when I grew up there. I used to sing slowly and sadly, as slowly as the glacier melts, about the steppe suffering from

drought. Like a shepherd I stood amidst the craggy rocks. And as before, the hollow sky was above me and long, dark nights were around me, and the women suffered, and my sister suffered and my mother suffered. . . .

And suddenly I began to sing with a young, gay voice.

The stone *balbals*[22] which had, like me, also stood for thousands of years, seemed to raise their stone arms in amazement and reach forward. Grazing lands moved and changed. . . . They disappeared and melted into beautiful cities, my cities. . . . And suddenly the Kazakh, who used to look to the mountains, which were always higher than his dreams, who once looked on the mountains with fear, saw at last that he was their equal. And suddenly the nomad, who had always thought the brooks faster than he, caught up with them. And suddenly the tent dweller rose into the sky and in one day—no, in less, in half day or in a quarter—traveled over the entire steppe! Man placed a bridle on the steppe, caught up with it, caught its head in a firm grip and now he is laughing and his face is covered with rosy color. . . .[23]

The Younger Generation of Poets

ASQAR TOQMAGAMBETOV. One of the most talented of the younger poets is Asqar Toqmagambetov, who was born in 1903 in Southern Kazakhstan in a poor cattle-herding family. It was not until 1928 that his first collection of poems, entitled *Collection of Labor* (*Änbek Žynagy*) appeared, followed, one year later, by another volume, *Songs of Labor* (*Änbek Žyry*). His vivid style immediately called attention to this newcomer on the Kazakh literary scene. He is today a recognized master of Kazakh poetry and is particularly known for his ability to report and interpret current events in his writings almost as quickly as history is made, a technique which he undoubtedly acquired during his early career as an *aqyn*.

Toqmagambetov's political interests soon drew him away from the *aul* into the city, where he became a journalist, creating for the Kazakh Bolshevik press a number of satirical pictures of the local bureaucracy, the *bajs,* and the clergy. Toqmagambetov

[22] *balbals:* the monuments erected by the early Turks over the graves of heroes.

[23] Auezov, "Ya, kazakhskaya pesnya, poyu," *Izvestiya* (May 23, 1936), p. 4.

soon turned to serious poetry, however, and also composed a number of popular songs, the best known of which are his "Red Army," "Budyonny's March," "Turksib." Toqmagambetov's poetry is not concerned only with political themes and we will see that he can frequently write highly lyrical, and even subjective, poetry. Of his longer poems the most significant are *In the Streets of Berlin* (1932), *The Guard* (1934), *The Cleaning Woman, The Stalin Way* (1937). In *The Cleaning Woman* he sings about the famous Chelyuskin polar expedition which is depicted as seen through the eyes of a simple cleaning woman on board the ice-breaker *Chelyuskin.*

Toqmagambetov's political poetry frequently shows considerable insight into human emotions and intense feeling. In this respect the two most interesting poems available are his long poem on Lenin's death, "Thirteen Years,"[24] and his highly lyrical poem, "Written in Blood."[25]

"Thirteen Years" is a realistic, and yet subtly lyrical, poem concerning Lenin's death as seen through the eyes of a young Kazakh boy. The poem utilizes again the typical method of contrast. The melancholy beginning tells of the impact of Lenin's death on the Kazakhs, while the second, less lyrical and less effective, part pictures Kazakh life in the thirties in highly optimistic tones.

The poem starts by giving the background of the sad news, a background in which nature imagery is utilized to set a mood of melancholy and foreboding. We have already seen such an approach, in a more stereotyped manner, in the old epic poetry and particularly in the old mourning songs (*džoqtau*):

> The broken window shakes,
> And the storm covers the ground like fog.
> . . . .
> Covered with thick hoar frost
> A melancholy old fir tree
> Stands near the broken window,

[24] Asqar Toqmagambetov, "Trinadsat' let," Drozdov *et al.*, eds., *Sbornik* . . . , pp. 260-64.

[25] Toqmagambetov, "Krovyu napisannoye," Sobolev, ed., *Pesni*. . . , pp. 540-47.

And the wind tears
At its needles; the tree is trembling sadly.

Like a hungry wolf in the darkness of night
The cold wind howls through the steppe;
It tries to tear off the door with its arms,
And the miserable cold
Penetrates through our tattered rags
Down to the very bones.

Then the scene shifts to the interior of the Kazakh hut into which the boy's father returns from town late at night. Here also is the strong folklore element of indistinct premonitions and undefined fears suggested by the sounds of the night. The tense scene of the return of the father acts as a prelude to the fateful message of death which he bears:

Snow on his eyebrows,
And icicles on his thick beard,
Father entered, grey from the cold,
And left our door
Open behind him.

Wiping the crackling ice from his mustache,
He stood, stroking his beard,
Mournfully he stood with sadness in his face.
"Father!"
I wanted to shout,—but Father was silent.

From his eyebrows the snow had melted,
And the icicles were disappearing from his beard.
Father no longer could bear it, he looked at us,
And suddenly tears,
Like heavy rain, fell from his eyes. . . .

"Lenin is no more"—Father said.
And then he cried. And I began to hear
How the wind beat against the window and moaned,
How it pulled at the door
And wolf-like howled and prowled through the steppe.

Although we may note a similarity to folklore motifs in the use of nature to create feeling of foreboding, in most respects this poem differs markedly from the old *džoqtau* with their traditional eulogies to the deceased. The short announcement by the father, which, in its intensity, recalls a similar scene in Mayakovsky's poem "Vladimir Ilich Lenin," is all that is said directly about Lenin's death. With sudden realism the author shows us that the impact of the news is not felt by the boy, who only feels the emotional tenseness and who turns to his father and asks if he has brought him something from town.

The second part of the poem, set thirteen years after Lenin's death, depicts the changes which have taken place in the lives of the Kazakhs during the Soviet period. The poet speaks of the radio and the airplane, with which the children in the poem are thoroughly familiar, and of trips to Moscow to the Komsomol Congress.[26] He refers to the literature which the young generation is reading:

> On my bookshelves
> There are Pushkin, Lermontov, Tolstoy,
> And Gogol talks with me,
> And Chekhov opens up before me.
> My soul burns when I read these books.

He talks of the gramophone, which has made its entrance into the home of the Kazakhs, about Stakhanov, the Dneprogez and the Karaganda oil fields.

In the second poem mentioned, "Written in Blood," the poet again uses the method of contrast. He tells of a young poet and a young girl rowing over the clear waters of a mountain lake, and seeing an inscription which had been chiseled in rock by a young *džigit* before dying in a last hopeless battle with the Russians during the 1916 rebellion. The young people learn from an old fisherman that this inscription was left by his son when he found himself surrounded by a Russian punitive battalion. The story of the young *džigit,* Tang-atar ("rising dawn"), is told by his aged father in the traditional oral style, which is contrasted with the less traditional purely lyrical nature depictions which precede it. The folk art element in an otherwise quite modern poem is in no way disturbing, but actually

[26] Toqmagambetov was a delegate from Kazakhstan to the 10th Komsomol Congress in Moscow in 1936. See *Pravda,* April 20, 1936, which carries a poem written by Toqmagambetov for this occasion, entitled "To Stalin" ("Stalinu").

increases the realistic effect of the poem since such a mode of expression is quite appropriate to the *aqyn*-like old man who tells the story of a twentieth-century *batyr*. There are elements of modern poetry even in the epic section in its pronounced lyrical qualities, and the evenly measured slow speed of the ancient epic form is almost completely lacking.

Probably the most effective parts of the poem are the lyrical descriptions of nature:

Here, over the waters, lies gray mist,
and through transparent smoke,
The lake gazes into the sky, like a solitary eye;
All tinted blue, it blinds the eye
And over it, the rustling silk of trees stands
towering high.

Surrounded it stands by aromatic and thick grass,
It seems to have lured the high arch of the skies
down to its very bottom;
All rivers speed to the lake, all springs run
down to it:
From times immemorial the lake has lured them on.

Even the moon has always wanted to be near the lake,
To rock in half-slumber gently on its waves,
And the dawn strews diamonds into its great expanse,
The stars dream nightly in its misty depths.

Eternally the same, the rocks guard the peace of these calm
waters,
And with its snowy heights, Mount Talgar guards them from
the sun.

Toqmagambetov's attitude toward Soviet society is more evident in his short poem "New Spring,"[27] in which the beauty of spring symbolizes the new conditions of his country:

The forest rustles, never silent,
Never silent, a freshet gurgles
In its nest of transparent and ever moving leaves,
Emerging in a pearl-like, sharp stream.

Before dawn breaks, the soul
Perceives only sounds—sounds of all shades.

[27] Toqmagambetov, "Novaya Vesna," Drozdov, *et al.*, eds., *Sbornik. . .* , pp. 265-66.

How beautiful are our nights
In their dress of silken winds!

The firmanment reflected in the waves
Is like a school of little fish.
The moon emerges silently,
Its face shining in golden hues.

Beautiful earth has clothed herself
In gowns of living flowers,
And in the hair of our maidens there shine
The diamonds of rain drops.

The earth is bathing in the rays,
And soon will be dried by the sun,
And summer through the hair so light
Runs like a little wind.

The clouds then send their bounty down,
In streams of golden rain
To make the roses bloom
Ever more proudly and more beautifully.

The face of lakes is trembling
Stirred by the blowing winds;
The wild choir of the geese and ducks
Sounds in friendly spirit here and there.

. . . .

I drink the air, as if 'twere wine
When before the morning dawn,
Into my opened window
The steppe aroma wafts. . . .

Open the doors more quickly, you,
Open your arms for embrace, oh, new year,
Oh, flaming sun, with it
All life blooms in my soul.

Oh, with my heart, I fly above,
I would embrace the whole wide world,
I pour out like a song, I bloom like the steppe,
And like the brook, I like to sparkle.

All life is singing, and I am singing too,
When I glance, like a lover into spring's face,
Into the space and freedom bright
In the bosom of Stalin's land.

Although Toqmagambetov is most noted for his political poetry, it appears that he is more successful when he draws upon his lyrical, many-shaded pictures in order to create the varied moods he wishes to express.

TAHIR DŽARUQOV. Undoubtedly one of the most significant Kazakh poets is Tahir Džaruqov, whose earliest works did not appear in print until 1927 and were not translated into Russian until 1938. Džaruqov, the son of a poor cattle breeder, was born in Western Kazakhstan in 1908. It was in this region of the steppes that the fiercest battles had ranged against the Russians, and from his earlier youth Džaruqov had listened to the *aqyns* sing of the glorious battles of the past. Džaruqov was educated at the Kazakh Pedagogical Institute at Alma-Ata, from which he graduated in 1931, and at the University of Leningrad.

In the poetry of Džaruqov there are reflected many of the trends which we have noted in the development of Soviet Kazakh poetry. The earliest collections of his works, *The Light of the Stars* (*Žuldyz žarygyn*) (1930) and *In the Dawn of Communism* (*Kommunizm Tanynda*) (1933), reveal the struggles of the literary apprentice. We can note again the schematism and sloganeering which were characteristic of early Kazakh Soviet poetry. It was not until 1934, after he came to Leningrad University, that the poet found his more mature style in *The Sun Has Spoken* (*Küntil qatty*), a long poem dedicated to four Soviet scientists who met death while exploring the stratosphere. With its appearance, Džaruqov became one of the acknowledged leaders of Kazakh poetry and one of the most prolific of the young Kazakh poets. By 1939 he had written eleven books of poetry. He is the author of a number of smaller poems on contemporary events, such as his "Song of the Motor," "Song about Ridder," "Five-Year-Plan Hammers," "The Caspian," "Karaganda," etc., as well as of a great number of larger epic-like works, as *The Sun Has Spoken, Khan Orda, Neftestan, The Kolkhoz Field, Prisoners of the Ice* (Džaruqov's contribution to the large number of literary works about the Chelyuskin expedition), *The Third International,* and finally his most famous long poem, *The Stream.*

In all these poetic works Džaruqov's ability to depict contemporary reality in a musical and lyrical style is evident. Although the influence of the oral tradition is apparent in his writings, the predominant characteristics of his work are the use of new subject matter and the influence of Russian lyric poets, particularly Pushkin. While Džaruqov most frequently writes of the past and present life of his people, he is also concerned with subjective reflections which demonstrate a quite new trend in modern Kazakh poetry. Džaruqov's impressive and tender love poetry is quite unlike earlier Kazakh poetry concerned with this theme, which was primarily influenced by the ornate love verses of Persian poetry. One of the best examples of the influence on Džaruqov of Western subjective lyricism is his poem "My Love,"[28] which seems to echo the delicate love songs of Pushkin:

> Under the shade of withering leaves,
> Under the arch of clouds, collecting for the night,
> You and I went far into the distance.
> And was I not ready then—hidden by foliage—
> To talk of love to you, my own?
>
> We could easily understand each other:
> Our hearts talked to each other
> Of sincere feeling, tenderness and strength.
> How could I refrain then from giving
> In silence—in the end—all my tenderness,
> All my strength—all at once—
> Everything!—to the gay, dark-eyed girl,
> With a glowing and passionate face
> And with little dimples! You are like that, all of you,
> And not to love one like you—that is impossible.

A more typical poem in which Džaruqov uses nature to create a mood of praise for the Soviet society is his "The Heart Is Singing":[29]

> My life is the proud current of the Darya,
> Wildly running into space.
> My life is wide like the limitless steppes.
> My gaze burns like the sun.

[28] "Moya lyubov'," Tahir Džaruqov, *Zolotaya step'*, ed. N. Sidorenko (Moscow, 1933), p. 24.

[29] Džaruqov, "Serdtse poyot," *Zolotaya step'.*, p. 9.

It is said that the mountains alone are beautiful,
Where they rise to the heights of eagles.
No, that is untrue! In these incredible days
Beauty is everywhere, it cannot be embraced.

Is not the wave in the fast current of the
stream magnificent,
As it angrily beats at the cliff? . . .
Is it not beautiful, when on a blue sky the moon
Swims, like a swan in the lake? . . .

Is it not wondrous, when at dawn's break,
Loving this clear morning,
A dark-eyed maiden gives her heart
And tenderly kisses her lover?

In the days when the earth grows beautiful,
The heart widens its range,
And our miraculous life
Burns in the soul with all its beauty.

The clearest examples of Džaruqov's close connection with the oral traditions emerge, as would be expected, in his songs about the past, particularly in those songs depicting the rebellions of the Kazakhs against the Russian colonizers. But even in these poems there are a great many realistic elements as in Džaruqov's song of a simple Kazakh *džigit*[30] who had participated in the uprising against the conscription decree of 1916 and had fought under Amangeldy:

Hoarfrost shines silvery, cold is the window,
In the steppe winter hut it is dark and crowded;
Poorly lighted by a miserable candle
Shines the *džigit's* face. In the fire of battle
He had been under Amangeldy's banner—
His uniform still hides the results of battle,
On his old cap, a star glimmers in scarlet,
And in his passionate speech Lenin arises.

Here we have the picture of a typical Kazakh *batyr,* but painted in quite realistic, untraditional colors against the background of the poverty of the Kazakh winter quarters. The

[30] Džaruqov, "Serebritsya inei. . . ," Drozdov *et al.*, eds., *Sbornik*. . . , p. 206.

džigit leaves his *aul* and goes to Moscow, where he and his companions are received by Lenin. The depiction of this meeting with the first Soviet leader, who by that time[31] had become part of the Kazakh legendary repertoire, is steeped in the old oral tradition. In contrast to the more realistic spirit of the lines quoted above, this scene takes on an almost epical character:

In the campfire heavy steppe-wood is burning,
The round-backed falcon has dozed off on the saddle,
And the hunters, forgetting about their *aul,*
Tell simple stories. . . .
The wind has died down, the howling has ceased.
And in the court of Moscow-beautiful
Lenin meets the steppe hunters.
He strokes the falcon and presents to them
His gun which never misses fire.
He spreads out the rug on the floor,
And fills the glasses with tea.
And till morning they talk in the Kremlin
Of herds, of grain, of land.

Džaruqov's use of folklore elements even in songs concerned strictly with modern phenomena can be seen in his poem about the Turksib railway.[32] While Muqanov's treatment of this theme shows the strong influence of Mayakovsky, Džaruqov reverts to the oral tradition to illustrate his observations when he depicts the railroad:

Out of the steel nostrils of the steam-wagon
Steam emerges,
And we fly on it more quickly,
Than in olden days the horse-*tulpar* would race.

Džaruqov's long poem *The Stream* (*Tysqyn*)[33] is probably the most successful of his works. The poem was written in 1937, at a time when Džaruqov was under the influence of Pushkin, and it is quite possible that the poem may have been inspired by Pushkin's *Bronze Horseman.* There are some obvious parallels, such as the depiction of the flood, which is taken from the flood

[31] This poem was written in the late thirties.
[32] Džaruqov, "Put' otkryt," Drozdov *et al.*, eds., *Sbornik. . .* , p. 209.
[33] Džaruqov, "Potok," *Zolotaya step'.*, pp. 34-90.

of 1921 which caused such havoc in the Alma-Ata region. In both Pushkin's and in Džaruqov's poems the depiction of the flood is of prime importance, but while Pushkin's flood destroys the happiness of Yevgeni, who becomes insane, the hero of Džaruqov's poem, while he loses his house and family in the waters, experiences a different fate, a fate which illustrates the optimistic and moralistic character of much of Soviet literature. He is saved by society, which takes the responsibility for his care and education.

The story of the poem is relatively simple. The family of the hero Qajsar is killed during the flood of 1921, and Qajsar, whose father had been a revolutionary guerilla fighter, becomes one of the countless wayward children who roam the country after the Civil War and is taken into one of the homes established for such destitute children. Here he falls in love with an orphan girl, Džamal ("Beauty"), and finally goes to Moscow to take up the study of architecture. After completing his studies he returns to his native Kazakhstan and to his Džamal.

In this poem there are united all the typical elements of Džaruqov's poetry. His use of folklore, his incisive realism, particularly in the scenes of the flood, and his lyricism revealed in the love scenes are all present. A skilful mixture of realism and the traditional folk art emerges most effectively in the depiction of the flood. In the first stanzas the tendency is toward a realistic treatment of the flood:

> The wind blew along, whistling.
> Night was howling, giving her signals
> To the evil spirits of the storm. And then there broke
> An impenetrable curtain of rain.
>
> . . . .
>
> Thunder beat hard and as if from close range,
> Mountains moaned under the furious attack;
> In raging fever
> The brainless monster hurtled bolders,
> And broke the aged granite rocks.
>
> The storm, freeing an evil force
> And breaking the pine trees on its road,

Crumbled the snows into the maelstrom,
The bottomless and limitless maelstrom.

. . . .

The water column flew steaming on the city.
The cold fog, cut by the rain as by a knife,
Twisted the night like a giant necklace.

Bridges crumbled as if
A gun's sights had been trained on them. Pine
 trees floated
In the stream, like candles. The wind chased
Clouds of siliceous dust from the foothills.

The darkness was fraught with sounds. It tore
 the doors from hinges.
The stream became a sea. Water beasts
Went mad in the huts.
—Flood!
—Flood!
Here everything went under. Who could count his loss?

. . . .

People drowned while eating,
Holding on to the walls; people yelled into the night.
And many, crazed, with shrieking laughter,
Threw infants who still sucked the breast into the stream.

Yet the flood is also referred to in the colorful folk imagery. The stormy night is compared to evil spirits, and the water, which tries to drag Qajsar to the bottom, is described in the following way:

Like forty falcons, filled with anger,
Mountains of sharp-clawed waves moved
The body of the boy, to tear it to pieces,
To fill their hungry stomachs with it.

The depiction of the storm is followed by calm and lyrical lines which contrast sharply with the tumultuous lines about the flood:

The sun was setting. Rose colored appeared
The little cloud-sheep. In the dust
A warm wind was playing. . . . And at the gates
Three old men were talking softly.

Again the oral tradition emerges as Qajsar is traveling by train to Leningrad. Džaruqov tells us that the railroad is

> Like a young *qulan* with his thick mane,
> Who jealously gathers his mares,
> Thus raced the train through the steppes;
> whinnied and beat
> With his miraculously rapid hoofbeats.
> . . . .
> In a *bajga*[34] it outstrips Taj-Buryl.[35]
> So great is the strength in its wheels!
> Akhan Säri![36] Your famous Qul Agyr[37]
> Would soon be exhausted and winded.

When the train bearing Qajsar arrives in Leningrad, the hero sees the statue of Peter the Great, which played so important a role in Pushkin's *Bronze Horseman* and which now reminds him of the disaster which befell him in his childhood.

> Immortal pages! The Bronze Horseman
> Was galloping along the pavement. Yevgeni, pale,
> Ran to the Neva, lost his mind;
> Behind him sounds victoriously the horse's
> snorting.
> . . . .
> Pushkin, beloved, with your magic lines
> You have brought nearer the events which years
> have pushed into the background. . . .

Some of the most lyrical lines are those which Džaruqov devotes to the young girl Džamal and to Qajsar's love for her. Qajsar, who now has returned to Alma-Ata as an architect, is walking with Džamal:

> After the performance of *Er Targhyn*
> Džamal and Qajsar walked. On the long path
> Midnight was pouring out its lights. Nearby the
> nightingale
> Grew silent and then again its voice was born.

[34] *bajga*-horse race.
[35] Taj-Buryl—a legendary horse from the heroic epic.
[36] Akhan Säri—a legendary epic hero.
[37] Qul Agyr—Akhan Säri's legendary horse.

The pattern of foliage, the gurgling of the fountains,
The moonlight on the tulip petals,
The play of shadows—all that disguised the park
Into a magical garden, into a dream from old Persia.

. . . .

Eye to eye, wordless, without assurance
They walked, their shadows flowing into one;
The great park hid in its embrace
The love and joy of two heart beats.

The Stream is the story of the new young Kazakh intelligentsia as symbolized by the wayward orphan Qajsar, who becomes a successful architect; it is also an encyclopedic tale of modern life in Kazakhstan. The picture of the new industrialized Kazakhstan is related as seen through the eyes of the returning Qajsar. He reflects as he looks at his country from the train window:

Yes, the steppe is no longer the same! And Alma-Ata
No longer resembles the decaying town:
Beauty lives in the large parks,
Multiplying its splendor with each year.

When Qajsar leaves the train, he enters a taxi and again reflects the new scenes.

Qajsar enters a taxi. Noisily the tires
Sing on the asphalt. Like a long line of stars
The long line of street lights stands.

. . . .

The driver turns into Tashkent Boulevard,
Where poplars stand silent and green.

. . . .

Houses and parks have embellished the capital.
The taxi flies. Friendly faces,
The Park of Federation, theaters, cafés. . . .
The asphalt sings, the car flies like a bird. . . .

How long since hovels used to stand here,
Their windows blinking, like trachoma-diseased eyes,
At the light of day. How long, since, calling his hens,
The rooster used to crow on the walls of clay?

The electro-station under the starry sky
Looked like a steamship to Qajsar:
Now it will hoot, lift anchor,
And move into the night on ocean's waters. . . .

Stop! The "House of Soviets."[38] How welcoming
and bright it looks.

In spite of the influence of Russian poetry, particularly of the poetry of Pushkin, *The Stream* has retained its national character and flavor. In form, it utilizes the metaphoric and hyperbolic language of the old folklore, as well as Western lyricism and realism. But even in the depiction of the new society, it has remained essentially Kazakh in spirit.

Džaruqov's poetry has brought him fame not only in Kazakhstan, but in all the USSR. In 1949 he received the highest Kazakh literary award, the Abaj Prize for literature for his poem *A Forest Rustles in the Desert,* which is dedicated to the new forestation program of the USSR.[39]

Since the war, Džaruqov has, like so many Soviet writers, fallen victim to the increasing strictures on intellectual and creative freedom, expressed in the party decree on literature of August 14, 1946, which defined political didacticism as one of the desirable aims for which the Soviet writer must strive. In harmony with this new line on the arts, Džaruqov's poetry has become permeated, in ever increasing measure, by that political and social incisiveness dubbed in Soviet writings *partijnost',* which might best be defined as signifying political consciousness in terms of the current political, social, and economic demands of the party. As a result, Džaruqov's postwar poetry is concerned, in large measure, with the economic drives for increased industrialization and higher agricultural yields which have characterized the Soviet scene ever since the end of the Second World War. The writing of this kind of "command" poetry has not been without adverse effect on the quality of Džaruqov's recent verse, which frequently bears more resemblance to a political newspaper editorial than to lyric poetry. In many of these postwar poems, Džaruqov's

[38] "The House of Soviets"—a hotel in Alma-Ata.
[39] *Lit. Gaz.,* January 4, 1950, p. 1.

truly fine poetic talent is almost totally buried. Typical of this new approach are such poems as "Temir-Tau" (1947),[40] which is concerned with a Kazakh steel worker-Stakhanovite. It is a grey, uninspired poem, prosaic to the utmost, but the content is "correct" and therefore the work found deep approval in the Kazakh party press.[41] Other poems on similar industrial themes are "Heroes of Coal" (1948),[42] written in honor of the celebration of Miner's Day in the USSR, and "Steelworker" (1947),[43] dedicated to the Kazakh Stakhanovite Altynbek Deribajev. Only occasionally, since 1946, has Džaruqov risen above the level of rhymed editorials, as in "Qaskelen's Herds" (1948),[44] in which the poet talks enthusiastically about collective farm achievements and "The Stormy Petrel" (1948),[45] written for the occasion of the eightieth anniversary of the birth of Maxim Gorky. It is these occasional reversions to Džaruqov's obviously fine poetic talents which give hope that, with a freer intellectual climate in the USSR, Džaruqov may again come forth as one of the most gifted lyricists of his young country. As it is, Džaruqov has not only contributed significantly to Kazakh literature, but he has also translated many works into Kazakh, including Griboyedov's comedy *Woe from Wit* (*Gore ot uma*), the epic poem *The Hero in the Tiger Skin,* by the Georgian poet Rustaveli, as well as many lyrics by Pushkin and Lermontov.

ABDYLDA TADŽYBAJEV. Abdylda Tadžybajev is another poet who has attempted to synthesize the traditional and the new elements in his poetry. He was born in 1909 in the district of Qyzyl Orda. His first published collection of poetry, issued in 1931 and entitled *New Rythms* (*Žana yrgaq*), was not at the disposal of this author, and we can only note that a number of critics have pointed out that this collection suffers from the same use of sloganized political material which characterized so much early Kazakh poetry. It was only in 1935, with the appearance

[40] In N. Sidorenko, ed., *Solnechny den'; iz kazakhshkikh poétov* (Moscow, 1949), p. 23.
[41] See *Kaz. Prav.,* August 15, 1947, p. 1.
[42] *Kaz. Prav.,* August 28, 1947, p. 2.
[43] Sidorenko, ed., *Solnechny. . . ,* pp. 30-34.
[44] *Ibid.,* pp. 24-28.
[45] *Kaz. Prav.,* March 28, 1948, p. 1.

of two of his important short poems, "Syr-Darya"[46] and "Conversation with Taras,"[47] that Tadžybajev finds his own style, which continues to be characteristic of his later works.

Lyrical qualities play an important part in Tadžybajev's poetry just as they do in the writings of Džaruqov. But Tadžybajev's lyricism is even more heartfelt and penetrating than Džaruqov's, and he has been called a "poet of great passions." Moreover, Tadžybajev draws inspiration from wider realms than does Džaruqov. He draws, in his own cultural heritage, not only from Kazakh folk art but also from the later nineteenth-century philosophical writings of such men as Abaj, and his writings show the influence of not only Russian literature but also the literatures of other European cultures. We can note particularly the influence of two non-Russian poets, the Ukrainian Taras Shevchenko and the German Heinrich Heine. Tadžybajev approached his foreign mentors first as a translator. His translations include many of the works of Pushkin (his most famous translation is that of Pushkin's *Ruslan and Lyudmilla*), and a number of poems by Shevchenko and Heine. Tadžybajev is particularly well known for his translation of Heine's "Deutschland."

Tadžybajev's tender lyricism as well as his ideology emerge most clearly in the poem "Syr-Darya." In the lines of this work we can sense the poet's love of the natural beauties of his native Kazakhstan as he describes the great river Syr-Darya, symbolically treated as his mother:

> I have fallen in love with you for ever,
> Old, grey mother mine;
> You used to sing me lullabies at night
> With the sounds of your transparent waters,
> oh Syr-Darya.

But for Tadžybajev nature is no longer merely an object of love, as it so frequently is with Džaruqov, nor is it an object of foreboding, as it was with so many *aqyns*. To him nature already appears in a new perspective, as is revealed in his numer-

[46] Sobolev, ed., *Pesni. . .* , pp. 521-22.
[47] "Rasgovor s Tarasom," *ibid.*, pp. 523-27.

ous reflections about the aid which nature can bring to modern man as he learns to subjugate his environment. Nature is undergoing constant change and participates in the socialist competition of his country. Kazakh nature has become rejuvenated, and the river Syr-Darya will soon bring to man the same benefits of electricity as the Dniepr does:

> You used to be old, but this era,
> Oh, my mother, has rejuvenated you,
> And now never again will the milk
> Dry out in your breast.
>
> But the powerful Dniepr, your old friend,
> Has outgrown you: along live wires
> The clear Dniepr waters
> Chase the mad power of lightning.
>
> And now I beg of you, oh my mother:
> Rise in all your gigantic size,
> Bring to earth for me
> The miraculous light of the unattainable stars.

The poem also reveals the close kinship which Tadžybajev feels toward other cultures and toward the poets who have so deeply influenced him. Thus, for example, he compares the poetic inspiration which he drew from his native river to the inspiration which the Rhine gave to Heine, the Neva to Pushkin, and the Dniepr to Shevchenko:

> If for Heine the free Rhine
> Was his real mother,
> Then you also, grey Syr,
> Have nurtured your own Heine.
>
> Of you, oh my land,
> Why shall I not sing,
> If Pushkin could sing of the Neva
> And Taras write about the Dniepr?

Tadžybajev concludes his poem by warning the Syr-Darya that only after it has made its great social contribution of providing electric power can the poet draw fullest inspiration from it:

Then, playing in golden rays,
You will flow eternally, Syr-Darya,
And then, taking pride in you, oh mother,
I shall become a true Heine.

We find the same mixture of lyricism and political and social content in Tadžybajev's poem "Conversation with Taras," in which the poet carries on a fictitious dialogue with Shevchenko. Shevchenko reminds the modern Kazakh poet of the melancholy past of the Ukraine and his own sufferings and tells him that he, during his lifetime, had been well aware that the Kazakhs were suffering as greatly as were the Ukrainians under tsarist oppression and Russification policies:

Listen . . . I was snuffed out
In terrible imprisonment—
That was a terrible
And difficult time!
In those days I cried my eyes out!
The past, like a shadow,
Passed before my eyes;
I remembered the former liberty
Of the free Dniepr,
I heard the sounds of shackles at night. . . .

. . . .

I marched under guard[48]
Through the unknown steppe:
Dusty space,
Yellow grass . . .
How far you were, oh Ukraine!
I went, a miserable wretch,
Rattling my chains,
And after me laughed a stupid owl.
How terrible the owlish laugh was for me then!

I learned to know the Kazakhs
I saw your fate,
Heard your moans,
The moans of poor men—
And I felt your bitter torture.
But I sat impotently,

[48] This reference is to Shevchenko's exile in Kazakhstan.

Imprisoned and chained,
And in vain
My hand strained for the pen—
They kept good guard over my song!

But then the spirit of Shevchenko greets the new era when both the Ukraine and Kazakhstan

Have forever become free—
Now its ever more joyful to live and more miraculous!

The strong influence of Shevchenko on Tadžybajev is felt as the poet pictures Shevchenko admonishing him:

Be, oh poet, fearless!
Be the people's singer!
Happy in the new life
Is the new man.
My son! I hand my songs down to you.

A poem which utilizes an approach similar to that of "Conversation with Taras" is "Two Worlds" ("Eki džihan") (1937). The two worlds pictured are the Soviet Union and Heine's Germany as seen by Tadžybajev and Heine as they travel together. Tadžybajev gives Heine a glowing account of the new land as he shows the German poet the achievements of the new times.

The varied sources from which Tadžybajev drew inspiration are revealed in all of Tadžybajev's poems. In a short poem he speaks of the inspiration he draws from Kazakh nature:

It was a marvelous summer when
I shared secrets with Mount Ala Tau,
Smelled its flowers, trod its grasses,
And climbed its icy rocks.
I built my *džurt* up on the heights
To rest in my native land.
Transparent air and the waters of streams
I drank, sinking my soul into them.[49]

The new enlightenment of his people also stimulates the imagination of the poet:

[49] Tadžybajev, "V obyatiyakh gor," Drozdov *et al.*, eds., *Sbornik*. . . , p. 250.

In the *džurt* I swung my cradle of songs,
Stringing rhymes like beads on a string.
Near me the voice of my wife
Repeated algebraic formulae aloud.

Busy with physics and chemistry,
She dug into her books
And succeeded, opening Abaj,
In learning a delicate verse.[50]

Tadžybajev's union with the oral tradition emerges most clearly, as it does in the songs of many of the modern Kazakh poets, in the depiction of times past. His poem written in honor of a famous nineteenth-century *aqyn,* Abyl, is so clearly steeped in the ancient oral tradition that, at times, it might seem that one is reading an ancient Kazakh epos, were it not for the new ideology contained in its lines.

During the Second World War, Tadžybajev's poetry was largely dedicated, as was that of all Soviet writers, to aiding the struggle against the Germans. In contrast to the war poetry of most Kazakh poets, however, Tadžybajev's war verses avoid the pitfalls of sloganeering. His war verses frequently stand out in their fresh and delicate tenderness and in the skilful drawing of elements from the traditional epos. The militant fighting spirit of the epical songs lent itself most facilely to depiction of the battles of the Second World War. Tadžybajev's verse is replete with the imagery of the traditional songs, as in his poem "Son and Mother"[51] (1942), where we meet a hero, like the legendary *batyr,* who,

Entering the field of battle, like a knight,
destroyed the enemy,
Always, as if untouchable by death, sped to the
spot where death threatened him most. . . .

The enemy also is depicted in traditional epic colors:

Like a cornered wolf, the enemy runs away wildly,
Races away to avenge and to save itself!
But a long, fiery whip lashes out at the condemned
beast.

[50] *Ibid.*
[51] Tadžybajev, "Syn i mat'," in Sidorenko, ed., *Solnechny*. . . , pp. 37-39.

The hero, who is compared to a young lion, has a machine gun, which, just like the weapons of the legendary hero, is personalized as his faithful friend and which, "like a living being," "sang out without refusing."

Quite a different spirit emanates from Tadžybajev's poetry of the postwar period. Much of it was obviously dashed off to satisfy the increasing demands for "party loyalty" (*partijnost'*) in art; and when Tadžybajev follows the politico-aesthetic party demands of the day and writes on purely political subject matter, as he does for instance in the poems "Before Mayakovsky's Portrait"[52] and "On the Top of the Mountain,"[53] his verse sounds flat and unimaginative, without a trace of the poet's usual delicate lyricism. However, there are also a number of poems written since the war in which the poet apparently paid less attention to the demands of the political theorists, and sings with his erstwhile simple and frequently touchingly musical lyricism about nature's beauties ("Ala-Tau," 1947)[54] or about the past ("Šolpan," 1946).[55]

There is little doubt that Tadžybajev is one of the most gifted poets of contemporary Kazakhstan. While he is sometimes banal and embarrassingly cheap in his political "command" poetry, he can also rise to heights of fancy and achieve depths of genuine emotion which no other modern Kazakh poet has yet attained.

In general, there can be noted in Kazakh poetry of the years of the Second World War and those immediately preceding it an increasing preoccupation with topical subjects reflecting the demands of the times. With the approach of the war, Kazakh poets began to concern themselves more and more with world themes. For example, in a short poem "I Sing"[56] the poet Qapan Satybaldin (b. 1917) contrasts the happy song of modern Kazakh youth with the sad fate of the youth of war-torn Spain. He paints the picture of two young girls, one a Kazakh at constructive work and the other a Spaniard who has lost her family in the fighting:

[52] "Pered portretom Mayakovskogo," *ibid.*, p. 39.
[53] "Na vershine gory," *ibid.*, p. 40.
[54] *Ibid.*, p. 41.
[55] *Ibid.*, pp. 41-43.
[56] Satybaldin, "Ya poyu," Sobolev, ed., *Pesni. . .* , pp. 508-9.

Sing of a heart, just orphaned:
Fighting perished her father and brothers—
Fighters for peace, for a gallant cause.
Fly, oh my verse, through the wolf-like fog of Europe,
Fly to my friends, into the trenches of Madrid,
Into the rocks of the mountains, where the red partisans
Like watchful eagles, stand guard over the path.

Similar in tone is also a poem by Dikhan Abilev (b. 1906) "The Spanish Girl."[57] Here again we note the same underlying idea of the Kazakh's song, winging its way to Spain to encourage the Spanish fighters:

Heart, touch the strings of the song,
Spread out, oh my songs!
With the cry of the eagle, with resounding voice,
Rise to the heights of the skies!
From the Kazakh steppes, from the yellow steppes
Fly to foreign lands,
Fly over the ocean's waves,—
To the mountains and steppes of Spain
And bring them my brotherly word!
Word of anger! Burst like a grenade,
Like a quick bullet, fly into the night
. . . .

Many poems concerned with the varying aspects of the war, are written in entirely untraditional style and sound modern and Western in their realism. Most of the war poetry is dedicated to the actual front-line fighting, as for instance Džumagali Sajn's "After the Battle"[58] (1948) and Bekkhožin's long poem "The Twenty-eight"[59] (1941). Many poems are devoted to the guerilla fighters behind the German lines, such as the poems of Džumagali Sajn, who was himself a member of a partisan detachment. Thus Sajn's cycle *Songs of the Partisan* (1943), and particularly the poem "I Longed For You, My Friends,"[60] from the cycle, expressed the poet-guerilla's longing for his comrades-in-arm, as he lies wounded in an underground guerilla hospital in the

[57] Abilev, "Ispanskaya devushka," Sobolev, ed., *Pesni. . .* , pp. 373-78.
[58] Sidorenko, ed., *Solnechny. . .* , pp. 70-71.
[59] *Ibid.*, pp. 84-86.
[60] *Ibid.*, pp. 68-69.

Ukraine. Pictures of the destruction wrought by the enemy are given with keenness by the poet Gali Ormanov ("The Little Flower," "The Oak").[61] Perhaps one of the most effective war poems is Bekkhožin's poem "A Voice in Oswięcim,"[62] in which the poet records his feelings of horror upon visiting the infamous Nazi death camp, where the ashes of the victims of Nazi brutality speak to him as a fellow-man and ask to be avenged. Several war poems expressing a more personalized feeling of grief over the parting of a soldier to the front, as for instance Abu Sarsenbajev's "The Apple Tree,"[63] or at the death of a comrade, as Qasym Amanžolov's poem "Abdulla,"[64] dedicated to the death in battle of the Kazakh poet Abdulla Džumagaliev (1915-1943), also deserve attention for their frequently delicate tone of desolation and mourning, suffused nevertheless with the ever-present optimistic faith in the future. The discussion of war poetry would not be complete without mentioning the large body of poems dedicated to the war effort at home. A typical example is Gali Ormanov's poem "Daughter of Balkhaš,"[65] a rather uninspired poem which calls the reader's attention to the homefront contribution to the war effort.

At the same time as Kazakh wartime poets wrote increasingly of topical themes, another trend could also be observed: we can note a marked revival of the epic spirit of old as in Qalmaqan Abdyqadyrov's "The Secret of Mukhambet"[66] and in Qalimžan Bekkhožin's "In the Hungry Steppe."[67] Frequently the poet acknowledges his debt to the oral tradition, as in the poem "Dombra"[68] by Bekkhožin and in a poem of the same name by Qasym Amanžolov.[69] Both poems pay enthusiastic and tender tribute to the singing of the *dombra*. Thus Bekkhožin writes:

[61] *Ibid.*, pp. 49-50; 51.
[62] *Ibid.*, p. 87.
[63] *Ibid.*, pp. 80-81.
[64] *Ibid.*, pp. 131-137.
[65] *Ibid.*, pp. 47-8.
[66] Abdyqadyrov, "Taina Mukhambeta," Drozdov, *et al.*, eds., *Sbornik. . .* , pp. 195-200.
[67] Bekkhožin, "V golodnoi stepi," *ibid.*, pp. 203-5.
[68] Bekkhožin, "Dombra," *Oktyabr'*, No. 8 (Moscow, 1947), p. 95.
[69] Q. Amanžolov, "Dombra," *Zvezda*, No. 5 (May, 1949), p. 113.

Your voice caresses my heart endlessly,
It seems that I was born with your sounds in my blood—
In it are the wind, the steppe and the sadness
of our fathers,
And the quiet tune of motherly love.
Your voice used to sing me to sleep as a child,
In it is all my life, turned into sound,

. . . .

Dombra, all my thoughts are devoted to you,
Dombra, all my songs are born by you,
My soul and my singing heart
Are forever united with you.

And Amanžolov sings:

The tune of the *dombra,* now quiet, now thundering
Agitates the hiding place of secret thoughts.
And soon within your very self there rings
The legendary source of miraculous songs.

Then take your paper and begin to write
And along the *aryqs* of shapely and measured verses,
To the voice of the *dombra,* from the bottom of your soul,
Let the river of songs flow quietly.

Poetry since the end of the war has stood increasingly under the shadow of the 1946 Party edict relating to literature, and consequently has been dedicated, to a large extent, to the theme of industrial and agricultural construction in Kazakhstan.

A notable new theme which has made its appearance in Kazakh literature since the war emanates from Stalin's well-known toast to the Russian people in 1945, in which the Soviet leader praised the Russian people as the most advanced fighters for liberty in the Soviet Union and the teachers and "elder brothers" of the other Soviet nationalities. We shall see later this new line is echoed very concretely in the prose works of this period. Two poems expressing this theme are Bekkhožin's "The Voice of Russia" and Satybaldin's "To the Russian People." Satybaldin, in his poem, speaks of the Russian as his "older brother" and praises him for having been so brave a soldier and for having saved the fatherland and describes him as now marching, shoulder to shoulder, with his Kazakh brethren, forward to new achievements.

Concluding Remarks

The poetic tradition in Kazakhstan is so strong and persevering that almost every Kazakh writer, no matter what his principal genre might be, has also written some poetry. Thus our aim in this chapter has been to give a picture of the more important trends in the ever-growing volume of Kazakh verse. Within the period of only a few decades the Kazaks have created a vital art which has drawn from their rich oral tradition but has also gradually encompassed the modern developments precipitated by the revolution and has become enriched by the influence of Western literature. This was, we have noted, a development not without severe birthpangs and bitter conflicts, and in many respects Kazakh poetry must still be considered in a relatively early stage of development. There is a long road of development from the formalized and stereotyped epic tradition to a sophisticated modern written poetry which concerns itself with all the varied complexities of human existence. Although we have noted the first attempts in Kazakh poetry to probe the individual, his motivations and emotions, most Kazakh poets are still more concerned with the external scene. In addition, we cannot observe, in the first decades of Kazakh poetry, any considerable experimentation with form itself. Although some poets have borrowed from Mayakovsky, the main influences remain the Kazakh oral art and the Russian poets of the nineteenth century. How much richer Kazakh poetry might have been, freed from its political harness, we can only surmise, and a full realization of its development must lie in the future. Nevertheless, it would seem that a significant basis for modern Kazakh poetry has been laid.

CHAPTER X

KAZAKH PROSE AFTER 1932

WE HAVE SEEN that Kazakh literature, while it was rich in poetic tradition, did not possess a comparable prose tradition. Apart from purely journalistic prose, the scientific writings of Valikhanov and Altynsaryn, and the philosophical prose writings of Abaj Qunanbajev, little prose had been written in the nineteenth century. The prerevolutionary twentieth century had seen only a few works of belletristic prose—Köbejev's novel *Qalym* and two unfinished novels by Toruaigyrov, *Whose Fault* and *The Beauty Khamal.* Even early Soviet Kazakh prose was extremely limited both in quantity and in quality.

In addition to the lack of prose tradition, Kazakh prose was held back by the long delay in the development of a large-scale program of translation into Kazakh of the Russian classics, as well as of modern Russian prose. It was not until the middle and late thirties that the translation program made significant headway. As would be expected, particular stress was first laid on the prose writings of Pushkin, whose poetry had already become popular in Kazakhstan. But even when the short stories of Pushkin were at last translated in the thirties, prose was still so unfamiliar a form to the Kazakh reading public that such works as Pushkin's *Dubrovski* and *Snowstorm* were first transformed into poetry.[1] It was felt that only by this means could the Kazakh reader appreciate Pushkin's works, and, moreover, the task was simplified for the Kazakh translator who was himself as yet relatively unfamiliar with prose forms. It was only in the middle thirties that prose translations of Russian and Western authors were seriously attempted.

[1] Neishtadt, "Na yazykakh narodov SSSR," *Lit. Gaz.*, February 10, 1937.

Since prose is clearly an innovation in Kazakh literature, which has developed almost entirely through the influence of Western—primarily Russian—literature, it is not surprising to note that Kazakh prose shows little influence from the oral tradition which had so marked an effect on modern poetry. In its stead, we can observe a much closer relationship to the realistic prose of nineteenth century Russia and to Soviet Russian prose.

In the twenties Kazakh prose was dominated by the simpler and shorter forms, the short story and prose sketches. The only full-length novel which was written during this period is Sabit Muqanov's *The Lost Ones* (1929), translated into Russian under the title *The Son of the Baj,* which is set in the Kazakhstan of the transforming years of 1928-29 and depicts the early struggle against the Kazakh *kulak,* the *baj*. Muqanov can be regarded as the first Kazakh prose writer of significant proportions. Among his works of the twenties there should be noted his short story "Balpom" (1927), which concerns itself with the problem of the conflict between the traditional Kazakh way of life and the new ethos which emerged under the impact of the new social relationships. The heroine of this work is a traditional Kazakh woman who overcomes the time-honored traditions which bind her to become an active combatant for the new way of life and, eventually, the political leader of her *aul*. Similar problems are treated by Muqanov in almost all his shorter prose works during the twenties. In his short story "Milk and Blood" (1929) Muqanov levels his attack at the traditional institution of the levirate and depicts in gruesome colors the punishment meted out to the heroine for refusing to submit to this custom. The repressed condition of Kazakh womanhood serves as the main theme of *Spouse and Housewife* (1928), while his short story "Myrzabek" (1928) takes up a totally new problem: that of the moral decline of a former Kazakh Communist after his marriage to the daughter of a Russian "white-guard" emigré.

After 1932 we can observe the emergence of somewhat more ambitious prose works, such as Muqanov's novels *Temirtas* (1935), *Friends* (1937), *Esil* (1938), and *Botagoz* (1939), Toqmagambetov's novel *Šaulder,* Mukhtar Auezov's novel *Abaj,* and the many short tales and short stories by Auezov, Musrypov, Omarov, and Tadžybajev. Since the end of the Second World War, there has again been a considerable increase in prose, represented by such works as the second part of Auezov's novel *Abaj* and its continuation, *The Road of Abaj,* Mustafin's novels *Millionaire, Šiganaq Bersiev* and *Life and Death,* Abdižamil Nurpejsov's *Kurlandia* and Muqanov's *Baluan Šolaq* and *Syr Darya,* which will be discussed in a later section of this chapter.

In the prose works which have appeared since 1932, two general themes, which have so continually preoccupied Kazakh thinking, predominate. On the one hand, there are the works which express the old Kazakhstan and which depict early Kazakh social relations in the critical light of the present. Common themes are the early rule of the tribal aristocracy, the oppression of women, and the struggle of the native intelligentsia against the Russian occupiers. On the other hand, there is the depiction of the new culture, which, as we have seen in Muqanov's work, is often contrasted with the old. In the majority of works concerned with the Soviet period we find the dominance of one general theme—the new agrarian society with all its implications. There is considerable interest in the new social relations in the *aul* and in problems of collectivization. Even the latest postwar prose works available are concerned primarily with agricultural and related problems. In contrast to the later poetry, very few of the recent prose works have been concerned with the industrialization of the steppes, and the few works which do attempt to deal with this development do not appear to be overly successful. As compared to the spread of collectivization and agriculture, the introduction of industry may not appear as problematic to some Kazakh writers, and its occurrence may well be somewhat obscured in the writers by the more fundamental problems of agriculture.

Bejimbet Majlin, one of the more talented prose writers as well as dramatists, is one of the Kazakh writers whose concern is primarily with the conflict between the old and the new. His first short story, "Šoga," is concerned with the ever-recurring theme of the restricted position of women in traditional Kazakh society. We will recall that this was the central problem in the first work of Kazakh prose, Köbejev's novel *Qalym.* Another early example of Majlin's prose is the small sketch, "Faithful Gun,"[2] which treats of the ill-fated return of a former *baj* to his lands, now owned by a collective farm. This tale shows Majlin's considerable mastery of his genre. It is concisely written, the action leads effectively to the climax, and the characters are well outlined. It seems that Majlin is at his best in the short, concentrated sketch or tale. Other prose works, which bear primarily on the Kazakh past, include Džansugurov's story "The Bill,"[3] which is concerned with the impact on early twentieth-century Kazakh society of the new mercantile economy, and Muqanov's novel *Botagoz,*[4] which is concerned with the 1916 uprising against the Russian conscription order and the subsequent period until the Civil War. This novel is particularly interesting since the author combines, with considerable skill, some aspects of the oral tradition with a realistic treatment of a definite and limited modern historical period. There are some excellently drawn realistic scenes of Kazakh *aul* life, of Russian officialdom and their Kazakh helpmates, and of the leaders of Kazakh opposition, particularly the hero, the revolutionary teacher Asqar, who is depicted as a typical Westerner of the school of Abaj and Altynsaryn, but who symbolizes nevertheless the fortitude and incorruptibility of the old *batyr.*

Another interesting prose work which deals with the past is Gabit Musrypov's short story "Mother."[5] Its central theme, well known in Kazakh folklore, is that of the constant intertribal struggle over pasture land and the consequent running attacks of one tribe on another. We find, however, a totally new attitude toward these old problems, for the author looks with censure on such customs of the Kazakhs, and decries the harm and misery which Kazakh women suffered when captured in a *barymta,* only perhaps to be sold again as a prize in a horse

[2] Bejimbet Majlin, "Vernoye Ruzhyo," *Nashi Dostizheniya,* No. 5 (Moscow, May, 1934), pp. 3-8.

[3] Ilyas Džansugurov, "Veksel'," *Novy Mir,* No. 5 (1936), pp. 95-104.

[4] Muqanov, *Botagoz* (Moscow, 1949).

[5] Gabit Musrypov, "Mat'," Sobolev, ed., *Pesni. . . ,* pp. 491-98.

race. No longer are these battles glorified, but rather inter-tribal warfare and the subjugation of women are condemned in sharpest terms. This is expressed in a rather moving speech of an old woman to the raiding *džigits,* in which she tells them of the suffering they bring on their own people and finally persuades them to return her daughter, whom they have captured. There is, in this short story, an unusual prevalence of formal elements of the oral art, but this is not surprising since the concern is with the distant past of the Kazakhs and the subject matter is clearly taken from the ancient epics.

During the thirties an increasing number of prose works begin to be occupied with more contemporary problems. Almost all the works of this period are concerned with the definition and depiction of a modern Kazakh hero image, so unlike, in character and appearance, the traditional image of the *batyr.* The model for the new hero is, as can be expected from reading Russian literature of the early Soviet period, the Bolshevik leader. Significant attempts to arrive at a definition of the problem of the hero image are made in two novels, *Temirtas* (1935) and *Esil* (1938), by the most prolific of Kazakh novelists, Sabit Muqanov. The somewhat schematically portrayed hero whose name is the title of the first work is a Kazakh Bolshevik who had passed through the battles of the Civil War and who now leads the battle against the survivors of the old order in the *aul,* the local *bajs.* The second novel, which is free from many of the schematic clichés which can be found in such abundance in *Temirtas,* again has as its central personage a Bolshevik, the Kazakh Ajdos, who carries on a relentless battle against the *bajs* during the Civil War.

Other works show more direct interest in the birth of agriculture, the destruction of nomadism, and the battle for collectivization of rural Kazakhstan. Such a work is Abdyqadyrov's short story "*Tulpar*—The Winged Horse,"[6] which is concerned with the new problem of horse breeding on a collective farm. There is first a traditional story of an ancient Kazakh and his horse as told by an old horsekeeper to his young *kolkhoz* com-

[6] Abdyqadyrov, "Tulpar-krylaty kon'," Sobolev, ed., *Pesni. . . ,* pp. 364-69.

panions, but the story points to a new moral, namely, that the modern Kazakh horse breeder must learn from the old Kazakh the art of treating horses. Only after he has learned to love the horse of the collective as the old Kazakh loved his horse will it be possible to breed real *kolkhoz tulpars,* akin in potentialities to the legendary winged horse.

A rather amusing short sketch about the new *kolkhoz* life is Gabit Musrypov's story "The Pig,"[7] in which the author tells of the introduction of pig husbandry on a Kazakh collective farm. The initial horror and disgust of the farmers at this new "unclean animal" is gradually overcome when the high fertility of the pig is recognized and it becomes clear that this animal provides a profitable enterprise for the farm. Here we find a rather rare example of a lighter tone and a humorous approach.

Prewar novels which have dealt with the problems of industrialization in Kazakhstan include *Friends,* by Sattar Erübajev (1937), which is concerned with the problems of the strengthening of Karaganda industry. The main protagonists are a Russian scientist, Voznetsenski, his daughter Liza, and a young Kazakh engineer, who are trying to work out their industrial problems. The novel ends with a picture of the possibility of a gigantic war between the USSR and the capitalist West. Another industrial novel is Gabiden Mustafin's *Life and Death,* which also is concerned with the Karaganda industries. This novel is closely related to the typical Russian Five-Year-Plan novel, with the ever recurring theme of the activities of the wreckers. The heroine is a young and beautiful Kazakh girl with the legendary name Džibek, who denounces her father, whom she discovers to be a wrecker.

In considering the prose of the thirties we can conclude with a remark made by Mukhtar Auezov in 1941:

> Despite the fact that during the last years there have appeared a great number of short stories and novels, the genre of prose . . . in Kazakhstan still remain[s] the least developed one in our literature.[8]

[7] Musrypov, "Svinya," *Nashi Dostizheniya,* No. 5 (May, 1934), pp. 9-12.
[8] Auezov, "Kazakhskaya literatura za 20 let," Drozdov *et al., Sbornik. . . ,* p. 388.

One might have expected that during the war years there would emerge a large body of works treating of the front-line battles in which so many Kazaks were taking part. Actually, however, relatively few prose works written during the war years concern themselves with this theme. Kazakh writers were repeatedly taken to task during the war for their failure to produce war works of significant proportions. When, in February, 1943, the Plenum of the Kazakh Writers Union met in Alma-Ata, the lack of enthusiasm for war themes preoccupied many of the discussions. It was pointed out at that time that, despite the fact that the war had already been raging for over a year, Kazakh writers had not produced a single significant prose work concerned with the war. The Kazakh daily press began to bristle with editorial blandishments addressed to the writers, who were exhorted to make up for their failings.[9] Despite all efforts, however, novels with the front-line war as the main theme did not begin to emerge until after the end of the war, under the compelling presure of the structures of the postwar party views on the literary arts. Typical postwar war novels are Musrypov's *Soldier from Kazakhstan,* Mustafin's *Life and Death,* and Nurpejsov's *Kurlandia.*

Most works written during, and since the war, however, continue to show a marked preoccupation with the problems of the economic transformation of the steppes. Again, with few exceptions, we find the same picture which had struck us during the thirties: although a few serious works have appeared which have been concerned with the industrialization of Kazakhstan, the great majority of postwar novelists continue to show a marked preference for the agricultural scene. There have also appeared, since the war, a number of significant historical and biographical novels.

Typical of some of the least successful postwar prose works which treat of the life on the Kazakh collective farm are the short stories of Sapargali Begalin. One may say, without exaggerating excessively, that most of Begalin's short stories are little

[9] E.g., *Kaz. Prav.,* February 23, 1943, p. 4; March 5, 1943, p. 2; March 28, 1943, p. 1; June 20, 1943, p. 3.

more than fictionalized, glorified economic reports, with lengthy speeches and statistical reports abounding. Thus, in the tale "The Sheep" Begalin reports the introduction to a Kazakh collective farm of a new breed of sheep. The tale begins with a detailed, almost zoological, description of the new breed and then shifts to a farm meeting, during which the reader is treated to a series of lengthy business reports and enthusiastic speeches, which make up the rest of the short tale.

A somewhat more significant example of collective farm literature is Mustafin's novel *Šyganaq Bersiev* (1945).[10] The hero of this novel, Šyganaq Bersiev, is a famous Stakhanovite pig breeder, an innovator who boldly stakes out new paths for more scientific pig production on his collective farm. Šyganaq is an outstanding organizer, a devoted, selfless worker, who spurs the other collective farm members on by his self-denying attitude towards the common task. He is opposed in his labors by a number of people, including the chairman of the local party committee, who fail to take part fully in the life of the *kolkhoz.* Essentially, Mustafin's novel already foreshadows many of the postwar novels concerned with similar themes; and it would not be a task of excessive difficulty to utilize the pattern of this novel as a schematic outline for almost all the postwar Kazakh works concerned with socialist construction. In almost every one of these novels, the actual hero of the story is not a human being, but rather the abstract concept of self-sacrificing labor and inventiveness, with which obstacles which seem well-nigh insurmountable are overcome by the sheer strength of superhuman efforts. Most of these works reveal only too painfully the Communist party pronouncements of 1946 on literature which were first expressed in Zhdanov's speech about the journals *Zvezda* and *Leningrad* and which, in essence, amounted to an admonition to writers to concern themselves, first and foremost, with contemporary problems of a political and economic nature and to make it clear in their works that Communism, the final stage of economic and political development envisaged by the

[10] Russian translation, Moscow, Sovetski Pisatel, 1948.

Marxists, is no longer a dream of the far distant future, but within the grasp of Soviet Man.

Two of the most significant novels, which are clearly a result of the Zhdanov policy, are Mustafin's novel *Millionaire,*[11] which was awarded the newly established Džambul Prize for Literature by the Council of Ministers of the KSSR,[12] and Muqanov's novel, *Syr Darya.*[13] *Millionaire* is concerned with the mechanization of a Kazakh collective farm. The treatment of this problem in this novel does not differ markedly from the treatment of modern collective farming in many Soviet Russian postwar novels. The main hero is a young Kazakh, Džomart, who at the outset of the novel is vice-chairman of the "millionaire" *kolkhoz* Amangeldy. As Džomart believes that the plans laid out for expansion of the farm by its chairman Džaqyp are not ambitious enough, he proposes a new plan which calls for the complete electrification of the *kolkhoz* and the exchange of the traditional Kazakh cattle for pure-bred livestock. After a long running battle against bureaucracy, his plan is ultimately accepted by the District Committee of the Party and by the Party nucleus of the collective farm and is carried into effect. As the novel ends, the collective farm is run entirely by electricity, cows are being milked by electric milking machines, and new roads are being built.

The characters in the novel are not convincing and their motivations are not apparent. Džomart's ambitious plans, despite the difficulties which are met, are realized too quickly for belief. The main obstacle appears to be the lack of working forces, but help arrives almost miraculously in the form of voluntary labor contributions both from Karaganda and from nearby collective farms which loan their workers for the construction of electric lines.

Even weaker is the attempt to develop the characters through a depiction of their personal lives. The subplot is concerned with the life of Džomart and his wife Alma. Neither Džomart nor Alma impresses one as a living human character. In addition,

[11] Gabiden Mustafin, *Millioner,* roman, *Druzhba Narodov,* No. 2 (1949), pp. 3-119.

[12] *Lit. Gaz.,* January 4, 1950, p. 1.

[13] Sabit Muqanov, *Syr Darya* (Moscow, 1953).

Mustafin employs a device which is little more than a trick to heighten the tragedy and courage of Alma. She is blinded in an airplane accident, but almost superhumanly overcomes her handicap, becomes an eminent musician, and eventually plays her own composition before a Moscow audience, which includes Stalin. The author presents us with a typical triangle situation. Džomart falls in love with Alma's friend Džanat, but the solution of the triangle is not very satisfactory and reveals clearly the new puritanical outlook prevalent in the Soviet Union. Alma declares that she cannot stand in the way of the happiness of Džomart, and Džanat foregoes Džomart's love since both Džomart and Džanat realize that they cannot achieve happiness by sacrificing the happiness of Alma. And the moralistic remarks of Džanat do not achieve their intended effect when she says:

What kind of passion wants to subdue us? A human or an animal passion? It is true that Alma with her own words has given us freedom, but we would be better off if she had not done so. She was able to tear out her heart and give it to us. Then, why cannot we take our hearts and give them to her? If our love is only a blind passion, then, like a carrion eagle, it will tear apart Alma's soul. And if our love is a true human passion, it should guard the clean soul of Alma. . . . I believe you. You are not lying and speak straight from the heart. But cannot passion make you drunk just like wine? There are many sinful passions, and what would become of people if there were no conscience in the world, if there were no will? I am afraid you have just forgotten about conscience and lost your will. You were ready to offend the clean soul of Alma.[14]

Džanat is, however, a more convincing character than Alma and the treatment of her inner struggle against her love for Džomart reveals more insight than the corresponding treatment of Alma's problems. The author is convincing also in his depictions of the representatives of the "old," such as the *kolkhoz* chairman Džaqyp, the swine-herd Bajmagambet, and the old *batyr*-like hunter Dos.

Much of the novel reminds us of the Russian novels of the period of the First Five-Year Plan. It frequently sounds more

[14] Mustafin, *Millioner,* p. 105.

like a textbook or a technical handbook on agriculture than like a work of literature. There are long and involved discussions about seed selections, the agricultural experiments of Academicians Vilyams and Lysenko, electric milking techniques, and road building, and the whole novel is pitched to the feverish speed which recalls such novels as Katayev's *Time Forward*. But at the same time the novel lacks the vitality and the skilful devices of Katayev's novel.

One great difference between this novel and the typical Russian novels of the First Five-Year Plan is the absence of the "wrecker" motif, which was almost never lacking in the earlier construction novels. True, there is the fraudulent bookkeeper, but his motives are not political and he is tried by the collective almost incidentally. In contrast to the typical Soviet approach of the early thirties, he is depicted rather sympathetically as a poor wretch, rather than as a hateful political enemy.

True to the recent resolutions, there is considerable talk in the novel about the dawning of Communism, which is symbolized in the attempts of one of the collective farmers to give up his private cattle, since their care interferes with his duties for the *kolkhoz*.

In general this is a novel of technical and political achievement, rather than of human conflict and drama. The constant optimism and endless successes of Džomart do not appear realistic, and he seems to serve primarily as a symbol of social progress. The main contribution of the novel lies in the information it provides concerning modern village life of Kazakhstan, the new role of women, and industrialization.

While Mustafin's novel is set in postwar rural Kazakhstan, the action of Muqanov's *Syr Darya* takes place shortly before, and during, the war. The novel, which is meant to present to the reader a panoramic view of Kazakhstan during the war years, is concerned with a somewhat broader problem than Mustafin's work. The subject matter is again the national construction effort, in this case the damming up of the Syr Darya River in order to provide large-scale irrigation for hitherto parched lands. The work on the dam, which is begun with great energy and speed, is threatened perilously by the outbreak of the war and the ensuing manpower and material shortages. It is this situation which represents the essential problem of the novel. Can the work be carried out despite the difficulties? And the answer is in the affirmative; for Soviet Man, we are told repeatedly, is capable of subjugating his environment, no matter what the obstacles. While the author is only somewhat more successful than Mustafin in creating living characters with convincing internal biographies and understandable motivations, he does succeed, to a considerably greater degree, in evoking the atmosphere of the strained, tense enthusiasm for the labor effort.

Muqanov, like Mustafin, has been somewhat more successful in his characterization of the older, tradition-minded Kazakhs, as the grizzled *kolkhoz* leader Syrbaj and his wife with their many traditional sayings and prejudices and their almost religious adherence to the time-honored traditions of hospitality. On the other hand, the younger generation in the novel remains only as a grey mass of ideal men and women, practically indistinguishable one from the other. The idealization of the labor effort has led Muqanov, as it has Mustafin, into the pitfalls of schematization, in which the individual participant is sacrificed to various principles of society. So greatly does the author idealize and romanticize that there remains little to remind the reader that he is watching an almost superhuman battle of men against nature. Everything flows with incredible ease and fluidity; and when the war interferes by taking away valued workers, the remaining workers simply redouble their efforts and the work is not perceivably slowed up; when the war needs require the withholding of much needed materials, again these shortcomings are rapidly and easily overcome. Bajžan, the chief engineer, reflects happily that there are actually no difficulties in the national construction effort when he says that "everyone works as if preparing for a holiday. And I feel only as if I were presiding at these festivities."

It is interesting to note that there are no significant negative characters in the novel. The single "wrecker," who attempts to slow the building efforts by demoralizing the participants, is quickly uncovered for what he is and dealt with by the courts. But again the "wrecker" episode is a most unimportant one and marks no serious interference with the successful execution of the construction plan.

Soviet critics have called this work a fine example of Socialist Realism. Yet the reader cannot but ask whether he is not presented here with a highly unreal situation. Can people truly be this good and morally impeccable? Are we not dealing here with an ideal behavior pattern, rather than with a normative one? The answer to this question, in terms of Soviet theory, can be found in the discussions which have been carried on, in recent years, over the question what actually is the "typical" for the representation of which the Soviet writer has been told repeatedly he is to strive. The answer given by responsible Soviet critics and political leaders is that by "typical" one must not understand the normative at all; rather, we are told to read into this term a form of idealized social behavior which does not necessarily indicate the "usual" or the "real." This probably was stated most concisely by Malenkov in his speech at the 19th Party Congress in 1952:

> The typical is not only that which is encountered with highest frequency, but that which expresses, most fully and most acutely, the essence of a given social force. . . . Under the typical we do not understand some kind of statistical average . . . . The typical is the basic sphere of the appearance of the party spirit [*partijnost'*] in realistic art. The problem of the typical is always a political one.[15]

While Mustafin's and Muqanov's novels are of interest primarily as sociological documents and as milestones testifying to at least technical progress in Kazakh prose literature, Mukhtar Auezov's cycle of novels concerned with Abaj Qunanbayev presents a totally different picture. For here Auezov is an author who is not only a novelist of distinction and talent, but also a literary scholar of no small merit. Auezov's *magnum opus* consists of the two parts of his biographical novel *Abaj* and its continuation, *The Road of Abaj*.

[15] G. Malenkov, *Otchetny doklad XIX s'ezdu partii o rabote Tsentral'nogo Komiteta VKP* (*b*) (Moscow, 1952), p. 73.

We have already discussed some of the earlier works of Mukhtar Auezov. We noted that his early works—plays and short tales—were primarily concerned with the Kazakh past and were quite close to the old oral art. After his early creative period, however, he embarked on far more ambitious adventures. The turning point in his career came in the middle twenties, with his studies in the Institute of Language and Material Culture of the University of Leningrad (1923-28) and his postgraduate work at the Central Asiatic State University in Tashkent in 1930. After completing his advanced studies, Auezov began to devote most of his time to the study of the founder of Kazakh written literature, Abaj Qunanbajev. However, Auezov's activities were not limited to his writings and research on Abaj's life. He also contributed, in this period, works concerned directly with the new era, such as his short story "Shoulder to Shoulder" dealing with the problems of socialist construction, and his plays depicting the Civil War in Kazakhstan (*The White Birch* and *Struggle*). In 1939 there appeared his monograph on the Kirgiz national epos *Manas* and his study on *The Epos and Folklore of the Kazakh People,*[16] written in collaboration with Leonid Sobolev. Auezov also contributed many translations of the Russian classics and of Soviet and Western literature including Shakespeare's *Othello,* Gogol's *Revizor,* and Pogodin's *Aristocrats.*

Auezov's dominant passion remained, however, the re-creation in his writings of the era dominated by Abaj Qunanbayev. Accordingly, Auezov undertook extensive research. He was fortunate in that he himself was born and reared in the very region in which Abaj had lived and worked, and thus he could interview people who had known Abaj personally or who had been at one time his pupils. He tells of his research and of his contact with former acquaintances of Abaj in an interview:

> Particularly in those years [1923-25] I met people who had known the hero of my future novel personally, and even today the conversations I had with Abaj's pupil Kökäj are alive in my memory.

[16] M. Auezov, L. Sobolev, "Epos i folklor kazakhskogo naroda," *Lit. Kritik,* No. 10-11 (November, 1939), pp. 210-33; No. 1 (January, 1940), pp. 169-80.

The memorable story teller Bajmagambet, luckily for us, has lived a long life. Even in my childhood I used to hear tales, many of which the story teller had remembered from Abaj's own words.[17]

Many of Auezov's critical and historical works have been devoted to a study of Abaj and the society in which he lived. In 1933 he participated in a joint project which resulted in the first complete publication of Abaj's works. Auezov's contributions to this project were invaluable and include a biography of the author. In 1934, he published another scholarly work, *History of Kazakh Literature of the Nineteenth Century.* In the next year his first independent article on Abaj, "Abaj, a Kazakh Classic,"[18] was publishsed, and a series of his studies dealing with various aspects of the art of Abaj appeared in the Kazakh periodical press.

Before Auezov completed his ambitious biographical novel of Abaj, he wrote, in collaboration with Leonid Sobolev, a tragedy on the life of the writer.[19] He also wrote a script for the moving picture *Songs of Abaj,* which was produced in the Alma-Ata film studios by G. L. Roshal, and contributed a libretto for the opera *Abaj* to the music of A. Zhubanov and L. Khamidi.

Part One of Auezov's novel *Abaj* was published in Kazakh in 1942, after running serially in Kazakh literary journals from 1939 on, and was translated into Russian in 1945.[20] Part Two appeared in Kazakh in 1947. In 1949, after certain revisions had been undertaken on the first part of the novel, both parts appeared in a new edition in Russian translation.[21]

Abaj is more than a biographical novel. It is a kaleidoscopic study of Kazakh society in the late nineteenth century against the background of the life of Abaj and the events in Abaj's tribe, the Tobyqty, from approximately 1858 to 1887. Side by side with the hero of the novel, Abaj, Auezov has pictured another

[17] "Kak sozdavalas' éta kniga. Beseda korrespondenta *Kazakhstanskoi Pravdy* s M. Auezovym," *Kaz. Prav.*, April 17, 1949, p. 3.

[18] Auezov, "Abaj—kazakhski klassik," *Literaturny Kazakhstan,* No. 2, (1935).

[19] Auezov, Sobolev, *Abaj,* Drozdov *et al.*, eds., *Sbornik. . .* , pp. 121-92.

[20] Auezov, *Abaj,* roman (Moscow, 1945).

[21] Auezov, *Abaj,* roman (Moscow, 1949). Henceforth all references to this work will be to the 1949 edition.

hero, the simple Kazakh man, in the setting of his traditional life. We might say that this novel is written on several levels. There is first of all the life of Abaj himself. Then there are the two aspects of Kazakh society: the old patriarchal order represented primarily by Abaj's father, the tyrannical Qunanbaj, and the new "Westernized" generation of young Kazakh intellectuals. Then again there are the two Russian strata in Kazakhstan, that of the rulers and that of the political exiles. Particularly impressive is the close connection of this work with the past and its tradition. Essentially, the author attempts to depict the first great contact between the cultures of the Russians and the Kazakhs. For all these reasons the novel strikes us by its breadth, and it might well be termed an epic of nineteenth-century Kazakhstan.

Abaj is written in a mature style. The imagery is poetic and colorful and material is presented with considerable realism. While certain criticisms can well be made concerning parts of the novel, for example the rather schematic treatment of some of the secondary characters, particularly the Russian exiles, most of the characters are handled with considerable psychological insight.

The first part of the novel is devoted to the years from 1853 to 1870 as the youthful Abaj is pictured in the circle of his father's family. The father is depicted as a strong-willed tyrant, a typical tribal leader, who does not hesitate at bloodshed in order to maintain his rule and the prestige of his tribe and who is merciless when dealing with any offenders of the customary law. One of the most powerful scenes in the novel occurs when Qunanbaj orders the execution of the old *batyr,* Qodar, because rumor has it that he has been living with his widowed daughter-in-law, Qamqa. In this scene there is revealed with particular intensity Auezov's mature attitude toward the tribal past from which he is willing to take inspiration, but which he does not hesitate to examine critically.

Among Auezov's most successful characters through whom he depicts the early times of the Kazakhs are the main women in the novel. There is the old grandmother Zärä, who, in her quiet, loving way, steers the young Abaj away from the autocratic ideas of his father and teaches him to love and help people and to admire nature. There is also Abaj's unhappy mother, one of the many wives of Qunanbaj. Again, there is the lyrical depiction of Abaj's first love, the young girl Togžan. In the description of the tender beauty of the young girl, Auezov comes closest to the oral tradition. We also find, in the passages concerned with Togžan, a few examples of the influence of the Persian poets. Thus, Abaj compares his love to *Zuhra*, the morning star, and to the moon in its pale and delicate light. But in striking contrast is Auezov's realistic handling of Abaj's emotional growth as he comes to love this young woman, a love which is answered with equal passion and which is clandestinely consummated.

The love theme was probably influenced by the lyrical epos *Qozy Körpöš and Bajan Sulū,* which is also concerned with the problems of two lovers who cannot marry without violating tribal traditions of exogamy. Abaj is forced by customary law to marry the girl whom his family has purchased for him, Dildä, and Togžan is forced to marry the man who has paid her *qalym*. "It is impossible not to go, not to marry him," she muses. "Such is the will of my parents." And Abaj, the otherwise headstrong young *džigit,* also bows to the customary law and pays the traditional premarital visit to his bride.

Some of the most colorful pages of the novel are concerned with Kazakh customs and traditions. There are detailed depictions of the nomadic migrations, of funeral and wedding ceremonies, of games of the children and the youth, of festivals, *ajtys,* horse races, etc.

In the first part of the novel we meet the young Abaj, who is gradually turning away from the traditional ways of his father. Through his acquaintance with the Russian exiles Mikhailov and Dolgopolov, he becomes more and more influenced by the ideas and the literatures of the West, and this new interest begins to replace his early preoccupation with Kazakh oral art and Persian and Arabic literatures. In the second volume we meet the mature Abaj, who is now a product not only of his Kazakh past but also of modern Russian culture. Here Auezov examines and probes the important problem of the influence of Russian culture on the growing Kazakh intelligentsia. We now see the Abaj whose views on literature have become shaped and who avidly studies the Russian classics:

During the whole winter Abaj, surrounded by his aids—dictionaries and textbooks—sat and pored over Russian books. And in spring, when it seemed to him that the light of the new world was already visible, he began to take up Pushkin. He began with prose and as he was reading he felt with great joy that he understood essentially everything. He was reading Pushkin's *Dubrovski.* Pushkin opened before Abaj all the richness of the Russian language —and it was only then that Abaj was able to understand all the implications of Pushkin's thought.

The deep emotional satisfaction and the particular clarity with which he was now able to sense all the life around him were evoked by his meeting with this book: this book proved to be like the companion one accidentally meets on the road, who suddenly and quite unexpectedly becomes one's best friend. It had been a long time since Abaj had felt such great joy. This day seemed to be the justification of his long seclusion, of his neglect of all domestic affairs and discussions. The ford for which he had looked for such a long time in order to cross to the other shore was now finally found.[22]

Some critics have held that Auezov was more successful when describing the ancient traditions of the Kazakhs,[23] but it would not seem that this point is entirely valid since Auezov has shown the reader, with admirable skill, what the new culture must have meant to the Kazakhs. We can feel the inspiration that it offered the intellectuals, but we can also feel, with the every-day Kazakh people, the amazement and confusion they must have experienced as they attempted to grasp the strange new concepts of nineteenth-century Russian culture.

The Marxist approach is clear in the social attitude of the writer as revealed in this book. Nineteenth-century Kazakhstan is pictured as composing two societies, the Russian society superimposed on that of the Kazakhs, both of which societies were themselves split by class conflicts. We see the struggle of the

[22] *Ibid.*, p. 522.

[23] See L. Severov's review of Part One of the novel in *Druzh. Nar.*, No. 12 (December, 1946).

poor Kazakh herders and intelligentsia against the forces of the Kazakh ruling aristocracy, and we see the division of Russian society into colonial administrators and tsarist officials on the one hand and the political exiles on the other. The author does not, however, slip into the pitfalls of schematization so common in many Kazakh novels. Although some of his minor characters are weak, in most cases the major characters are depicted with considerable grasp of the complexities of human nature.

A recent novel by Auezov, *The Road of Abaj,*[24] forms the last link of the Abaj cycle, carrying the life of the great Kazakh thinker to its conclusion. This novel has little of the power and convincingness of the earlier work. The characters are not as well rounded as they were in *Abaj* and their psychological make-up emerges almost solely in editorial statements by the author, rather than growing organically out of the dynamics of their personality. Unfortunately it appears that this author also has succumbed to the political criticisms which, in this case, held that his depiction of the role of the Russians in nineteenth-century Kazakhstan was not positive enough. Quite in contrast to the earlier novel, which presented a well-balanced picture of the contact with the Russians, *The Road of Abaj* presents an unconvincing picture, since there is almost no mention of any oppressive, or unpopular, Russian government policies. Furthermore, the author, at the slightest provocation, launches into lengthy editorials about the beneficial role of the Russians. We are witnessing here the tragic spectacle of a truly talented author following no longer the dictates of his mind, but rather submitting to the pressures of prevalent political attitudes. This is the last work of Auezov's which is available; and we can only hope a freer climate may again encourage the author to return to his earlier penetratingly realistic style.

Kazakh prose, which some thirty years ago hardly existed, has acquired an increasingly important position in modern Kazakh literature and has attained some memorable high points. Prose literature is, however, still young. Even with the constant

[24] Auezov, *Put' Abaya, Znamya,* Nos. 8-9 (1951).

strictures which are presently being imposed upon Soviet writers it appears quite evident that Kazakh fiction writers have traversed a long road in the development of the novel and the short story; and the foundations have certainly been laid for the development of a mature and rich literature. The shortcomings which have been noted, particularly in relation to the "economic" novels, can be attributed now, it would seem, more to an unfortunate political climate and somewhat less to the inexperience of Kazakh writers themselves.

APPENDIX

KAZAKH THEATER AND DRAMA

THE DEVELOPMENT of a modern dramatic tradition was considerably slower and more laborious, and considerably less successful, than that of other literary genres. The causes underlying the difficulties which lay in the way of the emergence of a dramatic tradition have their basis, first and foremost, in Mohammedan attitudes which regarded drama as a sinful occupation, and also in the lack, in nineteenth-century Kazakhstan, of an urban civilization or a court life which could have stimulated the emergence of a theatrical tradition, even in the face of Mohammedan interdictions. Not a single play was written in the nineteenth century, nor did there exist a single Kazakh theatrical establishment. As a result, theater and drama are the youngest, and as yet least fully developed, forms of art in modern Kazakhstan, and the number of plays which have been written is limited. Muqanov, in a recent survey of Kazakh literature, counts only eight Kazakh plays of significant proportions.[1] As the development of a significant dramatic tradition is still in the future, it is not surprising that relatively few Kazakh plays have found their way into Russian translation and practically no Kazakh plays are available in the West. We are thus forced into a very cursory survey of the development of the drama and a discussion of the Kazakh theater and its repertoire.

As the development of a network of playhouses as an indispensable prerequisite to the growth of a national dramatic tradition was closely related to the emergence of relatively stable urban and rural settled groups, it was not until the 1930's that any considerable growth of theaters could be observed. The first theater to be organized in Kazakhstan was the Kazakh

[1] Muqanov, "Kazakhskaya literatura no pod'eme," *Zvezda,* No. 5 (1949), p. 118.

Academic State Theater of Drama (in Kazakh *Drama Teatr,* for short), which was founded in 1926. The earliest Kazakh plays to be performed in this playhouse were dramas with themes harking back to the oral tradition, such as Auezov's *Änlik and Kebek;* but soon also plays with more contemporary and revolutionary themes could be observed on its boards, both by Kazakh authors, such as Sejfullin's *Red Falcons* and Majlin's *Majdan,* and translated plays by Russian authors. In 1933 another significant theater was founded in the capital, the Kazakh State Theater of Opera and Ballet (*Opera žane Ballet Teatr*); and in the same year there was created the first Russian theater in the republic, the Republican Russian Dramatic Theater, which produces not only Russian plays, contemporary and classical, but also Kazakh plays in Russian translation. The emergence of a significant number of good theaters, however, continues to be slow, particularly in the provinces.

No figures are available concerning the number of theatrical establishments in the 1920's and the early 1930's. By 1936, when more pertinent statistical data begin to become available, Soviet sources give the number of theaters, including semi-professional and amateur farm groups, as twenty-four, including eighteen theaters performing in the Kazakh language, four Russian theaters, one Uigur and one Uzbek theater.[2] This figure has since remained relatively stable and recent sources indicate a slower rate of growth, with forty-seven theaters in operation in 1947, of which twenty-one are Kazakh language theaters.[3]

Recently there has been a considerable increase in the number of moving picture houses. In 1917 there existed only twenty-two motion picture establishments, which were concentrated in the larger urban centers.[4] In 1936, a Soviet source[5] reports a total of 820 movie establishments, of which 536 were but traveling shows which toured the outlying districts and *auls.* Of the total number of motion picture establishments, only seventy-five were

[2] Kulumbetov, *op. cit.,* p. 46.

[3] See *Kaz. Prav.,* October 24, 1947, p. 1; Muqanov, "Kazakhskaya literatura . . . ," p. 117.

[4] Abdykalykov, Pankratova, *op. cit.,* p. 585.

[5] Kulumbetov, *op. cit.,* p. 46.

equipped for sound, while the rest showed only silent movies. By 1940, the last figures available to the author, Soviet sources claimed a total of 1,104 moving picture houses, of which 770 were equipped for sound.[6]

The principal theaters of the KSSR have absorbed a considerable amount from the predominant theatrical schools in Russia proper, and most of the leading actors have been trained in collective groups in the various Russian theatrical schools, such as the Central Theater Kombinat in Moscow or the various theatrical schools (*Tekhnikum*), attached to important Moscow theaters. Attached to the Moscow State Theater Kombinat there is also a Kazakh opera school which was founded in 1936 and which offers voice training to Kazakh students.[7]

The earliest plays produced on the Kazakh stage were the more traditional ones as Musrypov's *Qyz Džibek* and his play *Qozy Körpöš and Bajan Sulū,* as well as Auezov's plays *Änlik and Kebek* and *Ajman Šolpan.* The heroes of all these plays are the folklore *batyrs* of the past. It was only towards the end of the twenties that such Civil War and revolutionary Kazakh plays as Sejfullin's *Red Falcons* (*Qyzyl sunqarlar*), Kh. Khusainov's *Amangeldy* and Auezov's *Struggle* and *October* began to be performed on the Kazakh stage. But only towards the thirties do we find the gradual use of the Soviet themes of the Five Year Plan, collectivization, etc., as is evidenced in Džansugurov's drama, *Turksib.* Only after 1932 did the Kazakh State Theater of Drama begin to show translations of Soviet Russian plays, such as Kirshon's *Bread,* Pogodin's *My Friend,* Pogodin's *Aristocrats,* as well as Kazakh translations of the Russian classics (Gogol, Ostrovski) and works of world drama (Shakespeare, Molière, etc.).

By the 1940's theater programs in Kazakhstan, and particularly in the capital, Alma-Ata, had broadened considerably; and the repertoires of the three leading theaters of the city showed a considerable variety of Kazakh, Russian, and Western plays, operas, and ballets.

[6] Abdykalykov, Pankratova, *op. cit.,* p. 585.
[7] See "Teatralnaya smena Kazakhstana," *Lit. Gaz.,* May 10, 1936, p. 4.

INDEX

Abaj (novel), *see* Auezov
Abaj (opera by A. Zhubanov and L. Khamidi), *see* Auezov
Abaj Prize, 223
Abdyqadyrov, Qalmaqan, 189, 232; *Tempo,* 191; "*Tulpar*-the Winged Horse," 239-40
Abdykalykov, M., 153, 154
Abilev, Dikhan, 231
Ablaj khan, 87-89, 186, 187
Abu-bäkir, 97
Abū'l Gāzī, 111
Abyl (*aqyn*), 229
Academy of Sciences of the Kazakh SSR, 145, 152, 153, 198; Institute of Language and Literature, 152, 153; folklore section, 152
Academy of Sciences of the USSR, 145
'adāt, 14
"Address of the Hero Makhambet to Sultan Bajmagambet," *see* Ütemisov
adultery, 14
agglutination, 69
agriculture, xi, 4, 5, 7, 19, 24, 130, 133, 135, 163, 171, 223, 233, 237, 239, 241, 245
Ajman-Šolpan (epic), 61, 121, 151, 185; (play), *see* Auezov
ajmaq, 8; *see also* clan
Ajqap, 121, 123
ajtys, 29, 30-34, 170-72, 251
Akhan-säri, 97
Akhmatova, Anna, 152
Akmolinsk, 21, 23, 182
Aktyubinsk, xiii, 89
äl, see Kazakh Federation
Äl Aghasy, see Auezov
Ala Tau, 228
Alaš, 121
Alaš-orda, 134, 185
albasty, 52
Aldar Qos, 47, 50
Alibek (*aqyn*), 161
All-Union Congress of Soviet Writers, *see* Soviet Writers Congress
Alma, *see* Mustafin, *Millionaire*
Alma-Ata, 23, 121, 136, 152, 170, 215, 219, 221, 222, 223, 241, 257
Alpamyš-batyr, 60, 61, 72, 73, 81, 83, 154
Alqa, 189
Altai mountains, 9, 163
Altynsaryn, Ibraj, 101, 107-10, 113, 114, 121, 130, 235, 238; *Kirghiz Anthology,* 109; *Russian Primer for Kazakh Schools,* 109
Alymbetov, Sapargali, 169
Amanžolov, Qasym, 232, 233
ancestors, 7
Änlik and Kebek, see Auezov
aq süjök (white bones) 7; *see also* Kazakh aristocracy
Aq-tübe, *see* Aktyubinsk
Aq-Žunus (heroine of epos *Er-Targhyn*), 63, 64, 65, 66, 76, 77, 83
aqsaqal, 6
Aqša-khan (in epos *Er-Targhyn*), 62, 63, 66
aqyn, 26, 29, 30, 34, 68, 86, 87, 89, 90, 92, 102, 107, 113, 117, 121, 126, 146, 147, 148, 152, 156, 157, 158, 159, 160, 162, 163, 166, 167, 169, 170, 171, 172, 178, 183, 187, 195, 203, 209, 213, 215, 225, 229, 249
Arabia: art, 25; conquest of Central Asia, xii, 12; culture, 29, 111; language, 15, 27, 102, 120; literature, 15, 25, 98, 101, 111, 112, 113, 125, 184, 251
Arabic alphabet, 109, 121, 130, 140, 141, 188
Arabian Nights, 45, 113, 195
architecture, 25
artisans, 5
Asan Qajghy, 46, 50

"Asiatic School," 23
Asqar (in *Botagoz*), 238
aul, 6, 26, 39, 40, 94, 104, 108, 119, 126, 133, 144, 147, 149, 157, 160, 182, 187, 203, 207, 209, 218, 236, 237, 238, 239, 256
Auezov, Mukhtar, 33, 152, 153, 184-85, 208-9, 237, 240, 247-53; *Abaj,* 184, 236, 237, 247, 249-53; *Abaj* (libretto for opera), 249; *Ajman Šolpan,* 185, 257; *Äl Aghasy,* 184; *Änlik and Kebek,* 184, 185, 187, 256, 257; *Bajbiše Toqal,* 184; *Defenseless Woman,* 186; ***Epos and Folklore of*** *the Kazakh People, The,* 248; *History of Kazakh Literature of the Nineteenth Century,* 249; *October,* 257; *Qaraköz,* 185; *Road of Abaj, The,* 237, 247, 253; *Songs of Abaj* (script for moving picture), 249; *Struggle,* 248, 257; as translator, 248; *White Birch, The,* 248
Aulie Ata, 23
Averbakh, Leopold L., 179, 197
Azerbajev, Kenen, 159

Bābur, 111
Baghdad, 27
baj, 124, 127, 187, 203, 209, 236, 238, 239
bajan, see aqyn
baj-biše (first wife), 14
Bajbiše Toqal, see Auezov
Bajbolov, Qazangan, 159
Bajganin, Nurpeis (*aqyn*), 162, 167-69
Bajmagambet (*aqyn*), 249
Bajmuratov, Nurlybek, 169
Bajtursunov, Ahmad, 123, 128-31, 178, 188
Bajžan, *see* Muqanov, *Syr Darya*
balbal, 10, 11, 209
Balkhaš, 172, 232
ballet, 195, 256, 257
Baluan Šolaq, see Muqanov
baqsa, see shaman
"Barbara Allen," 67
bard, *see aqyn*
Barthold, V. V., 7, 11, 12
barymta, 137, 138
batyr, see epic hero
Bayan (in epos *Qozy Körpöš* ***and*** *Bayan Sulū*), 66, 67
bazar, 97
Bedny, Demyan, 194
Begalin, Sapargali, 241-42
Bek (*aqyn*), 160
Bekenov, 180
Beket-batyr, 93-95
Bekežanov, Nartaj, 169
Bekkhožin, Qalyžan, 231, 232
Belinski, V. G., 111
bet-ašar, 36, 40; *see also* wedding songs
betrothal before birth, 66
bi, 6, 16, 20
Bible, 73
Bilgä-Qaghan, 55
"The Bill" (Džansugurov), 238
"black bones," *see qara süjök*
Bleubajev, B., 170
Blok, Alexander, 181
blood revenge, 16
Bolshoi Theater, 195
book publishing, 120, 121, 128, 140, 156, 157, 176, 177, 178
Botagoz (Muqanov), 236, 238
"bourgeois nationalism," 153, 155, 178, 179, 180, 182, 185, 197, 198, 207
bride buying, *see qalym*
bride price, *see qalym*
Budyonny, Marshal, 210
Bukhar Džyrau, 42, 87-89
Bukhara, xiii, 97, 134
burial, 10, 11
Byron, George, 111, 118
Byzaubak (Bzaubak) (*aqyn*), 147, 148

Čagataj, 45, 101, 111, 125
camel, 3, 46, 51, 52, 62, 74, 81, 90, 91, 205
canning, 136
Carlyle, Thomas, 102
Catherine II, xiii
cattle, xii, 3, 4, 5, 6, 14, 17, 40, 82, 116; breeder, 7, 51, 133, 163, 171, 181, 183, 209, 215; breeding, 3, 130, 204, 207, 243
Caucasus, 206
census, 142
Central Asia, xi, xii, 133; Arabic conquest, *see under* Arabia; Chinese, 52, 60, 104, 105; southern regions, 5, 8; Sovietization, 133, 134
Central Asia State University, 184, 248
Central Theater Kombinat, 257
Chekhov, A. P., 121, 194, 212

Chelyuskin polar expedition, 198, 210, 215
Chernyshevski, N. G., 104, 111
Chimkent, 19, 23
China, 87, 141
Chinese, 55, 79, 109; chronicles, 55; Turkestan, 57, 60, 104, 105, 141
Christianity, 22, 106, 107
Chu River, xiii
cinemas, 256
cities, 136, 137, 183
Civil War, 134, 159, 180, 182, 186, 219, 238, 239, 248, 257
clan, 5, 6, 7, 8, 21
class struggle, 153, 252
clergy, 15, 23, 138, 141, 209
coal, 136, 164, 171, 172, 224
collective farming, 135, 136, 139, 157, 158, 164, 167, 190, 202, 203, 204, 207, 215, 224, 237, 238, 239, 240, 241, 242, 243, 244, 245, 246, 257
Communism, 196, 242, 245
Communist party, 123, 131, 135, 139, 159, 173, 190, 203, 239; All-Union, 152, 153, 154 n., 179, 193, 197, 223, 242, 247; Kazakh, 138, 139, 151, 153, 154, 155, 159, 170, 171, 176, 180, 181, 182, 186, 188, 189, 190, 198, 224, 236, 241, 242, 243; literary theory and policy, 173, 174, 175, 190, 195, 198, 223, 233, 234, 241, 242, 245, 247, 253, 254
Contemporary, The (*Sovremennik*), 102
Cossaks, 19, 20
Crimean khanate, 59, 62, 64
"crimes based on customs," 137-39
čybyzga, see musical instruments
cyrillic alphabet, 23, 109, 141

dangerous tasks, 48
Darwin, Charles, 111
Datov, Srym, 89
Davletbajev, 186
Defenseless Woman, see Auezov
Defoe, Daniel, 195
"Decree about the Struggle against Crimes Based on Customs," 138
deities, 10
Dickens, Charles, 102
ad-Dīn, Rašid, 111
divorce, 14
Dīvān lughāt at-Turk, see al Kāshgari, Maḥmūd
Dneprogez, 212
Dniepr, 212, 226, 227
Dobrolyubov, N. A., 111
Dolgopolov, Nifont, 111, 251
dombra, 29, 46, 232, 233
Dönentajev, Sabit, 127-128, 186
Doskej (*aqyn*), 162, 163
Dosqoža, 90, 92, 156
Dostoevski, Fedor, 99, 100, 103
dragon (*džalmaus*), 51, 53, 62
drama, 173, 183, 184, 185, 187, 194, 195, 198, 221, 237, 248, 249, 255, 256, 257
Džabajev, Džambul, 158, 163-64, 170
Džajyp, *see* Mustafin, *Millionaire*
Džajyq, see Ural
Džalbyr (Majlin), 195
džalmaus, see dragon
džalšy (hired worker), 8
Džambul Prize for Literature, 243
Džansugurov, Ilyas, 152, 186, 238; "The Bill," 238
džar-džar, 36, 37-39; *see also* wedding songs
Džaruqov, Tahir, 189, 199, 215-224, 225; *In the Dawn of Communism,* 215; *The Light of the Stars,* 215; *The Stream,* 215, 218-23; *The Sun Has Spoken,* 215
Dzhingiz-khan, 7, 35
džolbars, see tiger
Džoldybajev, 152
Džomart, *see* Mustafin, *Millionaire*
džoqtau, see mourning songs
Džumagaliev, Abdulla, 232
Dzungars, 42
džurt, see *yurt*
džüs, see Kazakh Hordes
džut, 3
džyr, see heroic epos
džyršy, see *aqyn*

eagle (as metaphor), 205, 206
Edige (in *Edige-batyr*), 72, 73
Edige-batyr, 59, 61, 72, 73, 105, 154
Edil, see Volga
education, 15-16, 22, 23, 24, 101, 107, 108, 109, 110, 111, 112, 113, 114, 122, 123, 129, 130, 135, 138, 139, 140, 141, 143, 144, 145, 165, 175, 177, 181, 182, 183, 184, 228; higher education, 143, 144, 145, 152, 156, 184, 215; price of, 14
electrification, 212, 243

Eleulov, Qošen, 172
Emba, 136
Enbekši Qazaq, 176
epic hero (*batyr*), 12, 26, 54, 58, 50 n., 60, 61, 63, 64, 71-75, 76, 77, 78, 79, 80, 82, 83, 84, 85, 95, 126, 147, 150, 159, 161, 165, 167, 168, 169, 204, 206, 221, 238, 239, 257; battle prowess, 74, 78; birth, 73, 160; family, 79, 80-82; friend, 74, 79; enemies, 79; horse, *see* horse; wife, 75, 76, 77, 78, 82, 83; invulnerability, 73, 167; modern hero, 159, 167, 168, 169, 213, 217, 218, 229, 230; praise of the hero, 74; youth, 72, 83
Epos and Folklore of the Kazakh People, see Auezov
er, see epic hero
Er-Kokča, 61
Erkokči-Erkosaj, 105
Er-Sajn, 61, 72, 73, 77, 78, 82, 84
Er-Targhyn, 61, 62-66, 74, 75, 76, 77, 83, 84, 221
Erübajev, Sattar, 240
Esil (Muqanov), 236, 239
estirtū, see songs of sad news
exogamy, 39, 251

Fadeyev, A., 194
"Faithless Lying" (*Opasyz Žalgan*) (Šortambaj), 96-97
falcon (as metaphor), 94, 150, 159, 160, 163, 205, 206, 218, 220
family, 5, 7, 8, 13, 17, 37, 40, 44, 49
fantastic stories, 26
Far East, xi
"Fellow Travelers" (*poputchiki*), 186, 189
Firdūsī, 45, 101, 111; *Šāhnāme,* 45, 113
fire worship, 11
Five-Year Plans, 142, 151, 173, 190-92, 193, 207, 215, 236, 244, 257
Friends, see Erübajev
friendship, 42
Frunze, 159, 160
Furmanov, Dmitri A., 194

Gabdulla (*aqyn*), 187
Ghaqlija, see Qunanbayev
goats, 3, 51, 53
Gogol, N. V., 194, 208, 212, 248, 257
Gök-tepe, xiii
Goethe, Johann Wolfgang von, 111, 118
Goncharov, Ivan A., 194
Gorky, Maxim, 151, 152, 194, 224
grave monuments, 10, 11, 209
grazing lands, 4, 46
Griboyedov, Alexander S., 224
Grimm's Fairy Tales, 52
Gross, Severin, 111
Gulyam, Gafur, 200 n.

Ḥafiẓ, 111
Happiness-Bringing Knowledge, see *Qutadghu-Bilig*
Hasford (Governor-General of Western Siberia), 102
heaven, *see tängri*
Heine, Heinrich, 111, 225, 226, 227, 228
heroic epos, 26, 28, 29, 41, 42, 54-85, 105, 107, 147, 150, 151, 152, 153, 162, 184, 248; antiquity, 54, 55-60; characters, 28, 71-85; clichés, 58, 69, 70-71, 149, 159, 167, 168, 187; description of battle, 56; distribution, 58-61; hero, *see* epic hero; Kirghiz epos, 56, 79, 102, 248; metric structure, 58, 69; modern epics, 157, 164, 229, 232; recital, 68; Soviet attitudes toward, 150-56; style, 56, 58, 68, 69, 147, 159, 160, 167, 203, 204, 210, 212, 230, 234; supranational character, 28; tradition, 25, 26, 167, 175, 201, 234, 238; Western European epic, 28
Herzen, Alexander, 111
Hibat al-haqa' iq, 88
hired workers (*džalšy*), 8
History of Kazakh Literature of the Nineteenth Century, see Auezov
History of the Kazakh SSR (Abdykalykov, Pankratova), 153, 154
Hodža Nasr-ed-Dīn, 47
horse, 3, 32, 42, 48, 51, 53, 207; as food, 3; as metaphor, 63, 74, 77, 78, 150, 159, 164, 169, 181, 204, 205, 206, 207, 221; as subject in folklore and literature, 3, 43, 50, 51, 62, 65, 69, 70, 73, 82-84, 90, 94, 95, 126, 150, 168, 181, 218, 221, 239, 240; biography, 83; endowed with human speech, 50, 82; magic horse, 50, 82, 83; milked, 3
husband, 14, 142; *see also* marriage

Ili River, 57
illiteracy, *see* literacy
illness, 11, 12, 13
Imambaeva, Solpan, 180
Imanov, Amangeldy, 149, 150, 217
Imperial Geographic Society, 28, 102, 103, 104
Improvisation, 27, 30, 33, 34, 44
In the Dawn of Communism (Džaruqov), 215
India, xi, 17, 45
Industry, 17, 133, 135, 136, 137, 139, 158, 164, 167, 171, 172, 177, 190, 191, 212, 215, 222, 223, 224, 226, 232, 233, 237, 240, 241, 245, 248, 257
infidels, 12, 62, 79, 95, 186
Institut krasnoi profesury, see Institute of Red Professors
Institute of Red Professors, 201
Iranian art, 25
Iranian cultures, 12, 29, 78
Iranian languages, xii, 120
Iranians, 4
irrigation, vii, 4
Irtysh, xiii, 163, 207
Ishim River, xiii
Islam, xii, 9, 11, 12, 13, 14, 15, 22, 29, 35, 36, 52, 57, 73 n., 75, 79, 80, 81, 88, 106, 107, 109, 111, 112, 113, 119, 120, 125, 138, 141, 154, 165, 166, 178, 180, 181, 183, 184, 186, 188, 209, 240, 255

Ja'qūb-Bek, 104
jär-sub, 10
journalism, 120, 121, 123, 128, 129, 132, 140, 145, 157, 176, 180, 195, 209, 224, 235, 241, 249

Kaigy, Asan, 30
Kaip-Nazarov, Mustafa, 179
Kalmyks, 61, 64, 65, 70, 71, 73, 74, 75, 77, 79, 80, 84, 89, 186, 187
Karaganda, 136, 171, 172, 212, 215, 240
Karakalpaks, 60
Karakhanides, 12
al-Kāshgarī, Maḥmūd, 27, 56-58
Katayev, Valentin, 245
Kazakh: aristocracy, 4, 7, 8, 17, 20, 21, 22, 102, 126, 127, 237, 253; ballet, *see* ballet; *dekada,* 195; economy, 3, 4, 5, 17, 133, 135, 238, 241, 242; federation, xii, 6, 7, 16, 28, 58, 87; history, viii, 7, 108, 184, 186, 187, 201, 248; Hordes, xiii, 32, 87, 126; hospitality, 47; humor, 47; intelligentsia, 24, 86, 99, 100, 101, 107, 108, 110, 122, 130, 132, 141, 146, 165, 173, 178, 184, 222, 237, 250, 252, 253; justice, x, 6, 16, 17, 20, 21, 96, 250; language, xii, 23, 100, 105, 109, 115, 120, 121, 128, 129, 130, 143, 144, 145, 176, 177, 256; literature, history of, 152, 153, 179, 180, 247, 248, 249, 255; nationalism, 24, 61, 85, 86, 90, 95, 107, 122, 133, 134, 135, 153, 154, 156, 179, 185; nationalists, 100, 112, 121, 122, 123, 128-31, 132, 134, 178, 181, 185, 188, 189, 192, 197, 207; oral art, history of, 184, 248; proverbs, 3, 7; rebellions, 89, 91, 92, 93, 95, 99, 146, 147, 148, 149, 155, 156, 212, 217, 238; religion, 9, 13, 84, 102, 106-7, 119; resistance to Russians, 86, 88, 89, 90, 101, 107, 108, 122, 130, 131, 146, 147, 149, 155, 156, 212, 237; social and political organization, 5, 7, 8, 9, 16, 19, 22, 95, 96, 110, 111, 112, 119, 133, 181, 237; social stratification, 7, 8, 16, 17, 106, 122, 126, 237; territory, xii, 18, 19; tribes, 16, 20, 21, 32; Westerners, 100, 101, 110, 112, 121, 122, 123-28, 129, 132, 165, 178, 238, 250; Writers' Union, 176, 183, 193, 194, 197, 241
Kazakh Academic State Theater of Drama, 195, 255-56, 257
Kazakh Academy of Sciences, *see* Academy of Sciences of the Kazakh SSR
Kazakh Association of Proletarian Writers, 183, 189, 190
Kazakh Pedagogical Institute, 215
Kazakh Philharmonic Orchestra, 195
Kazakh State Theater of Opera and Ballet, 256
Kazakh State University, 143, 144, 145
Kazakh SSR, 182; government, 143, 144, 170, 180, 182, 243
Kazalinsk, 23
Kazan khanate, 59
KazAPP, *see* Kazakh Writers' Union
Kenesary Nauryzbaj, *see* Nasynbaj
Kerimbekov, Sajadil, 158-59
Khamidi, L., 249

khan, xiii, 5, 7, 20, 38, 42, 43, 46, 48, 49, 88, 91, 93, 154, 186
Khanzada (in *Er-Targhyn*), 64, 65, 66
Khayyam, Omar, 101
Khiva, xiii, 134
Khludov, N. G., 100
Khomentovski, Col., 102
Khusainov, Kh., 257
Kirghiz, 25, 56, 57, 59, 60, 79, 134, 140, 142; Kirghiz epic *Manas,* 79, 102, 248; literature, 197, 200 n.; Republic, 134, 144
Kirghizstan, 102
Kirov, 198
Kirshon, Vladimir M., 257
Köbejev, Ispandiar, 127, 235, 238
Kökäj, 248
Kokand, xiii
Kolchak, 134
kolkhoz, see collective farm
Komsomol, 212
könül ajtū, see condolence songs
Koran, 15
Köroghly, 45
Korolenko, V. G., 194
Kremlin, 163, 218
Krylov, I. A., 111, 117, 127, 129
Kül-Tegin, 55, 56
küldirgiš, 53
kumiss, see *qumys*
Kurlandia, see Nurpejsov
Kustanai, 23

Latin alphabet, 130, 141, 165, 176, 177, 181, 189
legends, 26, 46, 150, 157, 164, 184, 187, 218
Lenin, 160, 161, 162, 181, 203, 206, 208, 210, 211, 212, 217, 218
Leningrad (city), 221; University of, 184, 215, 248
Leningrad (journal), 152, 242
Lermontov, M. Yu., 109, 110, 111, 117-18, 119, 204, 212, 224
levirate, 37, 40, 138, 236
Levshin, A. I., 29, 46
libraries, 176
Life and Death, see Mustafin
Light of the Stars, The, see Džaruqov
literacy, 23, 109, 140, 142-43, 157, 173, 181, 183
literary criticism, 123, 153, 179, 180, 182, 183, 185, 192, 193, 196, 198, 247, 249
literary history, 179, 180, 184, 193, 198, 247, 248, 249
literary theory and policy, 174, 195, 223, 241, 242, 247, 248, 249, 255
Literatura i iskusstvo Kazakhstana, 194
literature, Arabic, 15, 25, 98, 101, 111, 112, 113, 125, 184, 251; English, 102, 248, 257; German, 111, 225; Greek, 111; Persian, 15, 45, 98, 101, 111, 113, 125, 184, 216, 251; Russian, *see* Russian literature; Ukrainian, 99, 100, 225, 226, 227, 228; Western, 25, 110, 174, 225, 234, 235, 236, 251, 257; world, 176, 194
Lost Ones, The (Muqanov), 236
lungs, robber of, 52, 53; sacrifice of, 52; symbolism of, 12, 36, 52, 53
lyricism, 61, 67, 77, 80, 112, 127, 161, 202, 204, 205, 206, 207, 208, 210, 212, 213, 215, 216, 219, 223, 225, 230
Lysenko, academician, 245

Madrid, 231
magical healing qualities, 50
magical objects, 50
Maikov, A. N., 104
Majdan, see Majlin
Majlin, Bejimbet, 186, 237-38; *Džalbyr,* 195; "Faithful Gun," 238; *Majdan,* 256; "Šoga," 237, 238
Maldajev, Galim, 189
Malenkov, Georgi, 427
Manas (Kirghiz epos), 79, 102, 248
marriage, 8, 13, 14, 36, 71, 122, 127, 137, 236; customs, 36, 37, 39, 40, 137, 185, 236, 250, 251; songs, 36-41; *see also* levirate, exogamy, polygamy, *qalym*
Marx, Karl, 182, 203
Marxism, 174, 175, 190, 242, 252
Marxism and the National Question (Stalin), 135
Mayakovski, Vladimir V., 179 n., 191, 192, 199-200, 201, 202, 207, 212, 218, 230, 234
Mecca, 165
medrese, 15, 184
mekteb, 15
Mikhaelis, E. P., 111
Millionaire, The, see Mustafin
Mobilization Decree, 134, 146, 238

Mohammed, 13, 188
Mohammedanism, *see* Islam
Molière, 257
Mongolia, 54
Mongols, 11, 59, 61, 141, 181
Moscow, 162, 167, 212, 218, 219, 244, 257
mother, 37, 38, 80, 94
"Mother" (Musrypov), 238, 239
Mount Elbruz, 206
moving pictures, 149
mullā, 22, 87, 106
Muqanov, Sabit, 86, 152, 180, 183-84, 188, 189, 191, 192, 197, 199, 201-7, 218, 255; *Baluan Šolaq*, 237; "Balpom," 236; *Botagoz*, 236, 238; *Esil*, 236, 239; *Friends*, 236; *Lost Ones, The* (*Son of the Baj, The*), 236; "Milk and Blood," 236; *My Schoolyears*, 187; "Myrzabek," 236; *Poor Man of Yesterday and Today, The*, 183; *Spouse and Housewife*, 236; *Sulušaš*, 187, 188; *Syr Darya*, 237, 243, 245-47; *Temirtas*, 236, 239; *White Bear, The*, 198
Murat, 97-98, 109
music, 27, 33, 34, 47, 117, 195, 244, 257
musical instruments, 26, 29, 30, 46, 47, 68, 232, 233
Musrypov, Gabit, 189, 238; "Mother," 238, 239; "Pig, The," 240; *Qozy Körpöš and Bayan Sulū*, 257; *Qyz Džibek*, 195, 257; *Soldier from Kazakhstan*, 241
Mustafin, Gabiden, *Life and Death*, 237, 241; *Millionaire, The*, 237, 242, 243-45, 246, 247; *Šiganaq Bersiev*, 237, 242
My Schoolyears (Muqanov), 187
mysticism, 12, 113

Na literaturnom postu, see "On Literary Guard"
Na postu, see "On Guard"
Nasynbaj, 90, 92, 93, 156; *Kenesary Nauryzbaj*, 93
"National in form, socialist in content," 174, 175, 195
National Socialism (German), 232
Nāwā'ī, 'Ali-Šir, 45, 111
Nekrasov, N. A., 104, 111, 127
Neva, 221
New Economic Policy (NEP), 173, 186-90
new Turkic alphabet, 138, 139-42, 165, 176, 177, 181, 188, 189
Nizāmī, 111
Nogai tribe, 63, 64, 65
nomadic cattle breeding, 17; migrations, viii, 3, 4, 18, 157
nomadism, xii, 3, 5, 19, 133, 135, 204, 251
nomads, xi, xii, 3, 4, 13, 144, 151; settling of, 135, 163, 164, 239
"normative," *see* "typical"
novel, 127, 132, 139, 184, 186, 187, 235, 236, 237, 238, 241, 242, 243, 244, 245, 246, 247, 249-53
Nurpejsov, Abidžamil, *Kurlandia*, 237, 241

oasis regions, xi
oblast', 21
October, see Auezov
oil, 136, 164, 212, 215
Oimaut, 62
Oirat, 42, 60, 141, 154
Omsk, 23, 100, 102, 121, 182
"On Guard," 179, 188, 189
"On Literary Guard," 179, 189
Öngarbajev, Ötep, 159
Opan, 31, 32
opera, 249, 256, 257
oral art, elements in modern literature, 180, 184, 185, 186, 187, 191, 195, 196, 199, 201, 203, 204, 205, 206, 207, 208, 211, 212, 216, 217, 218, 219, 221, 223, 224, 225, 229, 230, 232, 234, 238, 239, 246, 251, 256, 257; research on, 152, 156, 183, 184, 193, 248; Soviet attitudes towards, 150-56, 176, 178, 179, 185, 192, 193, 196, 197, 198, 199
Orenburg, 20, 99, 121, 129, 183
Orkhon inscriptions, 9, 10, 54-56
Orkhon River, 57
Orlov, A. S., 59, 61, 152
Ormanov, Gali, 150, 232
Ostrovski, Alexander N., 257
Oswięcim, 232

Panfilov Division, 167
Pan-Islamism, 111, 178, 181
Pan-Turkism, 111, 131, 134, 178, 182
Pankratova, A., 153, 154
parents, 14, 17, 37, 251

partijnost', 198, 223, 224, 230, 241, 242, 243, 253, 254
Penkovski, L., 62
Perovsk, 23
Persia, 17
Persian literature, 15, 45, 98, 101, 111, 113, 125, 184, 216, 251
Peter the Great, ix, 5 n., 221
Petrashevski circle, 99
Petropavlovsk, 23
"Pig, The," *see* Musrypov
poetry, 173, 180, 182, 183, 186, 187, 191, 192, 193-234, 235
Pogodin, Nikolai F., 248, 257
polygamy, 13, 137, 138, 251
Poor Man of Yesterday and of Today, The (Muqanov), 183
Potanin, G. N., 28, 73, 100, 103
Pravda, 155
press, *see* journalism
proletariat, 136, 186
propaganda, 156, 157, 165, 167, 170, 171, 172, 180, 186, 192
prose, 107, 109, 112, 113, 120, 132, 173, 180, 183, 184, 189, 194, 198, 208, 209, 233, 235-54
puritanism, 244, 247; *see also* Soviet morality
Pushkin, Alexander S., 100, 109, 110, 111, 117, 119, 120, 121, 179, 187, 191, 195, 201, 204, 212, 216, 218, 219, 221, 223, 224, 225, 235, 252

Qajsar (in *The Stream*), 219, 220, 221, 222, 223
qalym (bride price), 13, 14, 37, 122, 137, 138, 185, 187, 235, 251
Qalym (novel by Köbejev), 127
Qambara-batyr, 61
Qanayev, Šortambaj, 96
qara süjök (black bones), 7
Qaraköz, *see* Auezov
Qarašev, Omar, 123, 125-26
Qart Qožaq (in *Er-Targhyn*), 63, 64, 76, 77
Qarynbaj, 50
Qasymov, Kenesary, 89, 92, 99, 156
Qazaq, 121, 129
Qazaqstan, 121
Qobdyqov, 169
Qoblandy (*Qoblandy-batyr*), 70, 71, 72, 73, 75, 76, 80, 167
Qoblandy-batyr, 59, 61, 70-71, 72, 73, 75, 76, 79, 80, 167
Qopejev, Mašqur Žusup, 123
Qorqyt, 47
Qošqarbajev, Šašubaj, 172
qostasū, see farewell songs
Qotybarov, Eset, 89, 95
Qozy, 66, 67
Qozy Körpöš and Bayan Sulū epos, 60, 61, 66-68, 121, 185 n., 187, 251; play, *see* Musrypov
qul, see slaves
Qulbaš (*aqyn*), 148, 149
qumys, 33, 172, 205
qūn, 16, 17
qūn alma (vendetta), 137
Qunanbaj, 250, 251
Qunanbayev, Abaj, 101, 110-20, 121, 125, 129, 178, 179, 180, 181, 191, 202, 204, 225, 229, 235, 236, 237, 238, 247, 248, 249-53; *Ghaqlija,* 113, 114, 115, 225
Qutadghu-Bilig, 88
Quwyršyq, 52
qyrq, 6, *see also* clan
Qyz-Džibek, epos, 68, 121, 151, 195; musical drama, *see* Musrypov
qyz-tanysū, 36, 39; *see also* wedding songs
Qyz-Žibek, see Qyz-Džibek
Qyzyl Orda, 224

Radloff, Vasili V. (Wilhelm), 4, 6, 7, 9, 11, 27, 29, 30, 37, 55, 62, 71, 100, 105
RAPP, *see* Russian Association of Proletarian Writers
realism, 125, 149, 164, 185, 204, 210, 212, 213, 218, 219, 223, 238, 250, 251, 253
Red Army, 134, 210
reincarnation, 11
Republican Russian Drama Theater, 256
Rhine, 226
rhyme, 55, 69
rhythm, 55
Road of Abaj, The, see Auezov
Robinson Crusoe, 195
Romeo and Juliet, 66
rū, *see* clan
rubber, 136
Russia: administration in Kazakhstan, 116, 135, 238, 250, 253; colonial policy, 17, 95, 96, 97, 106, 108, 113, 120, 131, 135; colonization of

Kazakhstan, 18, 19, 20, 21, 86-89, 105, 106, 122, 129, 130, 135, 238; conquest of Kazakhstan, xii, xiii, 5, 17, 25, 42, 61, 86, 87, 89, 154, 155; courts, xiv, 20; education, 22, 23, 24, 87, 99, 102, 107, 108, 109, 110, 111, 115, 182, 184; exiles in Kazakhstan, 87, 99, 119, 155, 250, 251, 253; governor, 20, 21, 119; land policy in Kazakhstan, 18, 19, 22, 89, 113, 130, 133, 135; language, 24, 90, 102, 115, 121, 142, 145, 176, 252; literature, 24, 25, 102, 109, 110, 111, 115, 127, 176, 177, 178, 191, 192, 193, 194, 195, 196, 197, 198, 199, 201, 216, 234, 235, 236, 239, 243, 244-45, 248, 252, 257; nationalism, 154, 155, 233, 253; philosophy, 24, 101, 199; religious policy in Kazakhstan, 106; Slavophiles, 101, 108; taxation, 18; trade in Kazakhstan, 5, 17; tsar, 21, 97, 119, 147, 148, 161; Westerners, 101, 108
Russian Association of Proletarian Writers (RAPP), 189, 193
Russian Colonization Authority, 19
Russians, attitudes toward, 22, 105-7, 154, 155, 156, 198, 252, 253
Russification, xiii, xiv, 19, 22, 24, 95, 98, 113, 133, 135, 139, 227
Rustaveli, 224

Šāhnāme, see Firdūsī
St. Petersburg, 28, 102, 104
Sajn-batyr (in *Er-Sajn*), 72, 77, 82, 84
Sajn, Džumagali, 199, 231 232
Saltykov-Shchedrin, M. E., 11, 115, 127
Saripov, 180
Sarsenbajev, Abu, 232
satire, 127, 128, 132, 165, 209
Satybaldin, Qapan, 199, 230, 231, 233
schools, 15, 23, 87, 99, 107, 108, 109, 142, 143
Schuyler, Eugene, 12-13
science, 215, 229, 235
secret language (in oral art), 48
sedentary societies, 12, 13, 24, 87
Sejfullin, Sakin, 152, 180, 181-83, 184, 186, 189, 196, 207-8, 256, 257
Selivanovski, A., 196
Semipalatinsk, 19, 21, 23, 111, 170
Semirechye, 18, 21
Semyonov (Tyanshansky), 100, 103
Serafimovich, Alexander S., 194
Serapion Brothers, 189
šeri'at, 138
Serkebajev, Beket, 89, 93-95, 156
settling of nomads, 4
Shakespeare, 66, 248, 257
shaman, 11, 13, 29, 52
shamanism, 9, 11, 27, 34, 35, 52, 102, 105, 137; shamanistic incantations, 52; shamanistic songs, 35
sheep, 3, 16, 46, 51, 74, 77, 92, 165, 242
Shevchenko, Taras, 99, 100, 225, 226, 227, 228
Sholokhov, Michail A., 194
short story, 189, 235, 236, 237, 238, 239, 241, 242, 248, 253
Šiganaq Bersiev, see Mustafin
slaves (*qul*), 8, 53, 187
Sobolev, Leonid, 152, 194-95, 248, 249
"social command," 191, 193, 200, 223, 230
Socialism, 123, 175, 196
socialist competition, 171, 226
Socialist Realism, 175, 180, 195, 196, 247
Society for the Study of the Kirghiz Region, 131
"Šoga" (Majlin), 237, 238
Soldier from Kazakhstan, see Musrypov
songs, 26, 29, 47, 102, 151, 157, 164, 208, 210; booksongs, 29, 98; ceremonial songs, 26; childbirth songs, 34; condolence songs, 34-44; songs "of contrast," 162, 203, 210; cursing songs, 34; farewell songs, 34, 41-42, 65, 80, 89, 92, 167; mourning songs, 34, 44-45, 92, 93, 95, 96, 149, 160, 162, 167, 169, 210, 211; religious songs, 35, 36; ritual songs, 34-35; singing games, *see ajtys*; songs of sad news, 34, 42-44, 92, 95, 149; wedding songs, 34, 36-41
Songs of Abaj (moving picture), *see* Auezov
Šora-batyr, 60, 61, 72, 73
Soviet, government, 136, 137, 143, 144; policy on literature, *see* Communist party
Soviet hero in literature, 242, 246
Soviet morality, 247

Soviet Writers' Congress, 151, 152, 194, 198
sovkhoz, see state farms
Sovremennik (Contemporary, The), 102
Soyuz Sovetskikh Pisatelei, see Union of Soviet Writers
Spanish Civil War, 230, 231
Spencer, Herbert, 111
Spinoza, 111
spirits, 10, 52; dangerous, 52; harmless, 52; in disguise, 52, 53; temptation by, 53
SSP, *see* Union of Soviet Writers
stakhanovite, 157, 204, 212, 224, 242
Stalin, Joseph, 135, 139, 140, 155, 160, 163, 181, 200, 201, 203, 205, 206, 207, 208, 210, 214, 233, 244
Stalin Prize, 178
state farms (*sovkhoz*), 135, 136, 158, 166 n.
Stepanov, B. N., 154
Stream, The, see Džaruqov
strikes, 133
Struggle, see Auezov
Ṣūfī, 12
suicide, 188
Šukasaptati, 45
sultans, xiii, 5, 6, 7, 20, 38, 94, 150, 187
Sulušaš (Muqanov), 187, 188
summer grazing land, 18
Sun Has Spoken, The (Džaruqov), 215
symbolism, 44, 51, 74, 85, 113
synsū, 36, 39; *see also* wedding songs
Syr Darya, xiii, 225, 226, 227, 237, 245
Syr Darya (novel), *see* Muqanov
Syzdyqov, Džahan, 180, 207; *The Fruits of Labor,* 191

Ṭabarī, 111
Tadzhik, 4; Soviet Republic, 134
Tadžybajev, Abdylda, 189, 198-99, 224-30; "Conversations with Taras," 225, 227, 228; *New Rhythms,* 224; "Syr Darya," 225, 226, 227; "Two Worlds," 228
taipas, 6; *see also* clan
Tajmanov, Isataj, 89, 90, 95, 156
tales, 26, 30, 45-53, 105, 109, 150, 157, 184, 187; animal tales, 51; children's tales, 51-52; comical tales, 47; demonological tales, 52-53; fairy tales, 50; historical tales, 46, 121, 184; love tales, 47-50; modern tales, 237
Tammersfors, 206
tängri, 10
Targhyn (in *Er-Targhyn*), 62, 63, 64, 65, 66, 74, 75, 83
Tarlovski, Mark, 76, 152
Tashkent, xiii, 97, 121, 184, 248
Tatar, 22, 60, 87, 95, 106, 107, 141 n., 150, 181; literature and oral art, 122, 125, 154
teachers, 15
Temirtas (Muqanov), 236, 239
Tempo (Abdyqadyrov), 191
"Temporary Rules for the Colonization of the Kirghiz Steppes by the Rural Population," 18
Temporary Statute, 18, 21
Teüke (khan), 5 n., 16
textbooks, 109
theaters, 255-57
theatrical schools, 257
Thomsen, V., 9
Three Epochs (Murat), 97
tiger (metaphor), 160, 203
Tiläp-Bergenov, 180
Till Eulenspiegel, 47
"Time of Lament," 95-98, 101, 116, 146
Timuride empire, xii
Tobyqty (tribe), 111, 249
Togžanov, G., 152, 193
Tokhtamyš, 72, 73
Tölegen (in *Qyz-Džibek*), 68
tölöngüt, 9
Tolstoy, L. N., 109, 111, 115, 121, 194, 212
Toqmagambetov, Asqar, 189, 198, 209-15; *Collection of Labor,* 209; "New Spring," 213-14; *Šaulder,* 236; *Songs of Labor,* 209; "Thirteen Years," 210-12; "Written in Blood," 210, 212-13
Torgaut, 62
Toruajgyrov, Sultan Mahmud, 123-25, 235
trade, 5
traditions, attitudes toward, 176, 178, 179, 180, 186, 187, 192, 193, 195, 196, 197, 198, 199, 201, 236, 237, 248, 250

translations, from Kazakh, 85, 105, 112, 115, 120, 127, 150, 158, 173, 176, 178, 182, 194, 195, 215, 249, 255, 256; into Kazakh, 98, 101, 111, 112, 113, 115, 117, 118, 121, 122, 129, 176, 194, 195, 224, 225, 235, 248, 256, 257
Tristan and Isolde, 67
Troitsk, 121
Trotski, L., 186, 198
tulpar, see horse
"*Tulpar*—the Winged Horse" (Abdyqadyrov), 239-40
T'ungan, 18, 134
Turgai district, 19, 21, 23, 108
Turgaiskaya Gazeta, 121
Turgenev, I. S., 194, 208
Turkestan Government-General, xiii
Turkic culture, xii, 9, 104; languages, xii, 27, 140; tribes, 47
Türkistan (town), 23
Türkmen, 25, 45, 134, 142; Republic, 134, 144
Turksib railroad, 164, 165, 192, 199, 207, 210, 218
Turmanžanov, 152
Turušbekov, Džusup, 200 n.
Tvardovski, A., 167
"typical" and "normative" (definition by Malenkov), 247
ubbe, 53

Uighur, 18, 60, 88, 134, 176, 256; language, 27, 176
Ukrainian, 155, 227; literature, *see* literature, Ukrainian
Union of Soviet Writers (SSP), 176, 178, 193, 194; Kazakh Branch, 170, 183, 193, 194, 197, 241
Ural district, 19; river, xiii, 62, 88, 97
Uralsk, 23
Uraq-batyr, 61, 105
Urda, 121
Urqumbajev, Teleubaj, 159
urū, see clan
Ütemisov, Makhambet, 89, 90, 91, 92, 95
Uzbek, xii, 4, 12, 60, 134, 142, 150, 176, 256; khanates, 17; literature, 197, 200 n.; Republic, 134, 144

Valikhanov, Čoqan, 10 n., 12, 28, 100, 101-7, 235; *Ablaj,* 104; *Arms of the Kirghiz in Ancient Times,* 104; *Dzungarian Sketches,* 105; *Kirghiz Genealogy,* 104; *Kirghiz Migratory Routes,* 104; *Notes on the Mountaineer Kirghiz,* 102; *Notes on Shamanism,* 105; *Report on the Situation of the Altyšar or of the Six Eastern Cities of the Chinese Province Nanlu (Little Bukhara),* 104; *Traditional Tales and Legends of the Large Horde of the Kirghiz-Kaisaks,* 105
vendetta, *see qūn alma*
Verne, Jules, 195
Verny, *see* Alma-Ata
Volga, 62, 168
vowel harmony, 140

War Communism, 173, 178-86
warfare, 8, 26, 54
weapons, 70, 71, 167, 168; personification of, 84, 230
White Bear, The (Muqanov), 198
White Birch, The, see Auezov
"white bones," *see aq süjök*
wife, 14, 40, 49, 91
winter grazing land, 4, 6, 8, 18, 217
wolf, 51, 52, 57, 74, 128, 211, 229
women, 13-15, 16, 75-76, 91, 108, 113, 114, 122, 127, 137, 138, 139, 142, 144, 181, 186, 187, 188, 208, 209, 236, 237, 238, 239, 243-44, 245, 251
World War, 133, 136, 137, 151, 152, 166, 167, 170, 198, 223, 229, 230, 231, 232, 233, 237, 240, 241, 245, 246
"wrecker" motif, 245, 246, 247

Yasenski, B., 195
yurt (džurt), 14, 37, 39, 76, 91, 119, 171, 172, 187, 228

Zaman Tili, 121
Žankhoža, 89
Zar zaman, see "Time of Lament"
žez-tyrnaq, 53
Zhdanov, Andrei A., 242, 243
Zhubanov, A., 249
Žirenše-šešän and Qarašaš, 48-49
Zoshchenko, Mikhail, 152
Žumabayev, 123
Župar-qoryghy, 47
žüs, see Kazakh Hordes
Zvezda, 152, 242